THE SCHOOL OF FAITH

TO
MARGARET

THE SCHOOL
OF FAITH

THE CATECHISMS OF THE REFORMED CHURCH

Translated and edited
with an Introduction by

THOMAS F. TORRANCE

JAMES CLARKE & CO. LIMITED
33 STORE STREET,
LONDON, W.C.1.

First published 1959

© THOMAS F. TORRANCE

Printed in Great Britain by
The Camelot Press Ltd., London and Southampton

CONTENTS

Preface   vii

Introduction   ix

Part I: The Larger Catechisms

Calvin's Geneva Catechism, 1541   3

The Heidelberg Catechism, 1563   67

Craig's Catechism, 1581   97

The New Catechism, 1644   167

The Larger Catechism, 1648   183

Part II: The Shorter Catechisms

The Little Catechism, 1556   237

Craig's Short Catechism, 1592   243

A Catechism for Young Children, 1641   255

The Shorter Catechism, 1648   261

The Latin Catechism, 1595   279

Index to Catechisms   291

PREFACE

THE purpose of this book is to gather together all the Catechisms officially authorised and employed by the Church of
Scotland since the Reformation, so that they may be studied
together. Two of them, *Craig's Catechism* of 1581 and *Duncan's Latin Catechism* of 1595, did not actually have *verbatim*
authorisation, but they were recognised and used by the Church
and have for long been acknowledged as authoritative instruments of instruction in the Faith. In all of them, we are given
theology in simple dialogical form as it is found in the living
stream of the Church's life and growth in history. It is theology
that has been moulded by that history, so that in its use today
the whole historical Church of Scotland continues to utter its
voice and to hand on its teaching. From time to time, however,
it is incumbent upon the Church to examine its traditional
doctrine, put it to the test of the Word of God heard anew in
fresh exegesis of the Holy Scriptures, and correct it where
necessary as an instrument for further teaching and instruction.
It is to be hoped that the republication of these historic Catechisms will enable the Church of Scotland through its ministers
and teachers to engage in healthy self-criticism in regard to
its teaching and preaching of the Gospel in order that it may be
enabled faithfully to fulfil its mission in the same Gospel today.

In preparing this volume I have had four classes of people in
mind: students of theology who require a handbook of authoritative Church theology for study and discussion; ministers
who require in simple form a doctrinal guide for their preaching and teaching of the Gospel and in their work of building
up the faith of the Church; teachers of young people in
Church and School who need to learn how the Church has

B

instructed its children in the past in order that they may fulfil their own duties today in faithful continuity with the past and new learning from the Word today; and finally that growing multitude of people in every Church who seek to understand the history and doctrine of other Churches in order that through common understanding of the faith and mutual learning in Christ they may strive for the unity of His Church in its mission of reconciliation. Although these Catechisms come from the Reformed Church in Switzerland, Germany, and Scotland, they are meant to contain, as Calvin put it, "articles of faith common to all Christians". They are offered, therefore, to that world-wide communion of God's people in which every Church needs and depends upon every other Church in Christ, and in which each Church is called to share what it has received with others, that in conjoint hearing and learning Christ we may grow up together in Him who is the Head of all.

The Introduction does not pretend to give an exhaustive analysis or account of the teaching of the Catechisms, but is intended only to initiate the various groups I have had in mind into study of this stream of Church doctrine, and to stimulate them to carry further the great task entrusted to us of handing on "like precious faith" to those who come after us.

I wish to acknowledge my considerable indebtedness to the publishers for their zeal and carefulness and to Mrs. E. R. Olbrycht for invaluable help in preparing the typescript for the printer. The Rev. G. B. Hewitt, Secretary and Director of Religious Education in the Church of Scotland, has very kindly read the proofs. For giving me so much of his time and help, I wish to thank him very warmly.

THOMAS F. TORRANCE

New College, Edinburgh
December, 1958

INTRODUCTION

Contents

I. *The Content and Form of the Catechisms* xii
   (1) Analysis of the Catechisms xii
   (2) Contrast between the Reformation and the
       Westminster Catechisms xvi
   (3) Criticism of their Content xx

II. *The Method of Instruction* xxi
   The Nature of Communication xxii
   (1) General Principles of Learning and Instruction xxiii
   (2) Particular Principles for Christian Learning and
       Instruction xxxii

III. *The Nature of Theology* xliii
   (1) Dialogical Theology xliii
   Contrast between Reformed and Mediaeval
       Theology xlv
   The Temptations of Dialogical Theology xlviii
   (2) The Systematic Interest of Theology l
   Contrast between the Covenant of Grace and the
       Sacramental Universe l
     (i) The General Principle—the Covenant lii
     (ii) The Particular Principle—the Doctrine of
          Christ lv
   (3) The Catholicity of Theology lxv
     (i) The Historical Interest lxvii
     (ii) The Ecumenical Interest lxviii
     (iii) Historical and Ecumenical Interests lxviii

IV. *Doctrinal Tendencies*   lxix

  (1) The Doctrine of God   lxx
    (i) Contrast with Latin Theology   lxx
    (ii) God in Christ   lxxii
    (iii) Implications of the Reformed Doctrine of
        God   lxxiii
  (2) The Doctrine of Christ   lxxx
    (i) Christ clothed with His Gospel   lxxx
    (ii) The Merits of Christ   lxxxiii
    (iii) The Threefold Office of Christ   lxxxvii

  (3) The Doctrine of the Holy Spirit   xcv
    (i) The Person of the Spirit   xcvi
    (ii) The Work of the Spirit   c
    (iii) The Communion of the Spirit   cvi

INTRODUCTION

THE Catechisms set forth Christian doctrine at its closest to the mission, life, and growth of the Church from age to age, for they aim to give a comprehensive exposition of the Gospel of Jesus Christ in the context of the whole Counsel of God and the whole life of the people of God. They sow the seed that germinates in the soil, brings forth living fruit, and provides good grain for use in the next generation. They shape the mind of the historical Church, building up its understanding of the Faith and directing its growth and development so that throughout all its changes from age to age it ever remains the same Household and Habitation of God built upon the foundation of the Apostles and Prophets, Christ Jesus Himself being the chief corner stone. While each Church provides this instruction in responsible fulfilment of its mission in its own place and time in history, the Catechism is designed, not for the self-expression and self-culture of a particular Church, but to serve the Communion of Saints, so that all who use it may worship one God, Father, Son, and Holy Spirit, and be schooled in one Faith in the unity of the whole Church of God past and present. It is for that reason that the common basis of the Catechisms has traditionally been the Apostles' Creed, the Ten Commandments, and the Lord's Prayer, and these have been expounded as far as possible in the universal language of the Church, and apart from the particular characteristics of any one Church and age.

The Catechisms collected here all belong to the Reformed Church, but they were not intended to be Presbyterian Catechisms; they were intended to be instruments of the Church reformed, that is of the one Church which puts its house in order in faithful conformity to the Apostolic *Kerygma* and *Didache*. It is for that very reason that we would not be using them aright if we did not put them to the test of the Apostolic *Kerygma* and *Didache*, and seek through such critical study ever new obedience to the Truth, continuing, as Calvin put it, "to be disciples of Christ right to the end" (p. 54). Moreover we keep faith with our fathers and show our thankfulness for the instruction which they have handed on to us, if we learn from their time-conditioned habits and modes of thought (which no generation can escape) how to distinguish more clearly between the heavenly treasure and the earthen vessel, and learn how to take out of that treasure things new as well as old. Again we show our respect for the treasure itself if we hand it on to our children only through further disciplined understanding of the Apostolic *Kerygma* and *Didache*, training them in their turn so to submit themselves to the critical and creative power of the Word of God that they may not only be "scholars in the household of God" (p. 12) but teachers in the School of Faith. It is in this way that the historical Church can more and more "attain unto the unity of the faith, and of the knowledge of the Son of God, unto a fullgrown man, unto the measure of the stature of the fulness of Christ" (Eph. 4:13).

I. THE CONTENT AND FORM OF THE CATECHISMS

1. *Analysis of the Catechisms*

All the Catechisms give an account of Christian doctrine, and then go on to speak about God's Law and the Lord's Prayer, that is, about Christian obedience and worship, but there are variations among them revealing significant differences in interest and emphasis which it is instructive to compare.

Calvin's Catechism falls into four main parts.

(1) *Faith*, which includes a short section on the knowledge

and service of God and then a full exposition of the Apostles' Creed, pp. 5-25.

(2) *The Law*, an exposition of the Ten Commandments as the rule directing our worship of God and love toward our neighbour, pp. 25-40.

(3) *Prayer*, an account of the meaning and way of prayer in the name of Christ, with an exposition of our Lord's pattern-prayer, pp. 40-51.

(4) *The Word and Sacraments*, the means through which we have an entry into God's heavenly Kingdom and by which we render worship to God, pp. 52-65.

All four are expounded as parts of our worship of God.

The Heidelberg Catechism is divided into three parts.

(1) *The Misery of Man*, a brief section on sin, the fall, and need of man for redemption, pp. 69, 70.

(2) *Redemption*, that is, man's comfort and salvation through Christ the Mediator and Redeemer, expounded on the basis of the Apostles' Creed, and including the Word and Sacraments, pp. 71-86.

(3) *Thankfulness*, an exposition of the Ten Commandments and the Lord's Prayer, that is of good works and the invocation of God, as the appropriate and required forms of our gratitude to God for redemption, p. 86-96.

The whole of this instruction is given in answer to the question as to our only comfort in life and death.

Craig's Catechism has a more complicated division but its essential pattern is similar.

(1) *The Three-fold State of Man*, pp. 100-5:

(*a*) His creation, and innocence, without death and misery.

(*b*) His miserable fall and bondage under sin.

(*c*) His calling to repentance and restoration in Jesus Christ.

(2) *The Four Parts of God's Honour*, pp. 106–27.

(*a*) *Faith*, an exposition of the Apostles' Creed in four parts, followed by a concluding section on faith and its fruits, pp. 106–26.

(*b*) *Obedience*, an account of the Ten Commandments, the summary of the Law and the relation of the Law and Gospel, pp. 127–36.

(*c*) *Prayer*, its meaning as the lifting up of our hearts and minds to God in thanksgiving and invocation, expounded on the basis of the Lord's Prayer, pp. 136–44.

(*d*) *Thanksgiving*, an account of the instruments in our service of God, the Word, the Sacraments, and the Ministry of men, concluding with sections on election and eschatology, pp. 144–65.

This represents a combination of features from the Catechisms of Geneva and Heidelberg, but the instruction is given with greater attention to the history of Redemption and the Covenant of Grace.

The New Catechism begins with a brief introduction (pp. 167–8) and then expounds the four principal parts of God's Service.

(1) *The Belief*, an exposition of the Apostles' Creed in twelve articles, pp. 168–73.

(2) *The Ten Commandments*, that is, an account of our obedience as duty toward God and duty toward our neighbour, followed by a section on the Word and Spirit who produce in us faith and repentance, pp. 173–7.

(3) *Prayer*, that is, a seeking from God of things needed to set forth His glory, and for the supply of our wants, pp. 177–80.

(4) *The Sacraments*, an account of the Sacraments as the rules of solemn thanksgiving in remembrance of Christ and His sacrifice, pp. 180–2.

The Larger Catechism, after a brief introduction on man's chief end and the Holy Scriptures, falls into two main parts.

(1) *What Man ought to believe concerning God*, which is distributed in the following proportions (pp. 185-203):

(*a*) Doctrines of God, the Trinity and the Divine Decrees (pp. 185-7), Creation, Providence, the Covenant of Life, the fall and sin of man and his punishment, pp. 185-90.

(*b*) The Covenant of Grace, its Mediation through Christ, His Three offices, Life, Death, Resurrection, Ascension, Heavenly Intercession and Coming again, pp. 190-5.

(*c*) The Benefits procured by Christ's Mediation, applied to us by the Holy Spirit, the Church, Effectual Calling, Justification, Adoption, Sanctification, Assurance, Communion in Grace and Glory, Eschatology, pp. 195-203.

(2) *The Duty of Man* required by the Holy Scriptures (pp. 204-34):

(*a*) The Moral Law, and its use both for the regenerate and the unregenerate, detailed exposition of the Ten Commandments, pp. 204-22.

(*b*) The Means of Grace through which Christ communicates to us the benefits of His Mediation, i.e. the Word and Sacraments and Prayer, involving an exposition of the Lord's Prayer, pp. 222-34.

The *Shorter Catechisms* follow very much the same patterns set by the *Larger Catechism*, but some interesting features may be noted. Although *Calvin's Geneva Catechism* is the longest the *Little Catechism* approved by him for examining young people at admission to Holy Communion is the shortest of all.

Craig's Short Catechism, which is perhaps the most Christological of them all, is set forth in twelve sections: (1) Our Miserable Bondage through Adam, (2) Our Redemption by

Christ, (3) Our Participation with Christ, (4) The Word, (5) Our Freedom to serve God, (6) The Sacraments, (7) Baptism, (8) The Supper, (9) Discipline, (10) The Magistrate, (11) The Table, (12) The End of our Redemption.

The A.B.C., or A Catechism for Young Children, clings to the traditional order, based on the Apostles' Creed, the Ten Commandments, and the Lord's Prayer, but no exposition of them is given, the main attention being given to Christ and His Gospel and the means of grace.

The Westminster Shorter Catechism is much the longest of the catechisms for young children, and is mainly concerned with the appropriation of salvation and with the Christian life. It has no section on the Church. Like *The Larger Catechism* it has little to say about the Holy Spirit, and is the only one of the smaller catechisms to give a detailed exposition of the Ten Commandments which gives it a distinctively moralistic tone. It is concerned above all with man's theocentric religion.

The *Rudimenta Pietatis* is distinctively a Catechism of the Reformation. It is concerned mainly with the Person and work of Christ, and our union with Him through the Word and Sacraments. It makes use of the Apostles' Creed, the Ten Commandments, and the Lord's Prayer, but the whole exposition is given under the rubric of the *Three-fold State of Man*: (1) In Sanctity and Sanity, (2) Under Sin and Death, (3) Under Christ's Grace. "Christ and His graces" is the dominant note throughout.

2. *The Contrast between the Reformation and the Westminster Catechisms*

The outstanding contrast which the above analysis reveals is that between the older Catechisms of the Reformation and those of the Westminster Assembly. That was well described as long ago as 1866 by Horatius Bonar in his *Catechisms of the Scottish Reformation*. "Our Scottish Catechisms", he said, "though grey with the antiquity of three centuries, are not yet out of date. They still read well, both as to style and substance; it would be hard to amend them, or to substitute something better in their place. Like some of our old church bells, they have retained for centuries their sweetness and amplitude of tone unimpaired. It may be questioned whether the Church gained anything by the exchange of the Reformation standards for those of the seventeenth century. The scholastic mould in which the latter are cast has somewhat trenched upon the ease and breadth which mark the former; and the skilful metaphysics employed at Westminster in giving lawyer-like precision to each statement, have imparted a local and temporary aspect to the new which did not belong to the more ancient standards. Or, enlarging the remark, we may say that there is something about the theology of the Reformation which renders it less likely to become obsolete than the theology of the Covenant. The simpler formulae of the older age are quite as explicit as those of the later; while by the adoption of the biblical in preference to the scholastic mode of expression, they have secured for themselves a buoyancy which will bear them up when the others go down" (p. viii).

In order to be more precise we may draw out the contrast along several lines:

(i) By keeping more close to a biblical mode of expression and to the Apostles' Creed the older Catechisms were more *universal* in their teaching, more in harmony with the theology of the whole Catholic Church from the beginning, and less marked by the idiosyncracies of their producers.

(ii) The Westminster Catechisms are markedly less Christological both in content and in outlook than their predecessors.

Thus in proportion they give less than half the space that the others give to the person and work of Christ. But the same contrast appears in the manner in which the other material is expounded. In Calvin's exposition of the Ten Commandments for example, there is much more evangelical teaching than in the *Larger Catechism*'s highly moralistic handling of them.

(iii) The Reformation catechisms are less rationalistic than those of Westminster. That is to say, they expound Christian doctrine in the light of its own inherent patterns, following the direction of the Apostles' Creed, whereas the Westminster divines abandoned that for a schematism of their own which they imposed upon the instruction they had received from their fathers. They schematised it to the scholastic pattern of the Federal Theology and thus expounded Christian doctrine from the point of view of a particular school of thought. There can be no doubt that this had many advantages at the time particularly over against the Counter-Reformation, but it led to serious difficulties in later generations when the Federal schematism was found to conflict with the results of fresh biblical exegesis and a more biblical theology.

(iv) There is also a clear contrast between the two in regard to objectivity. In the older Catechisms the focus of attention was directed toward the Incarnate Word as the object of theological activity, upon the objective person and work of Christ. In the Westminster theology the main focus of attention is upon man's appropriation of salvation through justifying faith and the working out of sanctification. Ultimately the main content of these Catechisms is concerned with man's action, man's obedience, man's duty toward God, man's duty to his neighbour, and man's religion, although undoubtedly all that is directed upward in a most astonishing way to the glory of God. But it is *man's* glorification of God that occupies most of the picture. In the older Catechisms man's obedience was regarded as part of his thanksgiving, but in the later it is schematised to the moral law as something that is partly revealed by "the light of nature". Here there is a very powerful objectivity of a different kind, an objectivity that is bound up with rationalised norms and patterns of thought and behaviour rather than with the nature of the object, that is to say, the subject-matter of theology.

On the other hand, there is a real contrast to be noted within the Catechisms of the Reformation, notably between that of Calvin and that of Heidelberg. The latter, as Karl Barth has pointed out (*Die Christliche Lehre nach dem heidelberger Katechismus*, p. 19), is mainly concerned with God's work in man. It is much more closely orientated than the other Reformed Catechisms to the religious needs of man, to the hunger of his soul, and its exposition at important points is given from the perspective of human experience of redemption. It is essentially an evangelical Catechism and because its account of evangelical experience was not divorced from a powerful Christology it exercised enormous influence.

When we turn to the two Catechisms of John Craig we find a theology in which the emphases of the Geneva and Heidelberg Catechisms are brought together in a remarkable way. This Catechism has three other features that deserve notice. (*a*) It is more concerned than any of them with what we now call the *Heilsgeschichte*, with the understanding of the Gospel in the light of the whole history of Redemption. (*b*) Its concern both for the doctrine of the person and work of Christ and for personal faith lays great emphasis upon union and communion with Christ in the Communion of Saints, that is in the mutual participation which all the members of the Church have with Christ and with one another. (*c*) The combination of the evangelical and sacramental "moments" in the teaching and the life of the Church. In Craig's theology we also find an increasing emphasis upon "conscience" and "religion" which later characterises the teaching of the Westminster standards.

3. Criticism of their Content

When we look at all of these Catechisms in the light of the predominant teaching of the Holy Scriptures, we are forced to offer some radical criticisms. None of them really gives us Christian doctrine in its inseparable relation to the whole history of redemption in Israel, to the whole life of the historical Jesus Christ, and to the Baptism of the Spirit at Pentecost and the founding of the Christian Church. Certain great moments of the *Heilsgeschichte* are singled out, the creation and fall of man, the giving of the Law, the birth of Jesus, His crucifixion and resurrection and ascension, but Christian doctrine cannot be abstracted from the whole course of God's intervention in Israel, and the whole course of the life and work of Christ, without alteration and misunderstanding. If in His infinite patience and forbearance God took such care and time to reveal Himself through Israel in preparation for the Incarnation, catechetical instruction cannot afford to bypass "the school of Israel" if it is adequately to fulfil its function.

More important than this, however, is the need to include in the Catechisms an account of the whole course of our Lord's ministry, in Word, and Deed, that is to say, to give the historical Jesus Christ His full place as God's saving action which He is given in the four Gospels. Moreover something ought to be included from the Acts of the Apostles of the launching of the Church upon its mission from Pentecost, while in the ethical section of the Catechism *The Beatitudes* and the *Hymn of Love* from 1 Corinthians 13 should be laid alongside of the Ten Commandments and our Lord's own Summary of the Law.

The major part of a Catechism ought to be concerned with instruction about the whole Christ, "Christ clothed with His Gospel". But if that is so, and if the other elements mentioned above cannot be neglected, then does this not mean that we have to reconsider the form of catechetical exposition, just because it is the content that must be allowed to determine the appropriate form in which it is to be presented? The great advantage of following the Apostles' Creed is that it does keep exposition close to the mighty acts of God in Christ, but the actual order in which the Gospel is presented is surely that of "the grace of the Lord Jesus Christ, and the love of God and the communion of the Holy Spirit". We cannot teach a doctrine of God and then add on to that a doctrine of Christ. It was for that reason that Calvin prefaced his account of the Apostles' Creed with a brief section which showed that "the foundation of true reliance upon God is to know Him in Jesus Christ" (p. 7), while Craig combined this with a more extended account of man's three-fold state and so recovered more of the setting of the doctrine of Christ in the history of redemption. The latter was achieved in considerable measure also by the stress upon the Covenant of Grace in the Westminster Catechisms, although they lost the strong Christological orientation of Calvin's teaching. We have much to learn from all of these Catechisms if we are to find the best way to sow the good seed in our own day.

II. THE METHOD OF INSTRUCTION

The nature of the content must be allowed to condition not only the form but the method of instruction. On the other hand, because instruction has to take into account the nature of the receiver, the mode of communication will be conditioned also by the mode of reception. How then is divine

Truth to be communicated to a human receiver? The answer to that question, so far as these Catechisms are concerned, is to be seen most clearly in their doctrine of sacramental communication. Behind everything lies the fact that the Word of God has become flesh, that the Son of God has become man, for it is this Word clothed with our humanity in the incarnate Son who is communicated to us. Communication takes place on the ground of a divine self-adaptation to our humanity which also lifts up our humanity into communion with God. Thus behind all Christian communication or instruction lies the supreme fact that when the Word became flesh, God accommodated or adapted His revelation to human form in Jesus Christ, so that the closer instruction keeps to the *humanity* of Jesus Christ, the more relevant it is to the humanity of the receiver. On the other hand, when this Word clothed with our humanity in Christ is actually communicated to us, that is done in a way appropriate to His nature as Word and human flesh, and He is to be received in a mode corresponding to the nature of the receivers as rational human beings, that is, as human beings with a rational and bodily nature. Therefore if Christ Jesus communicates Himself (the Word) to us in His body and blood, He is to be received correspondingly by appropriate response to His Word and His body and blood, that is by faith and by our senses. Communication is both spiritual and physical. It is in the unity of Word and Sacraments that the true nature of communication is enshrined, and the appropriate principle of instruction is revealed. But here it is very clear that we are concerned not only with the nature of the Teacher (Christ Himself) and with the nature of the receiver (the human being, young or old) but with the relation between Christ and the human receiver. The Sacraments tell us that that relation involves in inseparable intertwinement reconciliation and the communion of the Holy Spirit. Therefore a proper method of instruction will have to reckon with an event of communication which is also an event of reconciliation, and with the transcendent operation of the Holy Spirit who enables man to receive truth beyond his natural powers, and so to be lifted up above himself in communion with God.

Can this be applied to catechetical instruction? If it can, can we single out the main principles which must lie behind and indeed control the method of instruction? I believe we must answer these questions in the affirmative.

Because we have to be concerned in such communication or instruction with the nature of the human receiver and with the mode of reception appropriate to his human nature, there are general principles of instruction relevant to every field of knowledge where the human knower is involved; but because we have to be concerned with the nature of the Truth (Jesus Christ Himself) and with the mode of communication appropriate to His unique nature, there are particular principles of instruction relevant to this unique field of knowledge where divine self-disclosure is involved. We must beware, however, of separating these principles, the general and the particular, too sharply, for they only operate together, and the application of the general principles will inevitably involve some measure of adaptation to the particular field of knowledge in question.

1. *General Principles*

There is no need to discuss these in detail here, for that would involve a general account of the theory of education. It will be sufficient to single out only those matters of outstanding importance for the kind of instruction we are considering here. But before we do that it is necessary to give heed to the warning that modern educational theories cannot be applied without criticism to Christian communication or to catechetical instruction. Modern educational theory has been built up through a long tradition of thinkers from Aristotle in the ancient world and Comenius and Pestalozzi in the modern world, in which the idea of naturalistic development has tended to govern the whole concept of education. From the point of view of the Christian faith two primary elements have been neglected in this development, (*a*) the personal nature of the Truth, and (*b*) the radical nature of evil and the need for reconciliation with the Truth. Both of these demand a profounder conception of the "objectivity" of the Truth than modern educational theory has favoured—where by "objectivity" is meant that Truth is something that encounters us and even when we know it retains its objectivity over against us, resists every attempt to subdue it to some form of our own subjectivity, even when knowledge of it becomes inward and intensely personal. It is here that the teaching of Martin Buber has a great deal to offer to modern educational theory, as well as to the scholastic theories of instruction which work with a false objectivity.

The following general principles demand attention:

(i) All knowing involves an *adaptation of our capacities* in accordance with the nature of the object, and therefore instruction requires a specific adaptation on the part of the learner, a specific mode of rational activity determined by the nature of what is being taught or communicated. That of course has to be accommodated to the peculiarities of the learner in regard to age, previous education, etc., but whether the learner is old or young, well or poorly educated, he has to make an effort to relate his reason differently to different kinds of objects—that indeed is the very essence of rationality. It would be just as irrational to apply only the specific mode of rational activity which is required in mathematics to the knowledge of other human minds, as it would be to try to smell with the ear or see with the nose. Thus the communication of Christian truth requires like all other truth serious adaptation toward it on the part of the receiver.

(ii) Bound up with this is the question of *attitude*. One adopts a rather different attitude in biology from that required in archaeology. One does not adopt the same attitude toward a living thing as one does toward a piece of ancient pottery. In all scientific knowledge we must adopt a procedure of impartiality, that is, in this sense, of objectivity. In other words, we do not allow our presuppositions to dictate to us *a priori* anything about the "what" or "how" of what we are investigating. But that does not mean that we can be quite uncritical of our own attitudes in the research, for it would be quite unscientific to imagine that we the knowers can keep ourselves out of the picture altogether. It belongs to the scientific attitude therefore to learn humility and wonder, that is, how to be really open toward the disclosure of entirely new facts and meanings, but it also belongs to the scientific attitude to learn the appropriate attitude required by the nature of the field of study. Thus both learning and instructing require a disposition which echoes or reflects the nature of the subject-matter involved. No less than any other, Christian communication requires from the learner, not only an attitude of humility and wonder, but a disposition in receptivity corresponding to its material content.

(iii) It is an important step in any branch of scientific research to learn to ask the *right questions*. Of course to ask questions presupposes that you already have some knowledge, otherwise you would not know what to ask about—that involves an important principle we shall consider below. Nor would you really ask questions if you already had full knowledge, for then your questions would not be genuine. But in the progress of learning, it is essential to ask the questions appropriate to the nature of the object. If we ask only biological questions we can only expect biological answers, and if we ask only chemical questions we can only expect chemical answers. The really scientific questions are questions which the object, that we are studying, through its very nature puts to us, so that we in our turn put only those questions which will allow the object to declare itself to us or to yield to us its secrets. The more we know about a thing the more we know the kind of questions to ask which will serve its revealing and be the means of communicating knowledge of it. This scientific principle has to be applied to Christian instruction, and it is here that we see the fundamental importance of the catechetical method. The young learner does not know enough as yet to ask the right questions. We have to encourage him to ask questions, but also to learn that only the appropriate questions will be a means of knowledge. This is nowhere more true than in regard to Christian communication. Christianity does not set out to answer man's questions. If it did it would only give him what he already desires to know and has secretly determined how he will know it. Christianity is above all the question the Truth puts to man at every point in his life, so that it teaches him to ask the right, the true questions about himself, and to form on his lips the questions which the Truth by its own nature puts to him to ask of the Truth itself that it may disclose or reveal itself to him. Now the Catechism is designed to do just this, and it is therefore an invaluable method in instructing the young learner, for it not only trains him to ask the right questions, but trains him to allow himself to be questioned by the Truth, and so to have questions put into his mouth which he could not think up on his own, and which therefore call into question his own preconceptions. In other words it is an event of real impartation of the Truth.

(iv) You cannot think unless you have something to think about. It is difficult, perhaps impossible, to think about nothing. Unless the mind is given material to think about, it can only turn in upon itself and think about itself—and that is the mark of mental disease. No one more than a child needs to be fed with information, to be given food for thought, otherwise he cannot develop his mental powers or develop the modes of rational activity that are essential for his own independent learning. Educational theories that insist that teachers must concentrate on drawing out (*edu care*) the latent capacities of the child, and help him at every point to form his own judgements, without equal attention to the supply of information, are tragically mistaken. That is to work with the old Orphic myth that all learning is a form of recollection, or to hold that all truth is ultimately self-evident, and at the same time to inculcate the false notion of the autocracy of reason. If modern science has taught us anything about the reason, it has taught us that reason is nothing without its object, and that truly rational activity is inseparable from learning to behave in accordance with the nature of what is objectively given, for that is the only way to learning what we do not and cannot otherwise know. But there are whole branches of knowledge, such as history, where the sheer impartation of factual knowledge is a primary prerequisite. Christian Truth is essentially (but not only) historical in nature, and requires historical impartation. Thus it belongs to the fundamental nature of Christian instruction to impart to the learner a great deal of information which he does not have and could not acquire apart from receiving it from without and from others. Only with this Christian information can a child learn to think in a Christian way, and learn Christian Truth. This again is one of the important characteristics of catechetical instruction, for it imparts to a child at an early age long before his mental powers can grasp the meaning of it all, a considerable body of historical and doctrinal matter, and so provides him with something to think about in the years when he is developing his mental and spiritual capacities. Without any doubt it contributes to the success of this method that it imparts to the child more than he can grasp at the time, for it so stretches his powers that it helps him to reach beyond his grasp and then grasp beyond his former reach. But this has to be considered in conjunction with the next two principles of instruction.

(v) It belongs to the essence of good education *to hold together the realm of the image and the realm of the idea*. That is natural to the child who is at once both a born "realist" and a born "idealist", as it were. It is one of the most tragic features of modern occidental civilisation that the realm of the image is torn apart from the realm of the idea, and once that happens it is next to impossible to bring them together. Once this radical dichotomy becomes a part of our life, people divide into two main groups, those who think mainly in images, usually the more uneducated and less sophisticated people, and those who tend to think only in ideas and abstractions, and for whom the whole realm of concrete image, and therefore of event, is of secondary importance, and for some even ultimately unreal. In that radical dichotomy a peculiarity of our age is the forceful conjunction of material images with scientific abstractions which so radically characterises Marxist man, but a large part of the blame for that must rest with the idealist divorce of the realm of ideas from the realm of concrete events. Be that as it may, somehow modern education tends to perpetuate this rift between the image and the idea, and in so doing it creates a grave difficulty for Christian instruction, for Christianity, through its doctrine of the Incarnation above all, is committed to the healing of the rift between image and idea, and its whole method of communication involves the interpenetration of image and idea, the overlapping of the realm of events with the realm of ideas. That follows from the historical involvement of Christian Truth, which only can be known and communicated in a way corresponding to its nature as historical and spiritual Truth. This is of supreme importance for the instruction of the young, that from a very early age they should learn the Truth through both image and idea, and through image and idea in inseparable mutuality. Thus to teach only the stories of the Bible, that is only its dramatic images, to young children, and not to teach them the elements of doctrine, is to create in them the divorce of image from idea that proves so disastrous later on, when either they have to deny the world of imagery in order to think in ideas, or to repudiate the world of ideas in order to take seriously the concrete world of material images. Either way they are dwarfed and stunted in half of their natures. On the other hand to, teach them Christian doctrine from a very early age is both to preserve and cultivate wholeness in their life and to train their intellectual and spiritual capacities without damage to their natural life. There can be no question about the fact that the generations of people brought up on the *Shorter Catechism*, even though not otherwise highly educated, had powers of intellectual and spiritual grasp which the ordinary man markedly lacks today. Whatever some educationists may say the sheer success of Catechetical instruction for several hundred years proclaims it to be one of the great educational achievements of modern times.

(vi) You cannot make anything unless you have the tools with which to form and construct it. You cannot think unless you have tools with which to think and shape the thoughts in your mind and form your judgments. The tools that the mind requires are conceptions and categories and formulated ideas.

Nor can you make much progress in instruction and learning unless you have appropriate and adequate tools for rational communication. That is surely part of the immense significance of the Old Testament, that is of the whole history of God's dealings with Israel, for it was within Israel that there were shaped and formed the tools which were used in the New Testament to grasp and interpret the bewildering miracle of Jesus. Those tools needed recasting and reshaping in their actual use in the New Testament, but they did supply the basic material which the New Testament Revelation required for its communication. Is not that also the function of the Catechism? Just as we still need to be schooled in the Old Testament adequately to understand the New, so our children need to be schooled in the elements of the Christian faith in order to grasp for themselves the teaching of the New Testament when they come to read and study it. It is part of the purpose and function of the Catechism to put into the child's possession the basic tools which he needs in order to read and understand the Christian Revelation. But it is important that these tools should be given to him at an early age. Just as it is from the very earliest that we begin to form in our minds the categories of our understanding with which we interpret the natural world around us, so it is important that from the earliest the child should be trained in the rudiments of Christian doctrine, and have these built into his mind and soul, so that he has eyes to see, ears to hear, and a heart to understand the whole message of the Gospel. Train up a child in the Way and he will not depart from it, but deprive him of eyes and ears and a heart and you thrust him out into a world of darkness and stumbling and bewilderment. Give him the tools at an early age, and he will fulfil to the end his discipleship in Christ.

(vii) You cannot make much progress thinking on your own, in a vacuum. You cannot think unless you have something to think about. Nor can you think unless you have an environment, unless you have others with whom to think together. Likewise *Christian instruction requires the community of others*. It does not properly take place in isolation, but only in the midst of the Church, that is in the whole fellowship of life and mission and preaching and worship, for it is only in the essential integration of the Truth with being and action that it can be either received or communicated. The Truth has to be communicated to the learner in his setting in life where he has to adapt himself to the Truth in order to apprehend it, but strictly speaking that requires the adaptation of his setting in life to the Truth, for it is only in togetherness with his fellows that he can fully and adequately apprehend the Truth. Likewise the communication of it requires the community, for it is only in the manifold communication, that is in the Communion of Saints, that proper and adequate instruction can achieve its end. This belongs to the very nature of the reason, as we are learning again today, for the reason cannot, without damage and loss, be abstracted from the person and from personal life and fellowship. It is this interaction of minds, this dialectic of persons, that is so obviously important for real advance even in scientific and philosophical pursuits, which is required in every form of instruction, and not least in Christian instruction, because there, as we shall see, this is demanded from the side of the object as well as from the side of the knower and learner.

None of the seven principles we have been discussing is peculiar to Christian knowledge or instruction. They all obtain in every branch of science or knowledge in ways appropriate to each, but they have correspondingly appropriate application to Christian instruction and learning in accordance with the particular principles of instruction and learning demanded by the unique nature of Christian Truth.

2. *Particular Principles*

These principles derive from the very substance of the Christian faith, as the requirements of the unique nature and operation of the Truth as it is in Christ.

(i) *Jesus Christ is Himself the Truth.* As Kierkegaard put it, this is Truth in the form of personal being, Truth which is identical with the Person of the Teacher. But we must go further than that. It is Christ clothed with His Gospel who is the Truth, for this is unique Truth in which Christ's Person and His Message are inseparably one. It is this double character of Christian Truth which distinguishes it from all other truth. It is a Person, but in that it is also a message it is sharply distinguished from all personalism. It is a message, but in that it is a Person, it is sharply distinguished from all systems of ideas or truths or propositions. Christian doctrine is a communication of truths, but truths that cohere in the one unique Person of the Incarnate Son of God. Christian doctrine is a personal communication of life and being, but not in abstraction from a Message. It is this unique and two-fold nature of the Truth which gives to Christian knowledge and instruction their unique character. Christian instruction must be analogous to this two-fold nature of the Truth as Person and Message. That means that the message cannot be communicated except in personal relation to Christ the Truth, and that personal communion with Christ the Truth cannot take place apart from communication of the Message. Another way of putting this is to speak of the identity of the Word and the Person of Christ. He communicates Himself to us as the Word addressing us. This means that through the Word He communicates His Person to us, but it also means that when Christ comes to us personally, giving Himself to us in love, it is through the Word of address which asks of us the response of our love and obedience. In no other branch of knowledge is this the case, for nowhere else is truth in the form of personal being and nowhere else do truths cohere in a Person. What could be more appropriate in the communication of this Truth than instruction that takes place in a conversation of question and answer, of word and response, for here the personal mode of communication is analogous to the nature of the Truth? Truths are communicated in catechetical instruction, but their personal character is guarded by the personal mode of communication, for in the address where the appropriate questions are asked (questions put to us by the very nature of the Truth) it is Christ Himself who addresses His Word to us and asks of us a personal response in word. But here on the other hand, the response in word is put into our mouth by the Truth Himself. What could be more appropriate to the fact that Christ has come not only to bring to us the Word of God, but in our name and on our behalf to bear the Word before God, i.e. give to God an account for us, and so to be the true Word of man in response to the Word of God?

(ii) Kierkegaard has also reminded us that in the Incarnation the Absolute Fact has become a historical Fact, so that knowledge of it must be analogous to its historical nature. The Truth with which we are concerned is identical with the historical Jesus Christ, and therefore it is Truth that can be communicated only historically (that is not of course to deny that it must be communicated spiritually). The Truth is a historical Person, and must be communicated personally and historically. That is to say, the Truth must be communicated to us by other persons in time. It is not something that we can tell to ourselves, or to which we can relate ourselves timelessly. The truth comes to us and addresses us in history, using personal and temporal means, so that in order to learn the Truth we must allow others to tell it to us and to instruct us. Thus we cannot tell ourselves that we are forgiven. This has to be announced to us, for that belongs to the essentially personal and historical nature of this Truth.

We have a striking illustration of this in the Old Testament account of the child Samuel, to whom the Word of God came several times vertically from above, as it were, in the Temple at Shiloh, but who was unable to apprehend it or understand it except through the help of Eli. By himself Samuel could only interpret it as the voice of a man, and so could only misinterpret it. The Word of God required the agency of personal and historical communication, that is, to be conveyed horizontally, as it were, from one human person to another, before it was really received. Is that not also true of the communication of the Word since the Incarnation? The Word of God comes to us directly and personally, but it requires to come to us personally and historically through the communication of other historical persons. In other words, Christ communicates Himself personally in and through the historical Church where the Word is historically communicated to us by others, and where through them He comes Himself immediately in direct and personal address. Christian instruction must be analogous to that whole complex of Christ's self-communication. Hence we are to understand the use of catechetical conversation in the midst of the life and mission of the Church, and indeed, as the Reformers insisted, in the midst of its worship where Christ is really present through the proclamation of the Word and the administration of the Sacraments as the congregation gathers in His Name. Christian instruction requires as its medium a historical community of persons in fellowship with one another in Christ, if it is fully to achieve its end. Therefore catechetical instruction must not be divorced from the Communion of Saints, for its interrogations and answers, belong to mutual relations between Christ and His Church, and take place in the self—communication of Christ to His people, and in the corporate response of His people in prayer and praise and understanding of His Word.

(iii) True Christian instruction requires on the part of the learner or receiver *a response of self-denial and self-criticism.* To a certain extent this must be understood as an adaptation of the general principle requiring communication and learning to ask the right questions. In scientific activity it is the nature of the object that teaches us the right questions to put to it through which it is made to disclose itself to us—but normally "disclose itself" is too personal a way of putting it. Here, however, where we are concerned with Truth in the form of Personal Being, and with Truth as our Creator and Lord, the Truth does disclose Himself to us, and actively puts questions to us. Here our scientific questions are directed not so much to the object, Christ Himself, but are by Him directed back upon us, for we discover we are at the bar, and are being questioned by Him. The appropriate response to that questioning is one of self-questioning or self-criticism, for what hinders our knowledge is not Christ who communicates Himself to us, but we who are the knowers, the subjects to whom He reveals Himself. And therefore when the Truth encounters us He comes with the demand for self-denial on our part—we cannot otherwise follow Him and be obedient to the Truth. In other words, when we encounter the Truth in Christ, we discover that we are at variance with the Truth, in a state of rebellion and enmity toward it, so that the way of knowledge is the way of surrender and acknowledgement through self-denial and repentance. We bring to the knowledge of the Truth our own preconceptions and our own desires and seek to mould the Truth to our own ways, and to subdue it to our own satisfactions, but the Truth stands in our way and blocks us. He offends us, and there is only one way in which communication can take place, through yielding ourselves in repentant obedience to the Truth. Now this is in no sense a *sacrificium intellectus*—it is the only scientific and rational thing we can do, for if we are to know the Truth objectively, we cannot but adapt our rational activity to the mode of His encounter, and the mode of His self-revelation. To surrender ourselves in obedience to the Truth, to offer ourselves living sacrifices to Him, is the part of rational worship. Since that is the only way in which Christian instruction can achieve its end, the communication of the Truth cannot be divorced from the call for personal decision and obedience, involving repentance and self-denial on the part of the disciple if he is to follow Christ. Its reception requires on the part of the learner a decision against himself. This has to be understood in conjunction with the next principle.

(iv) Instruction in Christian Truth involves *reconciliation with the Truth*. Now to a certain extent this may also be looked on as a Christian adaptation of a general principle noted above, namely, the openness and readiness of man for new knowledge, and the requirement that he have an appropriate disposition toward it. No one can understand very well what he resents or opposes, especially in the realm of personal knowledge. But here we are confronted with something much profounder, that man is existentially severed from the Truth, as Kierkegaard once put it, and needs to be reconciled to the Truth. Revelation and reconciliation are inseparable, and communication and healing cannot be divorced from each other. Christian instruction has to reckon with the problem of evil, indeed with original sin. As John Craig put it, it is not that in the Fall we lost our minds and wills, "but we have lost a right mind and a right will" (p. 102); or as he put it even more sharply, there are "two contrary images in mankind, the image of God and the image of the Serpent" and between them there is "a continual battle" (p. 104). We are opposed to the Truth, and the

Truth is opposed to our untruth. Therefore reconciliation and healing have to take place if real communication is to be achieved. This is a two-fold reconciliation, between man and Christ and between man and his fellow-man. Here we return to the fact that it is only within the community of God's people that communication can take place, but now we see that this is the community of the reconciled where reconciliation between man and God and man and his fellow is actualised. It is in that community of reconciliation that the learner receives the required disposition toward the Truth, and himself enters into reconciliation with the Truth. This cannot be emphasised enough, but it has to be translated not only into fact in the life of the learner but into practice by the instructor, for reconciliation has to characterise his whole mode of instructing and catechising if he is to achieve true Christian communication. But now this carries us on to a further and a cognate principle.

(v) *Christian instruction involves renewal* on the part of the learner. If Christian Truth is Truth in the form of Personal Being in Jesus Christ, then knowing the Truth must involve a relation in being to it as well as a relation in cognition. Thus corresponding to the oneness of Truth and Being in Christ there must be a oneness of knowing and becoming on the part of the believer. Knowing the Truth and being recreated in the Truth are inseparable. "Except a man be born again", said Jesus to Nicodemus, "he cannot *see* the Kingdom of God". In no other sphere of knowledge does knowledge of the truth affect so decisively the being or the knower, but here knowledge of the Truth involves a radical change in being or a conversion. In some respects this also can be looked on as a Christian adaptation of the general scientific principle that rational knowledge of an object requires adaptation of behaviour in accordance with its nature. Because in Christ Truth and Being are one, adaptation to such Truth on the part of the knower

requires of him in the very act of knowing a radical reorientation in which knowing and being mutually involve one
another. In the language used at an earlier point, this will involve a reconciliation of idea and image, of truth and action,
and a renunciation of the radical dichotomy between a realm
of ideas and a realm of events. Reconciliation with the Truth
must be allowed to penetrate throughout the whole life and
being of the believer, so that reconciliation becomes an internal
truth of his own being and mind. It is only out of that wholeness of person and being that true knowing of the Truth can
be actualised. We must be aware of interpretating this psycho-
logically. Reconciliation has already taken place objectively
in Jesus Christ, for in Him our humanity has been apprehended
and has been converted back to union and communion with
God throughout the whole course of the Incarnation from the
birth of Jesus to His resurrection. That was the great *palingen-
nesia* in which we are given to share through the Holy Spirit, so
that conversion or renewal means a participating in the new
life and new obedience of man in union with God already
fulfilled in Jesus Christ. That demands the consideration of
another fundamental principle, but before then we must pause
to see what this involves for Christian instruction. Instruction
is not just schooling or indoctrinating, nor is it, as we have
seen, simply the developing of the powers and capacities which
the young learner already possesses, but it does involve a whole
movement of change and growth in the Truth. That is why it
is so important that it should begin very early, as close as
possible to his natural generation, so that his spiritual generation
may proceed *pari passu* with his normal growth and development, that from the very earliest he should learn to find his
spiritual life not in himself but in Christ, and so find the real
truth of his own personal being in union with his Lord and
Saviour. One of the great tragedies of modern life is that the

neglect of doctrinal teaching to children at an early age, has meant that their powers in other areas of intellectual life are often developed out of all proportion to their powers in Christian and spiritual understanding, with the result that they grow up desperately unbalanced, comparatively giants in certain areas of their personal life and dwarfs in other areas. The fruit of that is to be seen everywhere in the widespread malaise of tension, anxiety, frustration, and bewilderment—that is, in the lack of wholeness and reconciliation and equilibrium. Conversion in the psychological sense takes place when, as a result of such an unbalanced development and the radical dichotomy it involves, adaptation to the truth can only be a shattering experience. But that need not happen if Christian instruction and learning have been properly fulfilled.

(vi) Christian instruction can only achieve its end through *the demonstration of the Spirit*, as St. Paul called it. Jesus took care at the Last Supper to tell His disciples that He would send them "the Spirit of Truth", not in order to speak of Himself or teach them new things, but in order to reveal to them what Christ had already set before them in His Word, and Life, and Action. Jesus Himself is the Way, the Truth, and the Life, and no one can go to the Father but by Him, but we require the supernatural operation of the Spirit who proceeds from the Father and the Son in order to apprehend the Truth and to become sons of the Truth in apprehending it. In other words, Christian Truth is transcendent to us. It is other and higher than we are. It is beyond us, and we are unable to attain to it of ourselves. We need to be lifted up above ourselves, and enabled to grasp it beyond our natural capacities. For a man of earth to conceive the Truth is as miraculous an act as the Virgin Birth of Jesus Christ. We receive the Truth as it is announced to us, but it is only by the supernatural operation of the Spirit that we can really conceive it. Certainly it passes through all the rational processes of our own minds and knowledge of it is in no sense irrational, but the mind is adapted to the Truth by the Truth and only through that conformity to it can the human mind rise to know what is beyond it and is actually divine. In other words, the Truth acts creatively upon the knower who yields himself to the Truth, enlarges his powers and begets in him an understanding not otherwise attainable. All Christian instruction must reckon with this fundamental fact, and therefore it cannot be divorced from prayer and invocation of the Spirit and reliance upon His promised help in all our infirmity. This means also that we must never seek to do ourselves the work of the Spirit, as for example, by sheer force of indoctrination, to mould the mind of the learner by undue pressure. We may sow and plant and water, but it is God alone who gives the increase. Therefore Christian instruction has to learn how to wait upon God, for unless we do that we obtrude ourselves in place of the Holy Spirit and actually hinder His work. That which is spiritual cannot be carnally discerned or communicated; it requires spiritual discernment and spiritual communication. It requires the Holy Spirit.

(vii) Christian instruction has to reckon with the fact that the Truth may put the learner *at variance with the world*. The very fact that knowledge of the Truth requires reconciliation with the Truth, and renewal in the mind and life of the learner, means that he is singled out from the world, incorporated into a community of the reconciled and renewed and so belongs to the Communion of Saints over against the natural societies of the world. He does not come out of the natural societies for he has his natural life in them, but it does mean that his new life in the Truth creates a certain tension between him and the world. On the other hand, it must be remembered that the Truth into communion with which he has now entered is essentially reconciling Truth. Therefore he cannot have communion with it without entering into its reconciling operation, without being sent back to the world on a mission of reconciliation. Unless he really engages in that mission it is to be doubted whether he has really entered into communion with the Truth. We may state that in another way. Christian Truth, as we saw above, is by its very nature personal historical Truth that requires personal and historical communication; but it still requires personal and historical communication even when it is received, for to possess it truly means that we also communicate to others. We cannot tell the Truth to ourselves, but require others to tell it to us, but in accordance with its very nature the Truth requires of the receiver that he tell it to others as part of his communion with it and part of his understanding of it. Thus the Truth is really communicated to us when we can communicate it to others. Reception of the Truth reaches its fulfilment when from learning it passes in faithful discipleship to witness. This is all-important for the fulfilment of catechetical instruction. The teacher must never really cease to be a learner, for his teaching is the fulfilment of his learning, while the learner does not really learn unless he learns also from his learning how to teach the Truth to others. It is thus that catechetical instruction not only sows the good seed for future harvesting but ensures, as Calvin put it in a letter to Somerset, that good grain is provided for future sowing.

It cannot be said that all these principles were discerned or put into effect by the authors of the Reformed Catechisms, but it must be recognised that they did seek a way of communicating Christian Truth that was faithful to the nature of the Truth, and capable of effective use. Calvin was most clear-headed about what he wanted to do, but his answers were found to be too long by the Scottish Church, which preferred Craig's

method of brief questions and answers. That form of catechising was not meant to impart information in the first instance,
but to clarify in the minds of Church members their understanding of the teaching they received week by week in the
exposition of the Word and proclamation of the Gospel.
Craig's short Catechism was found too long for the use of
children of tender years and one still shorter was produced in
Edinburgh in 1641, but longer than that used in Geneva. When
we come to the Westminster Catechisms we find different
intentions mingled together: the Westminster *Shorter Cathechism*
was designed as a means of indoctrination, whereas the
Larger Catechism was rather a Directory for the use of teachers
—but both of them were concerned to give clear rational
summaries of the main points of the faith, and to provide
teachers and learners alike with the necessary tools for theological thinking. It cannot be disputed that they performed
magnificent service, but the question must be raised whether
they did not allow a more scholastic method to displace, at least
in part, the operation of the Holy Spirit, and whether they
really took as seriously as they ought to have the fact that
revelation and reconciliation are inseparable. Certainly it is in
the earlier Catechisms that the nature of Truth as Truth in the
form of personal Being (that Jesus Christ is Himself the Truth)
is best acknowledged. The Westminster Catechisms, however,
did set forth their instruction in accordance with their basic
teaching that it is through partaking of the benefits of Christ
that we partake of Christ, whereas the earlier Catechisms taught
that it is through partaking of Christ Himself that we partake
of His benefits. Thus the differences between the form and
method of instruction adopted in the later Catechisms and
those adopted in the earlier appear to derive from a difference
in understanding the nature of the content, that is, in the
substance of the faith.

III. THE NATURE OF THEOLOGY

We have already had much to say about this in the previous sections in discussing the nature of the Truth which must determine the form and method of Christian instruction. The main features of the nature of the Truth are that it is at once a Person and a Message, that this Person clothed with His Message has taken a historical form and is communicated personally and historically, and that this Truth encounters us in such a way as to reveal that we are alienated from it and need to be reconciled to it if actual communication is to take place. Communication of the Truth thus involves reconciliation and communion with the Truth. This manifold nature of Christian Truth as personal, rational, and historical means that a scientific theology, i.e. one faithful to the nature of its proper object, will be differentiated from other types of knowledge with which it certainly overlaps but with which it is too often confounded. Thus theology is not to be understood as a system of ideas, or as a sociology, or as a branch of historical science. On the other hand because Christian Truth is Truth in the form of personal Being, and because theological knowledge correspondingly involves knowing and becoming in inseparable unity, theology cannot be construed either in terms of an ontology or in terms of an ideology. How then are we to speak of the nature of theology?

(1) When we examine the Reformed theology out of which these catechisms sprang we see that it is essentially *dialogical*. That is to say, it is concerned throughout with the address of the Word of God and the obedient response of faith. It is essentially a theology of the Word. Reformed theology arrived at this understanding over against the philosophical theology of the Roman schoolmen, and that contrast is still illuminating.

Scientific theology in the modern sense began with Anselm

who may be said to have operated with two chief principles: (a) the conformity of reason with the Truth, and (b) the method of inquiry in which the Truth is addressed and interrogated in order that the reason may learn to conform to it obediently. That gave Anselm's theology its objectivity and its dialogical form which is most apparent in the many prayers to the *Veritas* interspersed throughout the theological dialogues. But with Abelard, Anselm's younger contemporary, early Mediaeval theology took another direction, for with him it ceased to be dialogical and became dialectical; that is to say, it concerned itself with the critical examination of truths by setting different opinions over against each other, and so arriving at a systematic presentation of truth through the principle of non-contradiction. But here the system arose not out of the nature of the Truth itself but out of the nature of the dialectical method. Mediaeval theology, however, also worked with another basic principle, the *sacramental universe* with its pre-established harmony between the visible and the invisible, the earthly and the heavenly. This had a general form and a particular form.

In its *general form* it stood for a correspondence between active thought and being, and therefore between the form-structure of knowledge and the form-structure of being; that is, it posited an inherent relation between logical forms and the nature of the truth. By means of this conception Mediaeval theology worked with an all-embracing system within which it brought its understanding of God and the creature, absolute and finite being, and their relations to one another. Even the Revelation of God in Christ was interpreted within this system, but that meant that Revelation was only filling out a conception of being already stabilised independently on the ground of natural theology.

The *particular form* which the principle of the sacramental universe took was the Church regarded as a sacramental institution of grace grounded upon and continuous with the Incarnation, as its extension into space and time. As sacramental institution the Church was related as redemptive microcosm to the macrocosm of the whole universe. Here Mediaeval theology posited an intrinsic relation of grace between the being and existence of the Church and the nature of the Truth of Revelation, so that the institutional Church was held to represent in its forms and dogmas the objectification of the truth in its institutional and rational structure, i.e. in the ordinances, decrees, and dogmatic definitions of the Church. It was on this ground that the Church itself came to assume supreme authority, for the expression of the mind of the Church in its dogmatic definitions was held to be the expression of the nature of the Truth.

The knowledge derived through both these sources was articulated in a grand synthesis through equating the conception of grace as the relation of the Divine Being as Cause to the creaturely being as operation, with the doctrine of the inherent relation of likeness between the Truth and the logical forms of the reason. In this way the element of dialogue was eliminated, and dialectics, that is the manipulation of the supposed norms or forms immanent to thought, came to exercise a determinative power over all the apprehension of the Truth, so that in the last resort Roman theology became subordinated to a philosophical ontology.

In recoil from this philosophical theology the Reformed Church returned to *positive theology* by concerning itself with the Word of God and obedient conformity to it in the faith and teaching of the Church. That is to say, it continued in the line of Anselm rather than of Abelard, but laid a more positive stress upon the Word of God which encounters and addresses us in and through the Holy Scriptures. In other words here we have a conception of theology as the conformity of thought with its object, but here the object is God revealing Himself in His Word, encountering us as Subject, and addressing us as subjects over against Him and in communion with Him. This had the effect of restoring to theology its dialogical character, and of restoring the centre of gravity to the objective Truth to which all human thought-forms are therefore subordinated. Indeed it is precisely because the Word addresses us, calls us to account, and summons us to penitent and obedient conformity to it, that here theology does not come under the domination of philosophical presuppositions but rather adapts and bends human thought-forms to the masterful use of Revelation as tools for its articulation in our understanding. Thus theological activity proceeds by constant reference to its source and sole norm in the Word of God, so that theological terms and formulations are ever brought to the bar of the Word for criticism and creative reorientation.

Reformed theology thus involves a way of knowing the Truth in which (a) the objectivity of the Truth is fully acknowledged, and (b) the knowing subject has full place over against the object in a dialogical relation. Nowhere is this more apparent than in the great Catechisms of the Reformation, which reflect in their very method of instruction the dialogical nature of theological knowledge. A true Catechism should be a conversation in the Word before the presence of God, so that there are really three parties in the conversation, for behind the conversation that the teacher and learner have with one another in their inquiry into the Truth there is the conversation which both have with the Truth, the Lord Himself. Since the Truth has assumed personal and historical form in the Incarnation and so requires personal and historical communication, God uses the human subjects as His appointed means for speaking the Truth, that each person, who cannot tell the Truth to himself, may have another to tell it to him. God used the aged Eli to speak to Samuel and to help Samuel hear directly for himself the Word of God, but God also used the little Samuel to communicate His message to Eli. Thus the Word of God always takes the field in such a way that it creates for itself a sphere of human and earthly conversation in which the Word has free course and each helps the other both in hearing and in speaking it. It is thus that dialogical theology arises within the Church as the sphere of the two-fold conversation between God and His people, and between members of the Church in the presence of the Word and Truth Himself. It is in this way that the Word of God stands the sons of men on their feet before Him that God may declare to them His Word and make them on their part not only objects of His address, but subjects responding to Him and to one another in the fellowship of the Church.

Now, however, we must note that dialogical theology is always open to a twofold temptation:

(a) There are two partners to this conversation, but just because the human partner is given his full place as a subject, he is constantly tempted to assume the major role and so to exercise a dominion in the realm of grace which he is given by creation to exercise only in the realm of nature. But that is to turn the Creator into a creature, and so to turn the Truth into a lie. It is to humanise theology by making anthropology the ultimate concern.

In this respect it is particularly instructive to examine the beginning of each Catechism and to ask where the main interest really lies, in God or in man. They all give God and man full place right at the start. Some of them begin with a question about the Creator (*Craig's Catechism*, 1581, *The New Catechism*, *A Catechism for Young Children*, *The Latin Catechism*), *Calvin's Catechisms* and the two *Westminster Catechisms* begin with a question about man's chief end, but *Craig's Short Catechism* begins with the question, "What are we by nature?" and *The Heidelberg Catechism* with, "What is your only comfort in life and death?" The last named reminds us of Luther's great question, "How can I get a gracious God?" and appears to have an anthropocentric interest, but on the other hand that tends to be offset by its doctrine of God and its Christology. The teaching of Calvin and of the Westminster divines begins with man but directs man's whole interest upward to God and His glory, and yet the Westminster Catechisms are inordinately interested in the appropriation of salvation by man. In the latter that emphasis upon man lies over against a very exalted conception of God which appears to put Him far out of reach. In Calvin's teaching, however, God is above all the One who has turned to man in His grace and brings man into familiar relation with Himself, who holds fellowship with man and who insists on being his heavenly Father.

There is a development here which is clearer when we set beside it the preaching that accompanied these Catechisms. At the Reformation preaching was concerned with presenting Christ and His graces and focussing the attention of the people upon Him, while in the application of the Gospel the people were directed toward their neighbours in Christian love and charity. In the Post-Westminster period, however, there is a change. Preaching is much more concerned with experience of Christ, with appropriation of His benefits, with attaining an interest in Him, while in the application the people were exhorted to be concerned with working out their own sanctification. There is a marked turning of the attention inward upon the self. This does indicate clearly the constant temptation of Protestant theology toward subjectivity and inwardness, toward religious experience and self-consciousness. For a while that was inhibited by Protestant scholasticism and rationalistic orthodoxy, but reaction to that lead straight into the subjectivist theology of the nineteenth century, aided and abetted by the great philosophical movement from Descartes and Kant, first in concentration upon the self and self-certainty and then upon the creative and legislative powers of the human mind over the objects of cognition. On the other hand, Protestant theology has always kept returning to the basic principle of the subordination of all tradition to the Word of God and of all its life and thought to God's self-revelation in Jesus Christ, so that it is constantly being called back out of its subjectivism, out of its monologue with itself, to dialogue with the Word of God.

(b) Dialogical theology is subjected to another temptation, to detach the human conversation from direct conversation with God, or to conduct the human conversation behind the back of God, as it were, as if He were not actually party to it. To do this inevitably means the transmutation of dialogical theology into dialectical theology, that is, to be more concerned with a consistent system of ideas than with real conversation with the living God. This step was taken early in Reformed theology in the seventeenth century which saw the rise of such a galaxy of Protestant schoolmen, particularly on the Continent. That is the theology that in part at any rate lies behind the Westminster Catechisms. It was partly in self-defence that this came about. Reformed theology had to be given firm and ordered expression in post-Reformation times, especially against the attacks of formidable theologians like Bellarmine, but in meeting these attacks it seized upon the prevailing philosophy and logic as weapons for battle and tools with which to build up its own structure. Hence in place of the more lively dialogical forms of the older Catechisms there were introduced more precise definitions and careful distinctions into the *Westminster Catechisms*. Once this happened it was inevitable that the human thought-forms, theological thought-forms, thus produced should come to exercise an unduly powerful influence over against the lively Word of God, and even to create a hardened and authoritative tradition which tended to control the interpretation of the Holy Scripture, and to inhibit advance in Biblical theology. The full understanding of this, however, requires consideration of another characteristic of theology.

(2) Inherent in the nature of theology is a *systematic* interest, for it is an attempt to give a coherent account of the whole of Christian doctrine. Everything depends, however, upon the kind of system involved and the use that is made of it. If theology is to be faithful to the nature of the Truth, it cannot schematise it according to some alien principle. The nature of the Truth itself must be allowed to prescribe the systematic principle to be employed in its exposition, and at no point must this systematic principle be allowed to assume an independent or authoritarian role; it can only be acknowledged as the servant of the Truth, and never as its master.

At this point also Reformed theology presents a sharp contrast to Roman theology. Instead of the systematic conception of a sacramental universe with its doctrine of an inherent relation between the structure of Being and the immanent forms of the rational understanding drawn from philosophy, Reformed theology substituted the doctrine of *the Covenant of Grace* drawn from the Biblical Revelation. This has supreme significance for the nature of theology in two chief respects.

(a) The Covenant which God in His grace has made with man calls man into fellowship and responsible relation with Himself, for within the Covenant God addresses man, bestows Himself in love upon him, and asks for his response in worship and love. Thus the Covenant establishes, confirms and preserves the dialogical nature of theology, and is indeed the form within which conversation between God and His people takes place. That we have already discussed, but the Covenant reveals another characteristic of theology, which we shall discuss below, namely, its historical character. That is to say, the Covenant marks out the sphere within Creation and history in which God's promises are given and fulfilled, and it is within that course of promise and fulfilment that conversation with God takes place, and therefore that dialogical theology arises as historical conversation with God.

(b) The Covenant embraces not only man but the whole of creation, so that the whole universe of creaturely existence, visible and invisible, is brought into a relation with God in which it is appointed to reflect His glory and be the sphere of His Revelation. Here there is a covenanted correspondence between the creation and the Creator; that is, not one which reposes upon some imaginary inherent relation of likeness and being between creation and God but solely upon the gracious decision of God to assume the created world beyond anything it possesses in itself into such a relation to Himself that He may use it as the instrument of His glory, and as the sphere within which He creates fellowship between man and Himself. This Covenant with its source and meaning in the free decision of God's grace manifests itself in one form of administration or economy before the Incarnation and another form of administration or economy after the Incarnation, but it is the one all-embracing Covenant of the overflowing love of God in which He wills to give Himself to His creatures and wills them to share in His life and glory. Over against the Roman idea of the sacramental universe this covenanted correspondence between the creation and God is construed in historical and dynamic terms, for it is concerned with God's real promise and fulfilment in which He actively intervenes in the history of the world and reconciles it to Himself.

In Mediaeval theology, as we have seen, the sacramental

principle had a general form, in the whole relation of nature and grace (the sacramental universe), and a particular form, in the sacramental institution of the Church as the extension of the Incarnation, and these two were interpreted in the light of each other through the integration of natural and revealed theology. The Biblical counterpart to that in Reformed theology is the One Covenant of Grace and its total fulfilment in the Person and Work of Jesus Christ the incarnate Son and Word of God. Thus if Reformed theology has a systematic principle it is to be regarded as deriving from this Covenant and its Fulfilment in Christ and as such derives from the very substance of the Gospel.

(i) *The One Covenant of Grace.* The Covenant embraces not only man but the whole of creation, for God has made the whole world as the sphere within which He may have fellow-ship with man and man may share in His grace and reflect His glory. As Karl Barth has interpreted it, the Covenant is the inner ground and form of the creation and creation is the outer ground or form of the Covenant, and the very centre of the Covenant is the will of God to be our Father and to have us as His dear children. Creation is thus to be understood as the sphere in space and time in which God wills to share His divine life and love with man who is created for this very end. Creation cannot be understood, therefore, in abstraction from God's Covenant purposes, but only as the instrument of His purpose in revelation and reconciliation. God does not reveal Himself in abstraction and emptiness, but reveals Himself to man within created existence in which He condescends to accommodate Himself to the creature through creaturely forms, appointing them as signs and instruments of His self-disclosure, veiling His truth in lowly forms adapted to creaturely apprehension. As Calvin used to put it, God wrapped Himself up in earthly signs and symbols and representations as the means through which in His mercy and gentleness He draws near to men, reveals His presence, and adapts men to receive His truth. Thus the whole of creation is a mirror, a theatre, a world of signs, which God uses in the fulfilment of His Covenant relations with men, as the tools and instruments of His Word. In itself, however, the world of creation is a labyrinth in which we are only lost and swallowed up, for only by the thread of the Word can we find our way through it to the Light of God.

In other words, the whole world of signs which God in His Covenant mercy has appointed to correspond to Him only has revealing significance, and therefore can be interpreted only, in relation to His Covenant will for communion with man and in the actualisation of that Covenant in the course of His redemptive acts in history. Thus while the whole of creation is formed to serve as the sphere of divine self-revelation, it cannot be interpreted or understood out of itself, as if it had an inherent relation of likeness or being to the Truth, but only in the light of the history of the Covenant of Grace and its appointed signs and orders and events in the life of the Covenant people, that is to say, according to its economy prior to the Incarnation and according to its economy after the Incarnation. And this means, further, that the whole of creation in its relation of the history of the Covenant can be understood only in the light of the Incarnation which is the goal of the Covenant, for in it creation is lifted up into the light and glory of God.

In this way Reformed theology certainly holds that God reveals Himself in creation, but not by some so-called "light of nature", and it certainly holds that God's revelation makes use of and is mediated through a creaturely objectivity, but it does not hold that an examination of this creaturely objectivity of itself can yield knowledge of God, for it can only yield a knowledge of the empirical world of nature. Reformed theology thus refuses to work with any doctrine of inherent likeness between creaturely being and Divine being, for such a doctrine inevitably means that the human knower interprets God in terms of his own inherent capacities and forms, while to make use of it as a systematic principle is to humanise divine truth, and to subordinate theology to anthropology, that is, in the language of St. Paul, to hold down the truth in unrighteousness, to change the glory of God into the likeness of corruptible man or to exchange the truth for a lie.

How far Reformed theology itself managed to escape this grave error is another story. Very soon in the Protestant Scholasticism of the seventeenth century the teaching of Calvin came to be amalgamated with what was thought to be a new brand of Aristotelianism, but it meant taking over first in a modified and then in a fuller form the old Roman doctrine that by nature man is intrinsically analogous to God and does not need to be made so by a special act of grace, and so by nature possesses in a relative degree what God possesses absolutely. When this was allied to the idea of a general Covenant of God with creation it began to operate as a systematic principle providing the general and universal conception of God in the light of which His special revelation of Himself in Christianity was interpreted. This laid the foundation within Protestant "orthodoxy" for the whole development of Neo-Protestantism in which man's self-understanding came to be employed as the ultimate criterion for the interpretation of all revelation and knowledge of God, and this meant the ultimate transmutation of theology into anthropology.

For a long time that development was hindered by the dominant place within Reformed theology of the doctrine of the transcendence of God and of a powerful Christology as well as by a scholastic doctrine of Holy Scripture. Such a stage we can discern in the theology of the Westminster Divines. But they were more involved in this development from another aspect of it, namely, through the clear-cut distinction between the Covenant of Grace and the Covenant of Works as the Covenant made with man in his creation apart from grace. That involved a separation between creation and redemption, so that creation came to be understood in terms of its own peculiar Covenant and laws and not in relation to the one all-embracing and historical Covenant of Grace. The Covenant of Works carried with it a doctrine of "the light of nature" and of a "religion" and "conscience" belonging to the natural man as such; and this was brought in from behind the Covenant of Grace to help interpret what was then called "the moral law", thus giving rise not only to the moralism and the moderatism of the eighteenth and nineteenth centuries, but to the widespread interpretation of "the Christian Religion" in terms of moral religion and moral judgements, that is to say, of the particular in terms of the universal already well-known to man because it is "revealed" in the roots of his human nature. Hence the invasion of humanism into modern Christianity. In our own day however this is being flung back by a massive return to Biblical theology, and a more Reformed and scientific approach to the proper object of theological studies.

(ii) *The Doctrine of Christ.* In Reformed theology the Covenant of Grace is regarded as completely fulfilled in Jesus Christ, so that the Covenant is not related to Christ as the general to the particular, but as the general to the concrete universal. In this way the Covenant idea is entirely subordinated to the doctrine of Christ, and cannot properly be erected into a masterful systematic principle within which alone Christ and His Gospel are to be interpreted. With the Incarnation the whole economy of the Covenant changes, for here in the Person and Work of Christ the Fatherly will of God for

communion with man is actualised in incarnation and reconciliation, and it is in the light of that fulfilled communion that
all else is to be interpreted. Hence Christian theology takes its
stand in the fulness of time *in Christ* and looks back from
there to interpret the previous history of the Covenant and the
creation itself with which it is bound up, and looks forward
to interpret the foundation and the life of the Church in the
economy of the Covenant in the last times between the first and
second Advents of Christ.

When the Covenant is actually fulfilled in Christ it takes a
new form in the New Covenant or Testament in which God
has poured out His Spirit, and through His Spirit pours out
His love into the hearts of His children and realises their relation
to Himself as sons of the heavenly Father. Here the bond of
the Covenant remains immutably steadfast, but as the inner
fulfilment of the Covenant God bestows upon us the Communion of the Spirit in which He not only restores us to
Himself but shares with us His divine life and love. The *outward form* which the Covenant takes in the new economy is
presented in the holy Sacraments as the signs which mark out
the sphere of God's self-revelation and self-giving to His people,
and the seals of His real presence and of His faithfulness in fulfilling in them all His promises, but the *inward form* which the
Covenant takes is the Communion of the Spirit, through
which we are taken up to share in the life and love of the
Father and the Son and the Holy Spirit. *The whole substance* of
this Covenant of Grace in its outer and in its inner form is
Jesus Christ Himself, so that it is in accordance with the Person
and Work of Christ, His Nature and His Mission, that the
whole life and faith of the people of God in the economy of the
New Covenant is to be understood. The New Covenant is in
the Body and Blood of *Christ*, the Communion of the Spirit
is Communion in the mystery of *Christ*, and the people of God,

in its covenanted communion in Christ through the Spirit, is the Body of *Christ*. Everything is directed toward *Christ* and in and through Him to the union and communion of Father, Son, and Holy Ghost.

For the Reformed Church dialogical theology is an essential element in this Communion of the Church with Christ, and cannot be abstracted from the Communion to be considered or carried on as an independent activity for its own sake. It belongs to the historical life and growth of the Church which we are to discuss below, but at this point we are concerned to discern the place which the doctrine of Christ has in the Church's systematic understanding and presentation of the Gospel. Once again we may set this forth in contrast to the teaching of the Roman Church.

(*a*) According to the Reformed Church the Roman Church had come to usurp the place occupied by Christ, so that the all-dominating concept in Roman theology was the institutional Church as sacramental organism full of grace and truth. The first and primary thing to be done in a recovery of true apostolicity and catholicity was to allow Christ to have His rightful place as sole Lord and Master in the life and theology of His Church. Along with this doctrine of *solus Christus,* and correlative to it, went the doctrines of *sola gratia, sola fide,* and *sola scriptura.*

This contrast may be drawn a little more and perhaps too sharply by saying that the Roman Church reinterpreted the Augustinian doctrine of *Totus Christus* (Christ and His members) to refer to the all-embracing *corpus mysticum,* that is to the Church in heaven and earth as embracing Christ and giving birth to Him, as it were, from age to age, and so mediating Him to the generations of His people. The Reformed Church interpreted the *Totus Christus* to refer to Christ who refuses to be without His Church but who in His sovereign grace assumes it into union and communion with Himself, as His servant, and as His body, and so gives the Church its life and place in history in the mission of the Gospel, that is, in the Communion of Grace reaching out to the Communion of Glory. The Church is in no sense an extension of the Incarnation, and is not therefore the continuation of the redemptive acts of God. The Church exists throughout history only through Communion with Christ bestowed upon it by the Spirit. The redemptive acts of God have been completely fulfilled in Christ, but Christ and His finished work, Christ clothed with His saving acts, remains enduring and everlasting reality, continuously and really present in the Church as its Lord and Master, giving it to participate in the fulfilled efficacy of His atoning reconciliation. Thus the *Heilsgeschichte* has been completed and only awaits its ultimate *epiphany* or *apocalypse* in the consummation of the Second Advent, but the Church has its life and mission on earth between the penultimate event of the *Heilsgeschichte* at Pentecost, and the ultimate event at the *Parousia*.

Certainly the *Heilsgeschichte* continued throughout the life of the people of God under the old form or economy of the Covenant of Grace, but with the Incarnation the redemptive acts were fulfilled and completed in Christ, so that with Christ the Covenant of Grace takes on a new economy or form, in which it does not operate through continuing redemptive acts but through the Communion of the Spirit once and for all poured out, through whom the people of God from generation to generation continue to participate in the once and for all events of the birth, life, death, resurrection and ascension of Christ. But the Communion of the Spirit means that the Church draws all its life and all its understanding from its sole source in the Person and finished work of Christ. Its whole existence and all its theology depend entirely upon its complete subordination to Him.

(*b*) This meant that the Reformed Church had to carry through a programme of reform in which all the doctrines inherited from the Mediaeval Church were subjected to Christological correction. The doctrine of the person of Christ had been fairly fully clarified in the Ecumenical Councils of the Church, although that had not been carried through into similar clarification of the saving work of Christ. But in whole areas of the Church's faith, there had been going on for hundreds and hundreds of years an unchecked and undisciplined development in doctrinal conceptions and formulations, unchecked and undisciplined except in so far as they did not detract from the growing importance and authority of the Church as the institutional sacramental organism and ark of salvation. Thus doctrines grew up out of the popular piety of the Dark and Middle ages, unchecked by critical reference to the doctrine of Christ, and only to be rationalised in the development of the systematic principles discussed above, until the whole understanding of salvation suffered through adjustment to the satisfactions of the natural man, and to a radical denial of the basic teaching of the New Testament Gospel.

The conflict arose over the question of an evangelical and faithful understanding of justification and grace, but behind all it was a struggle to give Jesus Christ His central place in the whole life and thought of the Church. It is in that light that the Reformation as a movement for theological reform is to be understood, that is, as a thoroughgoing criticism of all the received doctrines in the light of correspondence to the Gospel and coherence with the central doctrine of Christ, and a radical reforming and correcting of these doctrines by bringing them into obedient conformity to the doctrine of Christ. It was in that movement of faithfulness to Christ and His Gospel that Reformed theology came to understand both the nature of true theology and the nature of its systematic presentation

through consistent obedience to the Truth as it is in Christ
Jesus.

(c) What kind of system did this involve for Reformed
theology in its attempt to give coherent exposition of the
Gospel? It was inevitably a system determined by the nature
of Christ Himself. Thus as against the Mediaeval synthesis
which sought to give a coherent account of all being through
a system of rational ideas on the basis of a realist, philosophical
doctrine of universals, Reformed theology adopted as its
systematic principle consistent obedience to Jesus Christ. It
set aside any attempt to produce a logical system of ideas for
an attempt to expound the whole of evangelical doctrine,
which attained systematic form only as it allowed Christ to
impose Himself at every point upon the mind and teaching of
the Church. Thus theology was systematic only through
correspondence to the nature of Christ Himself, and through
a doctrinal coherence that grew out of correspondence with
the central doctrine of Christ. The "logic" was in Christ
before it was in the mind of the Church, for it is that objective,
material "logic" inherent in the unity of the Person of Christ,
that imposed itself upon the mind of the Church as it sought
disciplined conformity to Him in all its preaching and teaching
of the Gospel. Thus the pattern of the Church's knowledge
derives from the Form of Christ Himself, for He is the objective reality which the Church seeks to know and knows as it
orders all its knowing in accordance with the nature of the
object, that is in conformity to the nature of Christ.

Two important reservations must now be made with regard
to the deployment of the "logic" or "form" of Christ in the
interest of a systematic theology.

(a) The Church is confronted with the *mystery* of Christ,
and all its knowing must respect and conform to the nature
of that mystery, i.e. the mystery of Christ as God and Man in

the unity of one Person, the hypostatic union of divine and human natures in the one Person of the eternal Son and Word of God. It is the whole Christ in His divine and human natures who is the object of theological knowledge, and it is from the whole Christ that the pattern of that knowledge is derived, and upon the whole Christ that it ever reposes. Deployment of the form of Christ, or rather of obedient conformity to the form and nature of Christ as mystery, must leave room for mystery in the systematic presentation of theological knowledge—that means that in the nature of the case it must forego any kind of system that involves a principle of unbroken rational continuity behind its exposition, for that would be to "explain" the mystery, and so to "explain it away". Nothing could be more unscientific than to explain the mystery away, for scientific procedure requires of knowledge that it behaves consciously in terms of the whole nature of the object, so that if mystery reposes in the very nature of the object, corresponding mystery must characterise the nature of its knowledge. If mystery belongs to the nature of the object, it must also characterise the objectivity of the knowledge, for precisely therein lies its true rationality.

We can put that in another way by saying that the kind of connexion which theology must employ in its systematic presentation of Christ the Truth must correspond to the kind of connexion that inheres in His own nature as God and Man in the unity of One Person, that is to say, a transcendent connexion, a connexion in the Holy Spirit. It is that kind of transcendent connexion that a theology faithful to Christ must involve—and here once again we see how dialogical theology is a form of the Communion of the Spirit through which we participate in Christ and His Gospel. At no point can we allow purely logical connexion to displace the Communion of the Spirit. Logical connexion is involved, for the exposition of the whole Gospel must be made in an orderly way through the use of grammar and correct sequences in expression and thought, but these must never be allowed to determine the essential forms that theology shall take, nor allowed to cramp the expression of the Truth and so humanise and domesticate and distort it by thrusting it into the straight-jacket of fixed and necessary thought-forms. That would be an attempt to force the objective truth and being to conform to our thought about it, rather than to conform our thought to the objective truth and being we are seeking to understand and know.

(b) The "logic" or "form" of Christ in its subjective deployment by theology to give it a coherent pattern corresponding to that in the objective reality can never be absolutised or turned into an archetypal category by means of which all exposition of Christian doctrine is to be categorised or schematised. Thus even the "form" of Christ, truly and faithfully formulated as it may be, cannot be detached from Christ Himself and then used in any thoroughly schematic way in order to force the whole account of Christian teaching into a definite and necessary pattern. There can be no doubt that some formalism of this kind is as required as it is inescapable, but it must be handled only in abject subordination to the content, for its sole purpose is to serve the exposition of the content. If handled in the right way it can perform invaluable service in the interest of true consistency and genuine coherence.

In this way, for example, the doctrine of the hypostatic union, in so far as it is a faithful expression of the "form of Christ", can be deployed as a servant-category in the Christological correction of other doctrines such as the doctrine of the Sacraments. In such deployment it must be clearly and fully acknowledged that there is to be found in these other doctrines only a subsidiary reflexion of the "form of Christ", and that subsidiary reflexion consists in obedience and conformity to

Christ, and is in no sense a transference of "the hypostatic union" from the doctrine of the unique Person of Christ Himself to other areas of Christian teaching. The organic unity of all theological knowledge arises not from any categorisation and certainly not from the reduction of every other doctrine to Christology, but from consistent obedience to Christ. The way that the Word has taken in the Incarnation, life, death and resurrection and ascension of Jesus Christ, is the way in which God means us to apprehend and receive His Word. That is to say, it is in the obedient Humanity of Jesus Christ Himself that we are provided not only with the form of God's Revelation but with the true norm and pattern of all exposition of it. In this way dialogical theology participates in the obedience of the Son toward the Father, and is part of our continuing filial obedience to God in Jesus Christ.

How far did Reformed theology in the course of its development measure up to this conception of systematic theology? We have already seen how it revolted from the false objectivity and false systematisation of Mediaeval Roman theology, and we have noted that Reformed theology also had its period of great Schoolmen in the seventeenth and eighteenth centuries who tended to lapse back into the older categories and into the rational systematisation of Christian doctrine that they carried with them. It was in the course of that development that the *Federal Theology* arose, that is to say, a movement which tended to detach the conception of the Covenant and to make it into an abstract systematic principle. The Covenant came to be divided into two, the Covenant of Works made with the creation of man, and the Covenant of Grace which was expounded in terms of the Old and New Testaments or Covenants. But soon the Covenant of Grace came to be divided into two, the Covenant of Redemption concluded between the Father and the Son, and the Covenant of Grace concluded between the Father and the Son and all the elect in Him, through which the Covenant of Redemption was mediated in time to all who had an "interest" in it.

This is not the place to expound the Federal Theology—one of the best expositions of it in its earlier form will be found in the Westminster *Larger Catechism*. Our concern with it here is simply to note that in it the *federal idea* came to be deployed as a masterful systematic principle in the wrong way, for it provided the fixed scheme by means of which Christian teaching in the Reformed Church came to be categorised and systematised for more than two centuries. Calvin, Bullinger, and the Heidelberg theologians all made use of the conception of the Covenant of Grace (that was part of their faithfulness to the Holy Scriptures) but they never erected it into a masterful principle, for with them the Covenant, precisely through being fulfilled in Christ, is subordinated to Him. He is not only the Mediator but the Fulness of the Covenant, and it is Christology that occupies the masterful place in all their theology. But in historical "Calvinism", as Reformed theology came to be called, the Person of Christ frequently tended to be over-shadowed by the Covenant idea.

That is already apparent in the teaching of the Westminster Catechisms. We have noted how in them dialogical theology tends to become dialectical, while the proportion given to exposition of the doctrine of Christ is comparatively much smaller than ever in the Reformation documents, and the doctrine of the Spirit receives but scant attention. Clearly the systematic idea and its inherent rationalism left little room for the Holy Spirit. That is not very evident in the great champions of the Covenant theology, even in its developed post-Westminster form, namely, George and Patrick Gillespie, David Dickson and James Durham and Samuel Rutherford, for they operated with the powerful Christology and Soteriology embedded in the tradition of the Scottish Reformation, but later Christology came to receive comparatively such little attention that great reactions were provoked, such as in the work of Thomas Boston. However, it was only with the massive attention given to the historical Jesus in the nineteenth century that the hardened Covenant idea broke up, its formalistic grip upon Reformed theology was loosened, and the way was cleared for thoroughgoing obedience to Jesus Christ.

On the other hand, the employment of the Covenant idea by Reformed theology contributed to it, or confirmed within it, a two-fold characteristic. It gave Reformed theology a universal perspective, inasmuch as theology takes into account the whole economy of the Covenant before the Incarnation and the whole of its economy after the Incarnation. There can be no doubt that the Federal Theology achieved a magnificent and comprehensive unification of Biblical teaching. But it also gave theology its great historical perspective, as that which is concerned with the history of the people of God in Covenant relation and conversation with Him throughout all ages from the very beginning of the world to the present day, reaching out to the *Parousia*. It was indeed in the course of this development of the Federal Theology that there arose the conception of the *Heilsgeschichte* which has played such a significant part in modern Biblical theology.

(3) It belongs to the nature of theology to be *catholic*, that is to say, *historical* and *ecumenical*. This was an element of which Calvin was particularly conscious when he wrote his *Geneva Catechism*.

As we have just seen the relation of the doctrine of Christ to the one Covenant of Grace gives to theology its perspective in the whole history of God's people in Old Testament times and in New Testament times. It is essentially historical conversation between God and His Covenant people, i.e., dialogical theology that takes place in the historical Church. Theology is not correlative to a sacramental universe in the Mediaeval sense, but to the historical life of the Covenant people whom God has assumed into dialogue with Himself. It is within that Covenant that God imparts Himself and reveals Himself, entering into a subject-object relationship with man, and uses this subject-object relationship to be the sphere of His promise and fulfilment to the Covenant people.

This dialogue of God with Israel leads throughout the whole history of that people to its fulfilment in Christ who, as the Word of God made flesh, is both the embodiment of God's Word to man, and the embodiment of man's obedient Word to God. Within the dialogue of the divine-human life of Jesus, as the self-giving of God to man and the obedience of the Son to the Father, Revelation is both given and received, and as such is essentially historical and personal in nature. It is therefore communicable only in personal and historical ways. Thus from Christ there stretches out into history the Church as the people of the New Covenant, forming the sphere within time and space where God's fulfilled Revelation is met and heard and received and understood and obeyed in the Communion of the Spirit. Because this is the Revelation of historical and personal Truth it is met and received and understood and obeyed only through the historical and personal service rendered to it in the Church, that is only through historical mediation and tradition in the preaching and teaching of the Church. The Word and Truth of God in Christ remain transcendent to that historical mediation and tradition and can never be identified with it, nor can the Word and Truth of God suffer Himself to come under the authority of historical mediation and tradition, but He does not will to communicate Himself to us apart from that historical service.

This means that the theological hearing of the Word and

understanding of the Truth in each generation is always conditioned by the hearing and understanding of previous generations, the New Testament hearing and understanding by that of the Old Testament, the modern hearing and understanding by that of the fathers, in the Early Church, in the Middle ages, and in the Reformation. On the other hand each generation hears the Word and understands the Truth anew in direct confrontation with the Revelation once and for all fulfilled in Jesus Christ which takes place through the exegesis and preaching of the New Testament. Thus in each generation it is the whole historical Church that enters into conversation with God, not simply the modern generation, but that generation as conditioned by the hearing and understanding of all the generations that have gone before. Whether the modern generation is aware of it or not its hearing and understanding are predisposed and determined by the historical life and development of the Church. Therefore for the Church to engage in theological activity, blind to this conditioning, could only lead to self-deception on its part, and to loss in true objectivity through a failure to be critical of its own preconceptions.

In the light of this it is not difficult to see that by its very nature theology must be historical and ecumenical, and therefore catholic.

(i) Theology must engage in historical studies just because it is historical dialogue with God. It must seek to understand the mind of all the previous generations in the Church, and in the light of their hearing of the Word and understanding of the Truth hear the Word and seek to understand the Truth anew for itself. In this way it will be delivered from being a blind slave to traditional preconceptions, but in this way it will be enabled to engage in the growth and development of the whole Church in hearing and understanding, and will be better able to teach the rising generation and so perform the historical service required of it by God. It is only in this combination of historical theology and exegesis that the Church can be delivered from preaching its own private conceptions and carry through the disciplined self-criticism which frank and obedient conversation with God requires.

(ii) Theology must engage in ecumenical studies just because it is the dialogue of the one Covenant people with God, and therefore the exposition of theology as hearing of the Word and understanding of the Truth cannot be private to one particular Church any more than it can be private to one generation. By its very nature theology is concerned with the faith that is common to the whole Church in space and time, to the whole Church throughout history, but also to the whole Church living and working throughout the world today. A theology that is not essentially ecumenical is a contradiction in terms. We cannot engage in conversation with God by forgetting our fathers, or by separating ourselves from our brothers. It belongs to the very nature of the Church of Christ that we belong to one another, that each is imperfect without the other, that no one can comprehend the breadth and length and depth and height of the love of Christ except "with all saints". Thus each Church requires the aid of the other Churches in interpreting Holy Scripture and in the discipline of theological self-criticism and systematic exposition of the Gospel. Apart from the help it receives from other Churches each individual Church tends to choose its own private way, that is, to be heretical, but by engaging in theological conversation and communion with other Churches each Church is enabled to overcome its own private choice (*haeresis*) and to partake more and more of the fulness of Christ.

(iii) It is the combination of historical and ecumenical studies that is particularly valuable. Historical studies are necessary for the understanding of our brethren from another historical tradition, and yet it is only by engaging in conversation with those who belong to a Church that has embodied another historical tradition that we can fully understand the history of the Church. This applies not only to the separated Churches of the Evangelical world, but to the relations between so-called "Evangelical" and so-called "Catholic" Churches, between East and West, and indeed between the people of the New Covenant and the people of Israel who persist in living only according to the Old Covenant. It is thus that theological activity is enabled as fully as possible to engage still in conversation with the fathers of the Old Testament, with the Greek and Latin fathers of the ancient and mediaeval Church, and with the fathers of the Reformation in all its branches. We have to take very seriously the requirement of God to appear before Him, and to engage in conversation with Him, not alone, but with the whole company of God's people past and present. It is thus that it belongs to the very nature of theology to be essentially catholic, and it is enabled to be that by historical and ecumenical dialogue with the fathers and brethren alike.

IV. DOCTRINAL TENDENCIES

Every attempt to give systematic account of the Gospel is conditioned not only by what has preceded it but by the times in which it is carried out. Each Church and each movement in theology develops its own characteristics and peculiarities. Some of these are ephemeral, some are erroneous and have later to be resisted, and some are permanent contributions to the hearing and understanding of the Word by the whole Church. What are the doctrinal tendencies in these Catechisms of the Reformed Church, and what can we learn from examining and discussing them? Full answers to these questions can only be provided through long and careful study and through comparison of the teaching involved with that offered in other ages and Churches. We cannot undertake that in this introduction. It will be sufficient to discuss here only some of the main tendencies that appear in the Catechisms regarding the doctrines of God, of Christ, and of the Holy Spirit.

(1) *The Doctrine of God*
(i) *Contrast with Latin Theology*

The outstanding characteristic of the Reformed doctrine of God, in many ways, is its sharp departure from the Latin idea of God (*Deus sive natura*) which was taken up and after only partial correction given its great expression in the teaching of Thomas Aquinas. It was characteristic of this theology that it offered first a doctrine of God as the Supreme Being and Cause, infinite, eternal, omnipotent, omniscient, omnipresent, the Perfection of the Good, etc. This doctrine of God brought understanding of Him within a system in which the Supreme Being and creaturely being were brought together under the common concept of *being* and were therefore essentially analogous in being even with the infinite difference between them, God having His Being in a divine way, the creature having his in a creaturely way. This did involve some idea of an eternal positing or even co-existence of the creature with God's Being, so that if the *aeternitas mundi* could not be affirmed it could hardly be denied. Thus in spite of its efforts to assert the supreme and infinite nature of the Divine Being in His transcendence over all other being, in the last resort it was unable to make good this claim. The doctrine of the Being of God was formed through a philosophical ontology, and then the Biblical idea of God was added on to it, the God of the Old Testament, the *I am that I am*, and the Holy Trinity of the

New Testament. But here the *I am that I am* was interpreted only in terms of the aseity of God, and not also in terms of the God who alone can name Himself, and who is not known or knowable apart from His self-naming or self-revealing, while the doctrine of the Trinity had to be made to fit in with the basic ontology through alleged *vestigia Trinitatis* in creaturely being. The result was that the God thus conceived was a prisoner of a general concept of being. Even as First Cause He could not be conceived apart from His effects, but only as bound with them in the same conceptual system of necessary relations. Thomism may well be the most perfect system of ideas yet constructed but it is certainly the most determinist of all Christian theologies, resembling very closely the Arabian doctrine of God from which St. Thomas learned so much.

It was from this "frigid doctrine of the Sorbonne" that Calvin found himself in full revolt, as he turned to the Biblical Revelation, to the "familiar God" of the Old Testament and to the God and Father of Jesus Christ, and sought to know Him not through being and caused effects but in the way He actually has made Himself known in His revealing and reconciling work. The Reformed doctrine of God was not without its problems, as we shall see, but it did seek to be faithful, in its knowing of God, to the way in which He has willed to be known—that is the approach which characterises its whole theology.

When we turn to the teaching of these Catechisms, we find that most of them, which expound the Faith on the basis of the Apostles' Creed, begin right away with the doctrine of the Father, Son, and Holy Spirit. Why is it that we must begin in this way? To that the answer of the Heidelberg Catechism is clear and normative. "Because God has so revealed Himself in His Word that these three distinct persons are the one, eternal

God" (p. 73). In other words, the God of this theology, is the God who has revealed Himself in His Word, or as Craig put it, who has made Himself known to us through His promise and works (pp. 107f.). Calvin states explicitly that it is knowledge of God in Jesus Christ which is the foundation for faith (p. 7). God is the One who reveals Himself through His Word, Promises and Works, in Jesus Christ, so that we know Him as the God and Father of Christ, and as our Saviour. Because what we know of Him arises out of this His action, His self-revelation, His own presence in His Word and works, Calvin preferred to speak of His properties or perfections rather than His "attributes". It is not we who attribute these properties to God, but He who manifests them as the perfections of His own Person. Thus the whole problem of nominalism v. universalism that dogged Mediaeval theology, and even the subtle semi-nominalism in the Thomist doctrine of the divine attributes, is cut away in this doctrine of the living acting God who has come to us in Jesus Christ. Behind all those questions with which Mediaeval theology wrestled lay the problem of adding the Biblical revelation of God on to its philosophical conception of the Supreme Being, which ought never to have arisen.

(ii) *God in Christ*

In contrast, then, to Mediaeval theology, the Reformed doctrine of God can be set out in four main lines. (i) God is He who is known only through His Word, who is indeed unknowable except as He gives Himself to be known, but who has as a matter of fact condescended to reveal Himself to us familiarly in our human speech and in our creaturely world in such a way that we are drawn into conversation, that is personal relation, with Him. (ii) This is essentially the living, active, Creator God of the Biblical Revelation, who made the world out of nothing, so that all creaturely reality is utterly distinct from Him, though entirely dependent upon His goodness for its existence and being and order and goal. As such He is utterly free, transcendent and incomparable in His Divine Life and Being. He really is the Supreme Eternal, Infinite Being, and reveals Himself as such through His active intervention and works in creation and redemption. (iii) This God, is "a God in Covenant", as the Westminster *Larger Catechism* admirably put it (p. 207). He is not a God who wills to live alone but who has created man for communion with Himself and bound man in Covenant to Him, Himself entering into Covenant promises which He actively fulfils within creation and history. He is the God who intervenes in history, who is mightily active in the Covenant people, as well as the nations of the world, in the fulfilment of His redemptive purposes. (iv) He is the God and Father of Jesus Christ, the Saviour, to whom we in Christ may pray, "Our Father". It is this knowledge of God in Christ which governs all, which tells us that God is eternally Father, Son, and Holy Spirit, so that all the perfections of God are of the Three Persons of the Godhead, so that God's relation to the creature, in creation and in redemption, is the relation of this God who became incarnate and creaturely man, and yet remains very God on the throne of His Kingdom. There is no God except He who has shown us His Face in Jesus Christ, so that we cannot go behind the back of Christ to find God, or know anything about Him apart from this God, for there is no other God than this God. Here then, it is not some prior ontology, but Christology which is all-determining in our knowledge of God.

(iii) *Implications of the Reformed Doctrine of God*

Three issues arise out of this doctrine of God which must be noted.

(a) If God is really the Creator who created the world out of nothing as a creaturely reality utterly distinct from Himself, then the creaturely world, the whole world of nature, is entirely contingent upon God, and it cannot be known through knowledge of the Divine Being. In other words the co-relation or proportional relation between God and creaturely being, not only means that we cannot know God through an examination of His image embedded in the creaturely being of man as such, but that we cannot understand the creaturely processes of this world deductively from knowledge of the eternal, divine Reality. Hence nature can only be known through the observation and study of nature. This gave great impetus to the rise of empirical science in the modern sense. Reformed theology worked with a very clearly drawn distinction between a realm of grace in which God alone is Agent—that was defined by the doctrine of *sola gratia, sola fide*—and a realm of nature or creation in which man was appointed by God to have dominion, and to work with God as His partner. This helped to give rise to the activism of man in post-Reformation times, i.e. to the concept of *homo faber*.

This provided Reformed theology with both a problem and a corrective. It provided it with a problem, because the growing empiricism in all knowledge of created realities tended to extend its dominion over the realm of grace as well as the realm of nature, and so to subject theological truths to empirical assessment and criticism. That was of course to presuppose that empirical science was the only valid form of science. Now by its doctrine of creation out of nothing, and of the transcendence of God, and by renouncing the false idea that creaturely being is intrinsically analogous to divine being, Reformed theology renounced the attempt to prove the existence of God. In the course of the seventeenth century, however, Reformed theology began to change its ground by taking up again, as we

have noted, the rationalistic teaching of the Mediaeval schoolmen, and so laid itself open to these attacks from the empiri-
cists. In point of fact all they did, as we see so clearly in David
Hume's *Dialogues concerning Natural Religion*, was to destroy a
bad theology. But actually it was a very serious thing for
Reformed theology in that course of development in which
more and more it came to use man's self-understanding as its
criterion for theological knowledge. In the long run, however,
this empirical attack could only have a good result: it helped
to provide Reformed theology with a corrective. In other
words, it drove Reformed theology back upon its proper
object, and helped it to understand the proper procedure in all
scientific knowledge, the conformity of the reason to the
nature of the object, and so it helped Reformed theology to
find its principle of integration not in some general principles
of the human reason or some supposed norms or laws immanent in reason, but in the nature of the object, the incarnate
Word of God, that is, God's self-objectification for us in the
Humanity of Jesus Christ.

(*b*) How seriously did Reformed theology take the change
in the doctrine of God? How far did it allow its doctrine of
God to be determined by the doctrine of the Incarnation?
This is an old problem, although it became more acute at the
Reformation. Thus patristic theology, with some notable
exceptions, was dominated by the conception of the immutability of God which proved a real hindrance to it in understanding the atonement as act of God. Likewise Mediaeval
theology from Peter Lombard to Thomas Aquinas found it
difficult to take with entire seriousness the doctrine that God
the eternal Word *became* flesh, for how can the Eternal *become*?
Thus when it came to the doctrine of the atonement it did not
teach that God Himself in His deity descended into our death,
but that Christ suffered and died only in His humanity which

God used instrumentally while holding His Deity back. That may be consistent with the Mediaeval doctrine of God, but when that doctrine is given up for an essentially *Christian* doctrine, that is for a doctrine of God as revealed wholly and perfectly in Christ, so that we are to look for no other God than this one God who is found wholly in Him, how is the atonement to be construed? In reply to that we may cite an answer from *Calvin's Catechism* to question 68 (p. 15f.). "We must hold that it was according to His human nature that He was in that extremity: and that in order to allow this, His Deity held itself back a little, as if concealed, that is, did not show its power."

This is susceptible of two interpretations. It may mean only that the Deity and the divine action were hidden in the depth of humiliation Christ suffered, but it may also import a Nestorian tendency at this point, and really mean that it was not ultimately in His divine nature but only in His human nature that Christ suffered and offered Himself a sacrifice for us. There are undoubtedly tendencies in this direction in Calvin's thought, and they are understandable in view of Calvin's proper anxiety to teach that the Humanity of Christ was essential and integral and not merely instrumental in our salvation, but it is difficult to hold that in the last resort Calvin denied that the divine nature of the Son did not actively participate in the work of our salvation in offering atoning sacrifice. It was God Himself, God incarnate, who took our place, although that is necessarily veiled by His entry into our human death and human estate under judgement. The real test may be found in answer to the question whether Christ rose again from the dead by His own power, or whether He was only raised from the dead by the Father. Calvin does not deny that He was raised from the dead by the Father but he has no hesitation in stating also that He rose again Himself as

Conqueror. At this point, however, it is *The Larger Catechism* which says unambiguously "He rose again from the dead the third day by His own power" (p. 194). Be that as it may, there is clearly a problem here for Reformed theology. If we are to take the change in the doctrine of God demanded by the Incarnation seriously, then we must interpret "God was in Christ reconciling the world unto Himself" to mean, not only that God was at work *in man*, but that God came to work *as man*. This "humanity" of God is most apparent in the Catechisms of John Craig.

(c) A cognate issue in the doctrine of God is that of *abstraction*. This is particularly evident with regard to the doctrine of the divine decrees. Is election to be conceived as an act of God within His own eternity only in abstraction from the existence and life of Jesus Christ, or is it to be conceived only and fully in Jesus Christ? Again, there is a real problem here in regard to the teaching of Calvin. Karl Barth, for example, has not done full justice to Calvin in accusing him of abstraction at this point.

He has not taken into sufficient account the following. (a) Calvin not only thinks of election as in Christ, but thinks of Christ as the *Agent* and the *Matter* or *Substance* of election. (b) Calvin resisted the idea that election reposes upon some sort of darkness behind the revealed God, and therefore taught that at no point is natural theology more harmful than here, in its attempt to know God behind the back of Christ. Election reposes upon the mystery of God as revealed in Christ, but mystery there remains, and therefore we must not seek to rationalise it. (c) The positive will of God is unambiguously His will for our salvation. It is the nature of the Light to enlighten, not to blind, and of the Gospel to bring life, not to slay. Christ came to save, not to condemn. If therefore men are blinded by the Light, slain by the Gospel, or condemned by Christ, that can only be regarded, as Calvin put it times without number, as an "accidental" or "adventitious" result. There may appear to be a two-fold will of God for salvation and reprobation, but at the *Parousia* we shall see that there was only one divine will for our salvation. (*d*) We cannot, therefore, think of election and reprobation in any kind of equilibrium. In election we lay all the weight upon "the hidden cause", the grace of God, and not upon "the manifest cause", the faith of man; but in reprobation we lay all the weight upon "the manifest cause", man's rebellion or unbelief, and not upon "the hidden cause", the action of God. This deliberate unbalance means that Calvin refused to think out the problem of election logically or systematically. In the nature of the case that cannot be done without falsification. (*e*) Calvin therefore refused to agree that the negative result, condemnation or reprobation, should be inserted into Creed or Confession or Catechism where only the positive affirmations of faith belong. Nor does he obtrude the doctrine of election into the Catechism. It only comes in for incidental mention. But when all that is said in justice to Calvin, it must be admitted that there is a problem here, particularly in his polemical works in defence of predestination, for there is a tendency in them toward abstracting the work of God in election from the work of Christ. At any rate there is no outright identification of the eternal decree of God with His eternal Word. But what decree of God is there which is not also His Word, and the very Word who was made flesh in Jesus Christ?

It is in regard to this doctrine of election that we do note a process of abstraction developing in the Reformed doctrine of God; i.e. a doctrine of God tends to be formulated independently and then there has to be added on to it the knowledge of God revealed in the Person and Work of Christ. In the longer Catechism of John Craig election has a fuller place than in the

Catechisms of Geneva or Heidelberg, but it is election as taught by the *Scots Confession* of 1560 with which even Karl Barth did not disagree. In Craig's doctrine of God there is little or no tendency to abstraction, for he really thinks of God as He who has turned toward us in Jesus Christ and given Himself to us in union and communion with Him. This was the tradition up to the *Westminster Catechisms*, when a change was introduced into the doctrine of God. Here we have quite clearly and definitely a combination with the Reformed doctrine of God of more abstract conceptions derived from scholasticism, with correspondingly strong stress upon God's eternal and immutable decree.

It was in line with this element of abstraction that the Post-Westminster teaching (although it had earlier roots) made so much of the distinction between the Covenant of Redemption and the Covenant of Grace already noted above. That very distinction is a classic instance of the abstraction we are discussing, for it removes God's part in salvation into an area beyond time within God Himself, and makes use of a separate although related Covenant of Grace for its application within time. For this serious mistake some compensation might have been provided if there had been developed an adequate doctrine of the Holy Spirit, but that is just what is lacking, although the procession of the Spirit from the Son as well as from the Father is maintained. There can be little doubt that the conception of God in the Westminster theology suffers from some of the serious faults in the pre-Reformation teaching. Its "God" appears to lack the kindness, humanity, familiarity of the "God" of the Reformation, for tendencies toward impersonality, abstraction and even harshness are to be noted in the Westminster conception of God, although in the Catechisms there is a grand sense of the Holiness, Majesty, and Faithfulness of God coupled with that of His mercy to the elect.

(2) The Doctrine of Christ

Reformed theology, as we have seen, deliberately returned to the ancient Catholic doctrine of Christ and made it quite central. The doctrine of the Ecumenical Councils, notably of Chalcedon, was not taken over without further Biblical study and correction, notably in seeking to interpret the Person and Work of Christ closely together. Here for the first time since Athanasius and Cyril we have a really adequate doctrine of atonement, but here the *unio hypostatica* comes to be reinterpreted in the light of a *communicatio operationum* and greater stress is laid upon the *Mediation* of Christ. Care was taken to repudiate and avoid all the classical errors in Christology on both sides of the Chalcedonian fence, that is to say, anything that detracts from the perfection of His Deity, the perfection of His Humanity, or the Unity of His Person. In that development Calvin's doctrine of the atoning work of Christ, and the place he discerned in it of the obedience of Christ the Servant-Son, must be reckoned one of the greatest contributions to the whole history of Christology. It is in that rich inheritance that all these Catechisms came to be written. All that we can do here is to note some of the outstanding features of this Christology as a guide to its further study.

(i) Christ clothed with His Gospel

In a recent volume Professor G. S. Hendry has discussed "the problem of finding an integral place for the human life of the incarnate Lord within the framework of orthodoxy" which has haunted Reformed and Protestant theology since the time of Calvin (*The Gospel of the Incarnation*, pp. 35ff.). He directs attention to Calvin's awareness of this problem in the Apostles' Creed and the answer he gave to it in his *Geneva Catechism*. "Why do we go immediately from His birth to His death, passing over the whole history of His life? Because nothing is said here about what belongs properly to the substance of our redemption" (p. 13). Dr. Hendry shows that Calvin was not satisfied with this answer and points to three further facts in Calvin's teaching: that the whole life of Christ was to be regarded "as a perpetual Cross", that He made atonement by "the whole course of His obedience", and that "the teaching office of Christ" belongs to His saving work. This part of Calvin's answer has to be understood from his interpretation of Christ's life and work as that of the *Servant*, for it is essentially the servant-concept which, in Calvin's thought, integrates our understanding of His saving life and ministry. "From the moment when He assumed the form of a servant, He began, in order to redeem us, to pay the price of deliverance" (*Inst*. 2. 16. 5). To that we may also add one other factor which receives very full and powerful exposition in Calvin's writings, namely, the saving efficacy of the prayer-life of Jesus, a much neglected element in later doctrines of the saving work of Christ. In these Catechisms, however, that comes out most strongly in the teaching of John Craig who links together Christ's "obedience, prayer, and everlasting sacrifice" (p. 111).

There is another important element, however, which we must also consider in answer to this question, *the relation of Christ's human nature to our salvation*. Here we turn to Calvin's often repeated expression, "Christ clothed with His Gospel", "Christ clothed with His promises", "Christ and His graces", etc. By the "clothing" of Christ, Calvin referred not only to the flesh which He assumed, but to all that He in our flesh received for us and all that He in our flesh did for us, and therefore to what He was in Himself in the constitution of His incarnate Person and Life. This has to be understood ontically and noetically.

Ontically, the "clothing" of Christ refers to His flesh, to the fact that it was in His flesh (our humanity which He assumed) that He was anointed, and in His flesh that He has accomplished all the parts of our salvation. Thus in virtue of His incarnation and His saving work Christ has eternal life and salvation residing in Himself, that is, even in His human nature. Divine life resides in Him, and all the Blessings of God reside in Him, while it is in His human nature that He has perfected obedience and righteousness, that is in our human nature assumed by Him, so that our disobedience in human nature is redressed in Him. It is out of Christ's fulness of grace and truth, of life and righteousness, that we all receive. In this teaching Calvin followed very closely in the steps of Irenaeus and Athanasius. It is here that we have laid down the basis for a proper understanding of the saving significance of the Humanity of Christ. Calvin did not work that out in the detail that we would like, who have learned to concentrate so much attention upon the historical Jesus, but while the whole movement of research into the historical Jesus was ultimately unable to see the saving significance of the Humanity of Jesus, we do have that significance clearly and definitely laid down in the foundations of Reformed theology. It is however right here that we are faced with the deepest *scandalon*, that by His human nature Christ exerts saving influence upon us. This was the very point in Calvin's teaching so strenuously rejected by some of the greatest champions of the Westminster theology, such as William Cunningham. But that was equally a *scandalon* to the Liberal theology which talked so much about the historical life of Jesus. This, however, is fundamental to the teaching of the Reformation Catechisms. Christ is not only the Author and Agent of our salvation, but is in Himself, even in His human nature, the Source and Substance of it; therefore every one of the saving acts of Christ must carry with it, in our understanding, the whole substance of Christ's human life and nature. But that brings us to look at it from the other angle.

Noetically, the "clothing" of Christ refers to His promises, to His message which is proclaimed not only in Word but by His life and His deeds in the flesh. He does not come to us in the flesh apart from His own Word and self-revelation, or apart from all He both promises in His grace and actually fulfils in His love on our behalf. Christ cannot be separated from His mission of Revelation and Reconciliation or His Mediatorship, and therefore we cannot know Him "naked", as it were, without His "clothing". The only Christ we know is Christ clothed with His Gospel, and that is Christ with all His human life and historical acts and His self-communication to us through them. He the eternal Son condescended to enter into our lowly humanity, and so accommodated Himself to our weakness, and within our weakness He revealed Himself and fulfilled His promises of reconciliation. Thus His very flesh, His whole human life, was informed and determined from the start by the promises of revelation and reconciliation which He came to fulfil. It is only as clothed in that flesh that we encounter Him, and only as clothed in that flesh that we can know Him.

Thus the ontic and noetic aspects of this "clothing" cannot be separated from one another in our theology. It is precisely in that very togetherness of Christ and His graces in the constitution of His own Person as the incarnate Son and Saviour that we have the foundation for a full and proper Christology. Had Reformed theology remained faithful to this basic teaching, it is doubtful if it would ever have been at a loss in facing so many of the Christological problems of later times.

(ii) *The Merits of Christ*

This is a conception that finds not a little place in these Catechisms, but there is more to it than immediately meets the eye. We turn again first to Calvin, who was aware of the difficulty it raised. He recognised that if we set Christ over against the divine justice we could not speak even of Him as meriting the divine favour and so of putting God into His debt. The merit of Christ is to be understood only as correlative to His election, that is to say, only under the supreme decision of God's grace manifested in the assumption of our humanity. Within the Incarnation considered as pure act of God's mercy and condescension, the merit of Christ refers to the fact that in His human life and work He was not merely the instrument of God in our salvation, but was Himself the active Agent and Prince of it. In other words, by the term *merit* Calvin sought to give the Humanity of Christ its full and integral and essential place in His life and work as Mediator.

The older Reformed theology expounded this through a consideration of the active obedience of Christ, His passive obedience and His sanctification of human nature through union with His divine nature. (See *The Mystery of the Lord's Supper*, by Robert Bruce, pp. 33f.)

(1) By the *active obedience* of Christ is meant the positive fulfilment in the whole life of Jesus of His Sonship. From the beginning to the end He maintained a perfect filial relation to the Father in which He yielded to Him a life of utter love and faithfulness, and in which He received and laid hold of the love of the Father. This active obedience was therefore His own loving self-offering to the Father in our name and on our behalf, and also His own faithful appropriation of the Father's Word and Will in our name and on our behalf.

(2) By the *passive obedience* of Christ is meant His submission to the judgement of the Father upon our sin which He assumed in our Humanity and in His complete identification of Himself with us, in order that He might bear it in our stead and in our person. This is the passion He endured in the expiation of our sins, but it is also His willing acceptance of the divine verdict on our rebellious humanity.

(3) *By the sanctification of human nature* through union in Christ with His divine nature, Reformed theology asserts the saving significance of the Incarnation. In the very heart of Christ's atoning work we are concerned with the union He wrought out in His birth, life, death and resurrection between the human nature He assumed from us and His holy divine nature. That concerns the reconciling and sanctifying work carried on throughout the whole course of His human and historical life, but it also concerns the union wrought in the assumption of our fallen and estranged humanity which He sanctified in His very act of assuming it. Thus the incarnation, even in the narrower sense of that term, is redeeming event from the very birth of Jesus. In His holy assumption of our unholy humanity His purity wipes away our impurity, His Holiness covers our uncleanness, His divine life heals our corruption.

The distinction between the active and passive obedience of Christ is not emphasised in Reformed theology in order to distinguish or separate them but in order to insist that the whole course of Christ's active obedience is integral to His work of reconciliation, and that atonement cannot be limited to His passive obedience, that is to His passive submission to the penalty for our sin inflicted on Christ in His death. The active and passive obedience do not differ in regard to time for both extend to the very beginning of the Incarnation, to the birth of Jesus, and both reach out to its fulfilment in His death and resurrection. Nor do they differ with regard to their subject, for they are both manifestations of the one obedience of the Son of God in our humanity. They involve one another mutually in the unity of the one Person and in the unity of the whole life of Christ. This mutuality is very important, for it means that in our justification we have imputed to us not only the passive righteousness of Christ in which He satisfied for our

sins in suffering in His death on the Cross, but the active righteousness of Christ in which He positively fulfilled the Father's
Will in an obedient human *life*. In other words, justification
means not simply the non-imputation of our sins through the
pardon of Christ, but positive sharing in His human righteousness. We are saved not only by the *death* of Christ which He
suffered for our sake, but also by His *life* which He lived for
our sake.

Now in this active and passive obedience we are to think of
Christ as dealing with our *actual sins* through the atoning
exchange of His life and death and resurrection, but we cannot
do that without also thinking of His incarnational union of
our human nature with His divine nature as dealing with our
original sin, or as sanctifying our fallen human nature through
bringing it into healing and sanctifying union with holy
divine nature. This is also supremely important, for it is only
through this union of our human nature with His divine nature
that Jesus Christ gives us not only the negative righteousness of
the remission of sins but to share in the positive righteousness
of His obedient and loving life lived in perfect filial relation on
earth to the heavenly Father. If we neglect this essential element
in the obedience of the Son, then not only do the active and
passive obedience of Christ fall apart in our theology, but we
are unable to understand justification in Christ as anything
more than merely forensic non-imputation of sin. Moreover
if we neglect this essential element we are unable to see the
Humanity of Jesus in its saving significance, that is, to give the
whole life of the historical Jesus its rightful place in the doctrine
of atonement and recreation. It is necessary for us, therefore,
to give the fullest consideration to the place of the union of the
human and divine natures in the Being and Life of the Incarnate Son, for it is that saving and sanctifying union, in which
we are given to share, that belongs to the very substance of

our faith. In other words, what we are concerned with is the *filial life* which the Son lived out in our humanity in perfect holiness and love toward the Father and toward men, achieving that in Himself in assuming our human nature into oneness with Himself, and on that ground giving us to share in it, thus providing us with a fulness in His own obedient Sonship from which we may all receive.

(iii) *The Threefold Office of Christ*

An examination of the language used in the Old Testament and in the New Testament to express redemption shows that three major conceptions of redemption lie together in Biblical teaching, all very closely related, overlapping in their significance and converging in their fulfilment in the work of the one Mediator and Saviour.

(*a*) Redemption by the mighty hand of God and in sheer grace, at once out of the oppression of evil and out of judgement and death. But the mighty hand is the holiness of Christ, His obedience unto the death on the Cross. The mighty hand is the weakness of Christ, His blood shed freely for us on our behalf. Here the stress is laid on the nature of the redeeming act, and it is the *dramatic* aspect of atonement that is uppermost, the active and victorious intervention of God in rescuing and saving us.

(*b*) Redemption by an expiatory sacrifice for sin made in the offering of Christ's life for our life in obedience to the divine Will and Mercy. Christ is both the Priest and the Sacrifice in the one Lamb-and-Servant of God, shedding His blood in costly ransom or expiation, in order to remove the barrier of guilt and enmity between man and God and God and man, and so to effect reconciliation in a holy communion between them. Here the stress is upon the mode of the atoning redemption and on the restoration to fellowship with God that it effects. Here it is what we might call the *cultic-forensic* aspect of atonement that is uppermost, the priestly and judicial work of propitiation through sacrifice.

(c) Redemption through a Kinsman-Advocate, who acts out of a blood-tie or a covenant bond, or out of His pure love forging such a bond in Himself. Thus the Son of God by His Incarnation in our humanity makes Himself our brother-man, constitutes us His flesh and blood, and in His own body and blood forges the bond of the New Covenant, through all of which He takes over responsibility for us, stands in our place, takes our lost cause on Himself, makes sure our redemption in Himself, and so delivers us out of bondage into the freedom and inheritance of the sons of God. Here the stress is upon the nature of the Redeemer and our kinship with Him, and it is the *incarnational* or *ontological* aspect of atonement that is uppermost, that is the relation of our salvation to the nature and constitution of the Person of the Redeemer.

None of these three aspects anywhere stands alone in the Biblical teaching. They all overlap and depend on one another, and when one is removed or understressed, or one is over-stressed, the balance and meaning of the whole is gravely impaired or even destroyed. Now it was in correspondence to these three aspects of Christ's reconciling and atoning work that Reformed theology saw the saving import of the three aspects of Christ's life discussed above, His active and passive obedience, and His Incarnational sanctification of our human nature, and in that very order of correspondence. It was also in correspondence with both of these that it understood the doctrine of Christ's *Threefold Office* as King and Priest, and Prophet, but here too we must think of these three offices as overlapping each other and depending on each other, and never think of one without the other. And here again under-stress or overstress of one or more impairs and may even destroy the significance of the whole. At this point, however, Reformed theology usually preferred to consider the work of Christ in a different order, as the work of Prophet, Priest and King.

(a) The *Prophetic Office* cannot be understood only in the narrow sense of His teaching, although His teaching is an essential element of His atoning work, inasmuch as revelation and reconciliation cannot for a moment be separated from one another. The Prophetic Office refers above all to Christ's work as the Word made flesh, as He who brings the Word of the Father to bear upon man in his darkness and sin, but also as He who from within our darkness and alienation bears the Word before God, and in our name gives an account to God in the confession of our sin, and in acceptance of the Father's verdict upon us, and therefore also in hearing and appropriating God's Word of pardon and acceptance, all for us. He is not therefore only the Word of God to man, but the Word of man to God in perfect response and obedience, and in that two-fold capacity He is our Advocate. And yet He is this Advocate not because He steps in as a third party from outside, but because He is really and truly one of us, and very Man, our Kinsman, as well as really and truly one with God, and very God, God's Son. It is thus in the integration of the Prophetic Office of Christ and His incarnational union with us that the Prophetic Office is to be understood. When these have not been thought together there has inevitably been a failure to conserve the full integrity of Christ's saving work as Prophet, and His judicial work in passive obedience has been set over against His incarnational redemption in a false antithesis. The work of Christ cannot be divorced from His person. If the prophetic ministry of Christ is divorced from His person as the divine King, then the doctrine of His work quickly degenerates into some form of Socinian heresy or into some merely subjective theory of the atonement. On the other hand, if the element of incarnational redemption is divorced either from the teaching or priestly work of Christ, that is from His Word or Sacrifice, or both, it soon becomes transmuted into some doctrine of deification through union with deity, and that may take a Roman line of mystical absorption in God or a Protestant line of idealistic identity between the divine and the human. For the mystical and rationalistic mind the onto-logical aspect of redemption is particularly difficult, because when held properly together with the other aspects, it involves the finality of atonement as inseparably bound up with the particular and contingent which has definite place and date in time, in the historical Jesus. Therefore attempts by rationalists and mystics are made to reinterpret the historical particularity of Jesus symbolically. It is an offense to them that our salvation should depend upon the historical Being of Jesus, but this belongs to the very essence of the Christian faith.

(b) *The Priestly Office* of Christ cannot be understood in a narrow sense as referring only to His sacrificial death without serious error. If the priestly aspect of redemption is divorced from the prophetic and incarnational aspect, it degenerates into a legal and cultic fiction with no basis in actual existence and reality and therefore is without relevance to our actual humanity. Moreover if it were not grounded in the constitution of Christ as the divine King, the mighty Son of God become incarnate to deliver us out of pure love and grace, the priestly aspect of atonement would degenerate into a pagan notion of placating an angry God, and dwindle into a ritualistic superstition. This aspect of the saving work of Christ does involve a piacular act in which God reconciles Himself to man and reconciles man to Himself in Jesus Christ. That is to say, through the expiatory blood of Christ God draws near to man in mercy and forgiveness and draws man near to Himself in an unbreakable union of love and communion. But strike out of it the pure act of God, the sheer intervention in divine grace, strike out of it the primary fact that it is God Himself condescending to provide the sacrifice in His own free act of Incarnation, and it becomes a Pelagian sacerdotalist conception of appeasing an angry God through human mediation and human sacrifice. It is only on the basis of the divine act and of the incarnational union that the priestly work of Christ has its proper place, and then it must be construed not only as an act which God does for us *as God*, but also as an act which God does for us *as Man*.

It is the whole human life of Jesus, in His active as well as His passive obedience, that we are to see as the one perfect and sufficient sacrifice for the sins of the world once and for all offered through the eternal Spirit to the Father. Because it is rooted in His whole human life the priestly work of Jesus is to be understood not only as His self-sanctification and self-oblation to the Father, but as His redemptive impetration in obtaining the Father's acceptance of us and the Father's blessing upon us. It is on this very ground, as Mediator and Intercessor and Advocate, that He bestows upon us what He in our Humanity has received in the fulness of the Spirit. This mediation of the Spirit is an essential part of His atoning work in fulfilment of His Priestly Office. Pentecost is the mighty act of the risen and ascended High Priest who has opened the Kingdom of Heaven for all believers, opened a new and living way in His flesh to the Father, and opened the door for the pouring out of the riches of the divine Life and Love upon men.

(*c*) The *Kingly Office* of Christ is His Office as *Christus Victor*, but this cannot be isolated to form a so-called classical doctrine of the atonement without parody and depreciation of the other offices, and therefore without serious misinterpretation of Christ's Kingly Office. The idea of *Christus Victor* is easily related to the incarnational aspect or redemption, as we see in a number of patristic writers, but apart from the expiatory and forensic elements in the atoning work of Christ, it cannot avoid the charge of ultimate dualism, e.g. in the notion of ransom to the devil. In the Biblical teaching, redemption is both out of the judgement of God and out of an alien and oppressive power, which for its part is brought under the divine judgement. The signal instance of that in the Old Testament is the redemption of Israel out of Egypt, i.e. out of the tyrannical oppression of Pharaoh and from the avenging angel of death. Deliverance out of the former is only possible through sacrificial redemption from the judgement of God.

In the teaching of the New Testament, redemption is likewise regarded as both out of bondage of guilt and out of the thraldom of evil powers, but out of the latter only through the former. This is particularly evident in St. Paul's conception of redemption from the bondage of the law, that is, not from the law as such but from the régime of the law as it is used by sin. The law, which expresses God's Will, is Holy and exacts from us the judgement of death, and yet this same law can become an oppressive tyranny, for the powers of evil use its accusations against the sinner to bind him all the more in the slavery of sin. In this way the law becomes the strength of sin, as St. Paul put it. But when man is put in the right with the law, the law can no longer be the strength of sin, for sin cannot make use of the accusations and judgements of the law. Therefore redemption that involves the expiation of guilt and brings justification not only renders man free from the law but thereby also emancipates him from the thraldom of evil. This is especially important because it brings together the notions of redemption as expiation before God's holy Will and redemption out of the powers of darkness, in such a way that the whole notion of ransom to the evil powers, or ransom to the devil, is impossible and inadmissible. Here in this Biblical teaching, evil is revealed as having no right of its own over man, but to have usurped the right of the law of God and through that right to have robbed God of His inheritance in His people and His people of their inheritance in God. Therefore when a man is redeemed and justified through the blood of Christ, he is free from the power of evil, and the idea of ransom to the devil, in the nature of the case, cannot properly arise.

How then did Jesus fulfil this Kingly Office which was at once the work of *Christus Victor* and of *Christus Victima*? He overcame the powers of darkness by His Holy Life. Through His perfect holiness and obedience sin had no power over Him and therefore it was as the Holy One of God that He invaded the domain of evil and redeemed us out of the power of darkness. Here the mighty hand of God was the weakness of Jesus, His passive as well as His active obedience, in which He submitted to all that evil could do to Him, and broke its power by a meekness and obedience unto the death of the Cross. For by His holiness in our life and by His submission to the Father's judgement upon our sin He put us in the right with the Holy Will of God and so delivered us from the judgement of the law and its power in which evil seeks to clothe itself. So long as the Holy will of God exercises judgement upon sinners through the law, sin and evil embattle themselves behind the law and reduce man to bitter bondage, but in the redemption by the Holiness of Jesus in whom we are justified before God, we are no longer under the judgement or power of the law and are free from its tyranny, and from the evil that usurps its authority. Thus the redemption taught in the New Testament is redemption which robs the authorities and powers of darkness and evil of their vaunted right, and by expiation before the Holy Will of God reveals that they have no inherent right, and no claim to the price of ransom. It is through demolishing the usurped power of the law and the power of darkness over man that the Redeemer as a mighty Prince leads captivity captive and opens up an entirely new situation in which the old order is annulled and a new order of freedom in the Spirit is ushered in.

But now we have to note two other results of the isolation of the Kingly Office of Christ. If the royal or dramatic aspect of redemption is divorced from the incarnational aspect, it quickly dissolves into mere events, into the *beneficia Christi*, or into the timeless repetition of a mystery. On the other hand, if undue emphasis is laid upon the transcendent act of God, the factual focus of attention is laid upon man's response, and in the end this leads either to a sacerdotalist notion of ministry, for such a purely transcendent act requires some form of human mediation, or the attention to the human response leads to the notion of self-redemption through existential decision. Either way the lack of ontology, that is, the failure to integrate the dramatic work of *Christus Victor* with the living Being and obedience of the historical Jesus, is fatal.

Fuller account has had to be given of the *Kingly Office* of Christ not only because it is so misunderstood but because it is under the Kingship of Christ, the Royal Son of God, that His other offices are to be understood; that is, both of them have to be seen as offices fulfilled on the supreme basis of the Royal Decision of God to invade our humanity, and to work out the work of our salvation from within it, as work issuing out of our humanity, belonging to our humanity, yet arising to God the Father. It is thus in integration with the Prophetic and Priestly Offices of Christ that His Kingly Office comes to its fulfilment, for through them He triumphs as the Royal Son, the Only Begotten Son who carries back with Him to the throne of God many sons to glory. It belongs to one of the supreme contributions of Reformal theology that it saw this soteriological unity in the Offices of Christ and only out of that unity expounded the doctrine of the Mediator. That is the doctrine that lies behind and informs these Catechisms.

The counterpart to the doctrine of the Incarnation and saving work of Christ is the doctrine of union with Christ and of participation in Him and all His benefits—that takes place through the Communion of the Holy Spirit, and it is therefore to the doctrine of the Spirit that we now pass.

(3) *The Doctrine of the Holy Spirit*

It may be admitted that the doctrine of the Holy Spirit is the weakest of all the doctrines of the Church, for it has never been given the disciplined attention it requires. Perhaps the chief area in the history of thought where massive attention has been given to the Spirit (apart from the spiritualistic and pentecostal movements) was in the nineteenth century idealist theology but in that development the Spirit came to be identified with man's spirit, which is the exact opposite of the Christian doctrine of the Holy Spirit. The weakness in doctrine goes back, as Professor G. S. Hendry has shown in a book of rare power (*The Holy Spirit in Christian Theology*) partly to the inherent difficulty of the subject and partly also to the neglect of the Early Church. When the Apostles' Creed came to speak of the Holy Spirit, it passed on too quickly to the Church and the fruits of Christ's saving work in men. That was remedied to a certain extent by the Nicene Creed, but the fact that Catechisms are based as a rule on the Apostles' Creed has led them to devote correspondingly little attention to the Spirit. Nevertheless there have been great works on the doctrine of the Spirit from Athanasius' *Letters to Serapion* to Calvin's *Institutes*, book iii and even book iv, while in our own day Barth and Hendry have much to say to us. There is not a little of real importance in these Catechisms, indeed quite sufficient to show the tendencies at work in Reformed theology.

(i) *The Person of the Holy Spirit*

All the Catechisms set forth at the start the doctrine of the Holy Trinity and acknowledge the Person of the Spirit as co-eternal and co-equal with the Father and the Son. As *The Larger Catechism* puts it, "There are three persons in the God-head, the Father, the Son, and the Holy Spirit; and these three are one, eternal God, the same in substance, equal in power and glory; although distinguished by their personal properties" (p. 186). There are differences of emphases. *Calvin's Catechism* at this point speaks of the Holy Spirit as the virtue and power of God shed abroad over all His creatures but still perpetually resident in Himself, whereas the *Heidelberg Catechism* speaks of the Spirit only in terms of His sanctifying work. *Craig's Catechism* combines at the same point the relation of the Spirit to creation and to sanctification and stresses like *The Larger Catechism* the procession of the Spirit from the Father and the Son. For all of them the Spirit is the power and operation of God the Father and peculiarly the Spirit of Jesus Christ the Son of the Father, who is given to us on the ground of the saving work of Christ, so that through the Spirit we are renewed and sanctified, and are adopted to be sons of God in Christ.

The oustanding features here are directly related to the *Filioque* clause in the Western Creed, namely, the *Lordship* or Transcendence of the Spirit, and the Spirit of *Sonship*, that is of essentially filial and personal relation to the Father in and through His Son. The Holy Spirit is the lordly presence of God over the whole of His creation whereby He governs and disposes all things by His goodness, power, and wisdom, and whereby He curbs and restrains the powers of evil directing all to serve His glory. Thus in the scholastic language, the Holy Spirit is directly related to the decrees of God. In other words, the Lordship of the Spirit is the Kingdom of God, whether that is thought of as Lordship over nature, the nations, and the Church or over the ages. But this sovereign rule of God by His Spirit is associated with His Word. It is by His Word and Spirit that God rules and is exalted over all in His divine majesty and glory. The Spirit and the Word are, to use an old patristic expression, the two hands of God.

This relation between the Spirit and the Word is another way of expressing what is declared by the *filioque* clause in the Creed, and is reinforced by it. That the Spirit proceeds from the Son as well as the Father (that is from the Son who became incarnate and therefore also from the incarnate Son) means that the Spirit and the Word cannot be interpreted in terms of immanent principles or norms within the creaturely processes, but as the power and presence of God the Creator supervening upon the creaturely world in transcendent personal fashion, through the commanding Word of God, through the incarnate Person of the Son. Thus the mode of the Spirit's presence and operation is intensely personal. On the other hand, the operation of the Spirit is never merely instrumental in the hands of God—that is the danger in the old patristic image. He is God Himself personally present in this way, distinct from His Person as Father and distinct from His Person as Son, and yet as proceeding personally from the person of the Father and the person of the Son in the unity of the One God, and in the indivisible operations of the Trinity. He is essentially *Holy* Spirit, Spirit in all the Godness and Majesty of God, and only as such is He present to us.

The *filioque* clause, however, has a further importance, for it reminds us that the Spirit is essentially the Spirit of Christ. That is to say, His proper work toward us is in uttering Christ, revealing Him, creating communion with Him, as His proper work within the Trinity is the Communion of the Father with the Son and the Son with the Father. The Spirit has an essentially Christocentric relation. It was through the Spirit that Jesus was born of the Virgin Mary, by the Spirit that He was anointed at His Baptism, through the Spirit that He worked His miracles as with the finger of God, through the eternal Spirit that He offered Himself without spot to the Father, according to the Spirit of holiness that He was raised again from the dead, and it is this same Spirit whom Christ, after ascending to the Father, sends down upon us so that through the Communion of the Spirit we are made partakers in Christ and all His graces. It is through the Spirit that we receive and apprehend the self-revelation of God in Christ, and through the Spirit that the reconciling work of Christ is actualised within us so that we are restored in Christ to the Father, calling upon Him and acknowledged by Him as His beloved sons.

We cannot speak of the Spirit as poured out and as operative among men as if the Incarnation had not taken place, as if the Incarnation made no difference to His work, as if He may now operate behind the back of Christ. It was not of course the Spirit who was incarnated, but the Son, but now that the Incarnation has taken place, a theology faithful to Christ and to the relation of the Spirit to Him, is prevented from thinking of a relation of the Spirit to the creation or to men except in and through the Person and Work of Christ the incarnate Son. This does not mean that God is not present to us in His person and mode of Being as the Spirit as well as in His Person and mode of Being as the Son, but it does mean that we cannot separate in our thought the operation of the Spirit from the mighty acts of God in Christ.

This has a significant implication which we must note. The *filioque* clause implies the renunciation of a so-called natural revelation or natural theology. Whatever happened before the Incarnation now that the Word of God has once and for all become flesh, it is this incarnate Word of God who is uttered by the Spirit, for there is no other Word of God, simply because there is no other God. That is why Calvin was never tired of insisting that natural theology applied to the concept of election can only lead us into an inextricable labyrinth of error, for it would mean that we would be led to posit a Will of God other than His Will revealed and actualised in Jesus Christ. The *filioque* is another way of saying *solo Christo, solo verbo, sola gratia, sola fide*.

Why then does the Roman Church indulge in natural theology? One would expect this more naturally from the Eastern Church which was so hesitant about asserting the *filioque*, but not from the champions of the doctrine of the procession of the Spirit from the Son. But the truth is that the Roman Church has substituted at this point a secret *ecclesiaque* for the *filioque* on the ground that the Church is the extension of the Incarnation and as such possesses the Spirit dwelling in her as an immanent principle of life and truth. This enables the Roman Church to look to her own use of reason and to her own religious self-consciousness as sources of revelation, and indeed so to identify the truth with its own subjectivity as to claim for itself the ultimate court of appeal in all knowledge of Revelation. And yet, is this not precisely what Neo-Protestant theology has done, except that instead of operating with the *ecclesia* as the medium and channel of the Spirit, it has operated with the human spirit or reason, while in Schleiermacher, where this is corporately conceived in the consciousness of the Christian community, there is in fact a remarkable rapprochement with Rome? It is only by refusing to separate the Spirit from the Person and Work of Christ that we can avoid these errors.

(ii) *The Work of the Spirit*

It should be clear from the discussion above that for Reformed theology the work of the Spirit must be thought of in inseparable unity with the work of the whole Trinity, although it is regarded as especially related to Christ. In our Catechisms this is clearest in the teaching of John Craig who spoke of "the love of the Father, the death of Christ and the power of the Spirit" as working together (p. 119) and of the Church itself as "the good work of the three Persons" (p. 107). But within that perspective what are we to say about the sphere of the Spirit's operation, and how are we to describe the actual work of the Spirit? Here it may be helpful to speak first of His work in creation and then of His work in redemption, if we remember that no sharp distinction must be drawn between them.

(*a*) The Work of the Spirit *in creation* has already been noted above, but we may turn here to the way Craig describes it in question and answer. "What is His general office? He puts into execution all things that are decreed by God's secret counsel. What does He do in the order of nature? He keeps all things in their natural state. Where then do all these alterations come from? From the same Spirit, working diversely in nature. Is then the Spirit but nature? No. He is God, ruling and keeping nature. What does He do in the worldly kingdom? He raises them up and casts them down at His pleasure. Why are these things attributed to Him? Because He is the power and hand of God." (p. 118). To that we may add one other question and answer from the same Catechism. "Where does this difference (between the Law and the Gospel) come from? From the Spirit who is joined with the Gospel, and not with the Law"

(p. 135). Craig has already taught that the Spirit works in the order of nature, that He governs and rules over all, and executes God's decrees, so that when he speaks of the Spirit as joined with the Gospel and not the Law he has some special relationship in mind, clearly the relation of communion and participation in Christ into which we enter through the Gospel and not through the Law as such.

How then does the Spirit enact the Will of God as commanded in His Law? And how is there this difference? Craig does not say much to help us answer these questions, but this is an important issue that needs clarification. God's Spirit is poured out upon His creatures, as *Calvin's Catechism* puts it. What then is the difference between that pouring out of His Spirit and Pentecost? Here we have to take into account an element in Biblical teaching not very apparent in these Catechisms, namely, that the presence of the Spirit brings *judgement*, for it is His function to convict of sin, righteousness and judgement.

We may state the matter in this way. With the Fall of man the relation between the creation and God was thrown into tension. Man's disobedience against God met with the divine resistence, and as the theological narrative of Genesis so wonderfully describes it, he was put out of the garden of the Lord and even the ground was cursed for his sake. It does not mean that God gives man up and turns His back upon His creation, but that God holds Himself at a distance from man and keeps man at a distance from Himself, precisely for man's sake. With the Fall the presence of God's Spirit to His creatures brings the judgement of God to bear upon them, so that if the creatures are to have continued existence and are not to be destroyed, God must mercifully withhold the fulness of His presence from them, while nevertheless maintaining them in being and order in His creation.

Is it not in this sense also that we are to understand that "the Spirit is joined not with the Law"? When reconciliation between the world and God has taken place, and the enmity has been removed, then God may pour out His Spirit upon His creatures without consuming them in His judgement. Thus in a very fundamental sense there took place a real renewal of creation in and through the Incarnation, not only because Christ came to undertake a cosmic mission, to gather up all things and to be the Head of all things, but because following upon His atoning work, the Spirit was poured out on "all flesh" in accordance with the promise of God through the prophet Joel. He was also poured out in a special way upon the Church, the sphere where reconciliation was actualised, and was Himself the actualisation of that reconciliation in their midst. Only with the fulfilment of the atoning work of Christ was the Spirit thus poured out in fulness.

Now the operation of the Spirit in creation and in nature is to be regarded as the presence of God with the creation, to maintain it in being and order under God's government, a presence nevertheless in which God holds Himself at a distance from it lest He should destroy it. However, with the Incarnation and the finishing of Christ's work, we must think of the whole relation between the Spirit of God and His creation as undergoing a change—but that change has to be interpreted Christologically in relation to Christ the First-born and Head of all creation, i.e. it has to be interpreted eschatologically in terms of the new creation. Because we still await the redemption of the body, and the renewal of heaven and earth, we have still to interpret the presence of the Spirit to creation and nature as involving a measure of distance between it and God, in which He withholds the fulness of His presence until the appointed hour of final judgement and recreation. This doctrine, however, which Reformed theology has never fully

faced or worked out, depends upon the doctrine of the relation of the incarnate Word, crucified, risen and ascended, to the
whole creation, and that also has never been fully worked out.
In some real sense, as H. R. Mackintosh used to say, we have
to think of "the creation as proleptically conditioned by
redemption", but we must also say that in some real sense the
creatio continua is even now conditioned by the Incarnation and
Atonement, and that the whole universe pivots upon Jesus
Christ. It was to a certain extent the failure of Reformed
theology to think out the doctrine of Christ and the doctrine
of the Spirit in relation to creation, and therefore to nature,
that left the door open for a quick descent to serious error in
the tendency to do just what John Craig repudiated—namely
to identify the Spirit with nature.

(*b*) The work of the Spirit *in redemption* is to be considered
from two sides, from the side of Christ in the application of
His finished work, and from the side of man in receiving the
fruits of that work. In relation to Christ Himself from whom
the Spirit proceeds, as well as from the Father, the work of the
Spirit is to be understood as correlative to Christ's three-fold
Office as Prophet, and Priest, and King.

In regard to His *Prophetic Office* the Spirit is indeed the pro-
phetic Spirit who continues to utter Christ the Word and utters
the Word with all the quickening, life-giving power of God.
It is significant that the expression "quickening Spirit" is
applied in the New Testament both to Christ and to the
Spirit. It is here that the work of Christ and the work of the
Spirit cannot be separated out from one another in our
thought. But the Spirit is correlative to Christ's Prophetic
Office (as we have discussed it above) in another sense, as
Advocate; and here again it is significant that this expression
is applied both to Christ and to the Spirit. It is indeed through
the Spirit that Christ fulfils His Advocacy of us, binds us up

in the same bundle of Life with Himself, stands in for us, takes our cause upon Himself, and appears before the Father for us as our Intercessor—therefore it is natural that the term *intercede* or *intervene* should be applied to the work of the Spirit as well as to the work of Christ, as is done by St. Paul. It is in this two-fold Advocacy and Intercession that the work of Christ is not only fulfilled once and for all but applied to us who believe in Him, so that it is echoed in our invocation of God as our Father and echoed in our own intercessions in the name of Christ, because through the Spirit Christ dwells in us and we in Him in a new relation of being.

In regard to Christ's *Priestly Office* we must refer again to what has just been said, for Advocacy and Intercession belong to Christ's priestly work as well. But here we are to think also of the work of the Spirit as applying to us the blood of Christ. This is a conception which runs very powerfully through the Reformed theology. It means that the death of Christ on the Cross, the baptism of blood with which He was baptised, cannot be separated from Pentecost, the baptism with which the triumphant Christ baptises His Church, fulfilling on it and in it what He has already fulfilled in Himself. This teaching has powerful advocates in the early fathers of the Church, as we see, for example, in the recently discovered Homily of Melito of Sardis, in which he relates our sealing with the Spirit to our sealing with the blood of the Covenant as one and the same thing. It is for this reason that the work of the Spirit is so closely concerned with the Sacraments in applying to us the propitiation of Christ and in giving us communion in His sacrifice.

In regard to the *Kingly Office* of Christ, the Spirit works as the power and operation of God, effectively applying Christ's victory over the powers of darkness to us, and so delivering us from bondage into the freedom of the sons of God. Through the Spirit Christ clothed with His victory and power is present to us, so that His triumphant work is ever operative and bearing fruit in us. It is through the Lord the Spirit that the Kingdom of God comes upon us although we do not in the least deserve it and gathers us into the realm where grace reigns. It is through the Lordly presence of the Spirit that Christ clothed with His graces so gives Himself to us that He remains the Lord the Saviour, the King who does not come under our control but who is freely and unstintingly the Lord the Giver of life. It is just because He does not come under our control that He remains our Saviour. In the New Testament grace is spoken of as the grace of Jesus Christ, not as the grace of the Spirit, but in the history of the Church the conception of "the grace of the Spirit" did arise and is even found frequently in the writings of Calvin and in the Westminster theology, as well as in the teaching of Rome. It was through the association of grace with the Spirit that grace came to be detached from Christ and thought of as "something" communicable and transmissible and which can be channelised and infused. But that deterioration would not have taken place, if the doctrine of the Lordship of the Spirit had been properly maintained, and the inseparable association of the Spirit with the Royal Person and Office of Christ carefully preserved.

The work of the Spirit in relation to redemption has to be considered also from the other side, not only from the side of the objective work of Christ but from the side of the subjectification of revelation and reconciliation in the life and faith of the Church. Here we are to think of the Spirit as creating and calling forth the response of man in faith and understanding, in thanksgiving and worship and prayer. It is one of the notable features of the earlier Reformed Catechisms that they expound this whole aspect of the Spirit's work under

"Thanksgiving". We cannot enter into this in detail here, but we must turn now to consider the basic question that underlies this whole relationship.

(iii) *The Communion of the Spirit*

The Reformed doctrine of the Communion of the Spirit is not a doctrine of communion in spirit or even simply a doctrine of communion in the Spirit, but a doctrine of Communion in Christ through the Spirit, or, to put it otherwise, of *union with Christ through the Communion of the Spirit*. Thus the Communion of the Spirit has to be understood as correlative to the union of God and man wrought out in the Life and Work of Jesus Christ. This is fundamental to all that these Catechisms have to teach about the work of the Spirit in God's people as actualising subjectively in them what has been accomplished for them once and for all objectively in the Incarnation. This is a spiritual work *in man* and carries with it the promise of ultimate fulfilment in the redemption of the *whole man*, body and soul, in the new creation. It is this combination of the Communion of the Spirit with union with Christ that lies at the foundation of the Church's hope and so forms the very heart of its eschatology.

Because the Communion of the Spirit is correlative to the incarnational union in Christ, we have to think of it as twofold, in relation to the human life and the work of Christ.

(*a*) John Craig in his Catechism of 1581 spoke of this in terms of what he called "our carnal union with Christ" and "our spiritual union with Him" (p. 113). By "carnal union" he referred to Christ's union with us and our union with Christ which He wrought out in His birth of the Spirit and in His human life through which He sanctifies us. He was made man like us that He might die for us. Thus "life and righteousness are placed in our flesh", for in Him "our flesh is joined personally with the Fountain of life" (ibid.). But in taking our flesh or humanity upon Him Christ was also "filled with the Holy Spirit without measure that He might bestow the Spirit upon us". Therefore "those who are joined with Him spiritually" are sure of this life.

That is very clearly stated, but there is one question which has to be raised. Is the spiritual union another union, a union in addition to our carnal union with Christ, or is it a sharing in the one and only union between God and man wrought out in Jesus Christ? That is a very important question, for if the spiritual union is an additional union, then our salvation depends not only on the finished work of Christ but upon something else as well which has later to be added on to it before it is real for us. That was in fact the idea taught by Romans for example, in their doctrine of baptismal regeneration and *ex opere operato* sacramental incorporation into Christ, but it is the same idea that is taught also by Protestants in their doctrine of a union with Christ which is effected by faith or by conversion through which alone what Christ has done for us becomes real for us. Both these forms of the same error lead to a doctrine of man's co-operation in his own salvation; and so involve a doctrine of conditional grace.

This doctrine is unfortunately found in the Westminster Catechisms. It is particularly clear in the later Covenant theology in which a man was said to acquire "a saving interest in Christ" through entering into a personal covenant with Him in addition to the Covenant of Grace sealed to him in baptism and proclaimed to him (on this condition) in the Gospel. As against that grave aberration it must be insisted that there is only one union with Christ, that which He has wrought out with us in His birth and life and death and resurrection and in which He gives us to share through the gift of His Spirit. The difference between these two views may appear very

slight indeed at this point, but the implications of this difference
are very far-reaching especially in the whole sphere of the life
and work of the Church, in the doctrine of grace, and in our
understanding of the Sacraments.

(b) What Craig called "our carnal union" with Christ must
be understood, however, to include explicitly what Christ has
done for us in His and our flesh. It is here that we may turn
back to Calvin who was particularly concerned with this in
his doctrine of the Lord's Supper. Through the Communion
of the Spirit we are given to partake of the body and blood
of Christ, that is to share in His whole human life and in His
death on the Cross, i.e., in His obedient self-oblation and self-
sanctification which He fulfilled for our sakes. In answer to
the question, "Do you mean we must truly communicate in
the body and blood of the Lord?" Calvin gives this answer:
"I understand so. But since the whole affiance of our salvation
rests in the obedience which He has rendered to God, His
Father, in order that it may be imputed to us as if it were ours,
we must possess Him: for His blessings are not ours, unless He
gives Himself to us first" (p. 60). In other words, what Craig
described as the carnal union wrought out between us and
Christ includes His whole life and work of saving obedience
so that when we speak of a spiritual union with Christ, that
means that through the Spirit we are given to share in the
covenanted obedience of Christ—the term that Calvin used
for that is "affiance". In His obedient human life Jesus Christ
was not only the Son of God drawing near to us in the flesh,
but in and out of our flesh He lived a life of perfect obedience
and trust and confidence toward God the Father, a perfectly
faithful life, in which His obedience and faith toward God were
part of His vicarious and atoning life, part of His sanctified
human nature. It is in that very human nature, with its faith
and obedience, that we are given to participate through the

Communion of the Spirit, and that is the very foundation of our faith in Him and the ground of our obedience to the Father.

We are not saved by the act of our believing, but saved in the very act of believing by the faithful and obedient life of Jesus Christ on whom we rely, for He has already bound us up in covenant and "carnal" union with Him. When we understand the Gospel in this way we cannot seriously talk about "justifying faith" as a condition of our salvation, for this is the kind of faith in which we rely wholly upon the vicarious faith of Christ and not upon ourselves even in the act of faith. It is only on this basis that we are really free to believe and have faith in Christ without the ulterior motive of using faith to secure our salvation. Only on this basis of thanksgiving for what Christ has already done for us in His finished work (finished from the side of God but finished also from the side of man in whose place He stood and stands) can we really and fully speak about our own living and active faith in Christ.

This comes out remarkably well in another series of questions and answers found in *Craig's Catechism*. After speaking of the union wrought out by Christ in which He was made flesh of our flesh, and of the corresponding union in which we are made flesh of His flesh through being united to Him spiritually as members with the Head (p. 12), Craig went on to ask "What do we get from this union?", and answered by speaking of justification through the perfect obedience and justice of Christ. Then the Catechism continued: "How can another man's justice be made ours? Christ is not another man to us properly. Why is He not another man to us? Because He is given to us freely by the Father with all His graces, and we are joined with Him. How is justification offered to us? By the preaching of the Gospel. How do we receive justification? Only by our own lively faith" (p. 125). Christ and His people are properly

One Man—that is the very heart of the doctrine of the Church. As George Gillespie put it half a century later, echoing the words of Augustine and Calvin, "There is but one Christ. Yes, the Head and the body make but one Christ, so that you cannot divide the body without dividing Christ". This is the Pauline teaching which spoke of One Christ, One New Man, One Body and One Spirit. It is in that Oneness that the Communion of the Spirit is to be understood.

Arising out of this there are at least three major implications that we must note.

(1) It is through partaking of Christ Himself that we partake of His benefits and blessings. As we have seen, Christ and His graces, Christ and His merits, Christ and His benefits, Christ and His promises, are all ways of speaking of the impossibility of separating Christ's life from His work or of separating His work on the Cross from His atoning life. Faith is concerned here with the whole Christ, and union with Christ is with that whole Christ. If there has to be a priority in our understanding then we must say with Calvin and Craig, in the passages cited above, that it is through participating in Christ that we partake of His benefits, for unless He gives Himself to us first, His blessings are not ours. This means that the forensic element in the atoning work of Christ rests upon the basis of His Incarnation, upon His Person and Human life, and therefore that the forensic element in justification reposes for its substance and meaning upon union with Christ. It is through union with Him that we enter into the blessing of justification, because it was through His becoming one with us first in His Incarnation that Christ wrought our justification for us. Once again, the difference between this view and the view that we first share in the benefits of Christ and then through them come to share in His life and have union with Him, may seem very slight and unimportant, but the reverse is the case.

It is the clear tendency of the Westminster theology to reverse the role, and to insist first on judicial justification and justifying faith and then on that basis to speak of our entering into union with Christ. But two things happen here. First, the meaning both of justification and faith changes, and second, the forensic and believing element is uppermost, and so a judicial and cognitive relation tends to displace the Communion of the Spirit. That is why the doctrine of the Spirit has so little place in the Westminster theology, and the work of the Spirit is only brought in incidentally and regarded instrumentally. It was this change in emphasis from the teaching of the Reformers that tended to oust the doctrine of union with Christ from its place of central importance, and so made the whole doctrine of the Sacraments problematic, for the Sacraments cannot be understood in terms only of judicial and cognitive relation without evacuating them of their main substance. That is the process that we can see going on in the *Westminster Catechisms*. When we compare their teaching on Baptism, for example, with that of the *Westminster Directory*, the difference is very obvious; it was this Catechetical teaching that came to exercise so much influence in the eighteenth and nineteenth century until there came a switch back to the teaching of the New Testament and the Reformers.

(2) How wide is the range of "the carnal union" which Christ has effected between Himself as the Incarnate Son and human flesh? Does this include all men, or does it refer only to the elect? This is of fundamental importance for the doctrine of the Spirit. If Christ's incarnational union with us involves all men, then we must give a proper interpretation to the pouring out of the Spirit upon "*all* flesh", but if Christ's incarnational union only involves those who believe in Him or only some out of the human race, then the doctrine of the Spirit's work must be changed accordingly. The question to

be faced then is whether Christ only entered into a generic relation with men through becoming one particular man, or also entered into an ontological relation with all men in the assumption of our human flesh. Two caveats against the former ought to be stated right away. If Christ only entered into a generic relation with men then (*a*) the saving union of men with Christ must be regarded as an additional union added by the Spirit on to the union which He has perfected in Himself; and (*b*) the Church can only be construed in terms of an extension of the Incarnation, both of which we must reject as erroneous.

This problem cannot be discussed fully here, but in line with what has already been said above about the relation of Christ to the creation, we may remind ourselves that the eternal Son and Word of God is He in whom all men cohere for He is the Creator who gives them being and through His Spirit holds them in being. There is thus an ontological relation between the creature and the Creator reposing upon His sheer grace, in which He gives them being as realities distinct from Himself, so that the ontological relation, as Barth has so clearly and decisively shown, is not reversible. That is, the Son and Word of God became man by becoming one particular Man, but because He is the Creator Word who became Man, even as the incarnate Word He still holds all men in an ontological relation to Himself. That relation was not broken off with the Incarnation.

It may be argued that this applies only to the eternal Son, but if we really hold that the human nature and the divine nature share in one hypostasis or person, it will be extremely difficult to maintain that Christ has only generic relation to men. In any case it belongs to the very essence of the Incarnational life and work of the Son that in Him redemption penetrates back to the very beginning and reunites man's life to God's creative purpose. Redemption is no mere after-thought on the part of God, for in it the original creation comes to a transcendent realisation, and the one Covenant of Grace made with all creation is fulfilled. The Biblical teaching is quite explicit that in Christ all things are really involved in recon-ciliation, that He is not only the Head of believers but the Head of all creation and that all things visible and invisible are gathered up and cohere in Him—from which we cannot exclude a relation in being between all men and Christ. The teaching of the earlier of these Catechisms is that Christ is the Head of men and angels, the Head of all men, and as the Head of all men died for all men, so that all men are involved already objectively in His human life and in His work in life and death, i.e. not only on judicial and transactional grounds, but on the ground of the constitution of His Person as Mediator.

Now this carries with it the implication "that human beings have no being apart from Christ as man" (which Dr. Henry rejects, *The Gospel of the Incarnation*, p. 5). If Christ had not come, if the Incarnation had not taken place, and things be-tween man and God had been and are allowed to take their course as a result of man's estrangement from God and God's judgement upon man, man would disappear into nothing. It belongs to the nature of sin that it is alienation from God, and therefore that it is alienation from the source of all being in the Creator. There is nothing that the rebel or the sinner wants less than to be laid hold of by God in spite of his sin and be restrained from his sinful movement away from God, but that is precisely what happened in the Incarnation. The Incarnation means that God refused to hold back His love, and His loving affirmation of His creation, that He refused to let man go the way of his sin, from alienation to alienation, and so ultimately into non-being. The Incarnation means that God Himself condescended to enter into our alienated human existence, to lay hold of it, to bind it in union with Himself; and the consummation of the Incarnation in the death and resurrection means that the Son of God died for all men, and so once and for all constituted men as men upon whom God had poured out His life and love, so that men are for ever laid hold of by God and affirmed in their being as His creatures. They can no more escape from His love and sink into non-being than they can constitute themselves men for whom Christ has not died. How can God go back upon the death of His dear Son? How can God undo the Incarnation and go back upon Himself? How can God who is Love go back upon the pouring out of His love once and for all and so cease to be Himself? That is the decisive, final thing about the whole Incarnation including the death of Christ, that it affects all men, indeed the whole of creation, for the whole of creation is now put on a new basis with God, the basis of a Love that does not withhold itself but only overflows in pure unending Love. That is why creation still continues in being, and that is why man still exists, for God has not given him up, but on the contrary poured out His love upon him unreservedly once and for ever, decidedly and finally affirming man as His child, eternally confirming the creation as His own handiwork. God does not say Yes, and No, for all that He has done is Yes and Amen in Christ. That applies to every man, whether he will or no. He owes his very being to Christ and belongs to Christ, and in that he belongs to Christ he has his being only from Him and in relation to Him.

All this is not to say that a man may not suffer damnation, for he may in spite of all reject Christ and refuse God's grace. How that is possible, we simply cannot understand: that a sinner face to face with the infinite love of God should yet rebel against it and choose to take his own way, isolating himself from that love—that is the bottomless mystery of evil before which we can only stand aghast, the surd which we cannot rationalise, the enigma of Judas. But it happens. Just as it is by the very breath God gives us that we sin against Him, so it is by the very being that a man is given in and through Christ that he may yet turn his back upon Christ and deny Him, and so shatter himself against the love of God that will not let him go just because it does not cease to love. But this does mean that if a man irrevocably chooses the way of his sinful self-will and suffers damnation, he does not and cannot go into non-being, disappearing into annihilation, for the Incarnation and death of Christ cannot be undone. The sinner cannot undo the fact that Christ has gathered him into a relation of being with Him, and has once and for all laid hold of him in His life and death and resurrection.

This may be stated in another way. The sinner cannot isolate himself from God by escaping into an area where God's love does not love and where he can be left to himself. Even in hell he cannot be left to himself for there he is still apprehended by the fact that God loves, that His love negates all that is not love just by being love, that His love refuses to allow the sinner to escape being loved and therefore resists the sinner's will to isolate himself from that love. His being in hell is not the result of God's decision to damn him, but the result of his own decision to choose himself against the love of God and therefore of the negative decision of God's love to oppose his refusal of God's love just by being Love. This negative decision of God's love is the wrath of the Lamb, that is to say, the once and for all fact that Christ has died for the sins of the world, the finalising of the love in an eternally decisive deed, which just because it cannot be undone stands irresolutely opposed to all that it is not love, or that resists it. Just because the love of God has once and for all drawn all men into the circle of its own loving, it has thereby rejected all that rejects God's love. It does not reject by ceasing to love but precisely by continuing to love and therein rejecting all that rejects love. Therefore the sinner in hell cannot escape the fact that he is loved, cannot escape into being left to himself, and therefore even in choosing himself so as for ever to be himself, he cannot escape from himself as one loved, so that he is for ever imprisoned in his own refusal of being loved and indeed that is the very hell of it.

Words and thoughts fail us when we try to think like this. We can only stammer for we hardly know what we say, but must we not ask what is the relation to Christ of those who ultimately refuse Him? And since we cannot think it out to the end, if only because the end, the *eschaton*, is still to come, must we not yet say, that ultimate refusal of Christ cannot undo the fact that the sinner was made brother to Christ by His Incarnation, and bought with the blood of Christ, and in that He died for him and even rose again for him, must we not also say that when he stands before God at the final judgement it is what Christ has done for him that raises him to judgement? Such implications may baffle us until we clap our hands upon our mouth, but whichever way we turn we are still faced with the inescapable fact that the Incarnation and the Cross involve the being of all men, so that they have their humanity only from Him.

Is that not part of the mystery of the Kingdom of God at work in the world, that is, not only among those who hear the Word, in the Church, but really beyond it, out in the field of the world? According to the teaching of Jesus it is at work in the world, but it is at work as mystery which cannot be discerned by observation, so that the result will be apparent only at the end in the judgement and consummation of the world. In the language of Ephesians, Christ is the mystery in whom all things are involved and gathered up, so that He is the Head of all things and all creation. There is a sense, there-fore, in which we must speak of all men as ingrafted into Christ in virtue of His incarnational and atoning work, and we must consequently speak of those who refuse Him and ultimately prove reprobate as those who break themselves off from Him. In Calvin's words, "that very relationship of the flesh, by which He has allied us to Himself, the ungodly break off and dissolve by their unbelief, so that it is by their own fault that they are rendered utter strangers to Him" (*Comm. on Ps.* 22:23).

It is in correlation with this relationship of Christ with all men and indeed all creation that we are to think of the whole range of the Spirit's operation. The "carnal union" effected by Christ between Himself and all men supplies, as it were, the field of the Spirit's activity, so that in a profound sense we have to take seriously the fact that the Spirit was poured out on "all flesh" and operates on "all flesh." But now we must consider the concretion of this operation in the community of those in whom the reconciliation is subjectively actualised through the Spirit.

(3) Because the Holy Spirit is sent *in the Name of Christ* He operates especially wherever that Name is heard and wherever people gather together under that Name, that is within the sphere of the Church founded by Christ upon Himself as the new people of God to whom He committed the Gospel of the New Covenant and upon whom He breathed His own Spirit sending them out in the mission of forgiveness as He had been sent into the world by the Father. In considering the relation of the Communion of the Spirit to the Church we have to take into account two factors, namely, that Christ is related to the Church as a whole, as a Body, and that He is related to each member of the Church singly and individually.

In the heart of Christ's relation to all men the Church occupies a central place, and describes the inner circle of His identification with men where His own Sonship toward the Father is made consciously to echo within mankind in a filial relation of obedience to God. The Church is the point or the sphere in human flesh where the personal union in Christ between God and man creates for itself a corresponding personal fellowship ·between man and man, within which the relation between the Father and the Son and the Son and the Father is folded out horizontally in history, or (to put it the other way round) within which men in their relations with one another in creation are given to share in the life and love of the Father and Son and the Holy Spirit, that is in the Communion of the Spirit. The Church is thus the way in which the Communion of the Spirit functions within the social relations of creation by creating a supernatural fellowship in their midst through which, while still within creation, they share in the divine life and love poured out upon them from above in and through Jesus Christ.

This Church Jesus Christ related to Himself corporately. It was the Church as Church that Christ bound to Himself in His incarnate mission. As the Epistle to the Ephesians describes it, "Christ loved the church and gave himself for it, that he might sanctify and cleanse it with the washing of water by the word, that he might present it to himself a glorious church, not having spot or wrinkle, or any such thing, but that it might be holy and without blemish" (Eph. 5:25f.). The same focussing of Christ's work upon the concrete community formed immediately round Himself is apparent in all the four Gospels. He became incarnate in the midst of Israel, the Covenant people of God, and within Israel He began His work within the people prepared for the Lord by the Baptism of John, and within that messianic discipleship He chose a discipleship of His own and formed them round Him as the nucleus of His new people with whom He inaugurated the

New Covenant in His body and blood at the Last Supper. Throughout His ministry He created this inner discipleship as a fellowship of love, loving them as the Father had loved Him, and creating within them love toward Him and the Father. And having loved these His own who were in the world, He loved them to the end. Then after cleansing them with water and the Word, and binding them into one body with Himself in His body and blood He went forth to give Himself for them, that through His own self-sanctification He might sanctify them and present them to the Father as His own, that they and He might be one, as He the incarnate Son and the Father were one and that through them all the world might believe.

It was to this same inner group that He returned on Easter Evening reconstituting them as the nucleus of His Church, breathing upon them the Spirit whom He had covenanted to give them at the Last Supper. In that Communion of the Spirit, and therefore in His union as the crucified and risen Saviour with them, He sent them forth on their mission to bear the treasure of the Gospel of forgiveness and reconciliation to all men. What happened to the Twelve in the Upper Room happened to the whole Church of the one hundred and twenty on the Day of Pentecost when the Spirit was poured out in fulness, once and for all baptising them as the Church which Christ had loved and for which He had given Himself and which He now confirmed as the one People of God in whom the promise of the fulness of God's presence through the Spirit was fulfilled, and sent them out into all mankind as the means through whom the mystery of His Kingdom, the Word growing and increasing and multiplying miraculously, would work in the field of the whole world until the end.

It is important to remember that this Church was already in existence as Church when Christ died and rose again. The

Church was not founded with Pentecost; nor indeed was it first founded with the Incarnation. It was founded with creation, with the establishment of the One Covenant of Grace and its operation through the calling out and forming of the Covenant people, although that was proleptically conditioned by the Incarnation and Redemption. It was into this people that the Son became incarnate, and within it that He was the true Vine and the disciples were the true branches of this Vine, He and His disciples together building the new Israel, the new people in whom all peoples are to be blessed. It was only as Christ gathered up in Himself the ancient Covenant people, and as He established in Himself the new Covenant people, that He went forth to finish His work once and for all. It is upon this Christ who will not be without His ancient people or without His new people, that the Church is founded from age to age, ingrafted, that is, into Christ the true Vine, and therefore into the stock of Israel, the old as well as the new Israel. The Church on earth and in history does not have the promise of the fulness of Spirit apart from this ingrafting, apart from Israel old and new, apart from the One Covenant as it moved from its old to its new economy in Christ and in His Spirit. The Communion of the Spirit is strictly correlative to this Covenant Community, One Spirit and therefore one Body, One Christ and therefore one Church through the one Communion of the Spirit with Him.

The Christian Church is formed through the change in the economy or dispensation of the Covenant and is thus to be distinguished from the Church in the old Israel, but the Covenant remains the same, and the "economic" purpose (the dispensation, *oikonomia*, and stewardship, *oikonomia*, of the mysteries of God) remains the same, the Covenant of Grace with creation. The "economic" purpose of the old Covenant was the election of one people in place of all for the blessing of God upon all. That was wholly fulfilled in the "economic" condescension of the Son in the Incarnation, and now that fulfilled "economy" is communicated to the world through the "economic" purpose of the Church, the election of one community in place of all for the blessing of God upon all. Within this Church we are given to share in "the fulfilled economy", the mystery of Christ, that through the Church the one "economy" or "dispensation" of the ages may be fulfilled among all men and in the whole creation of things visible and invisible.

The Church has its very being and life in this new form of the "economy" of the Covenant in which through the Spirit the Church shares in the New Humanity of Christ in order that through the same Spirit at work in the fellowship of the Church mankind as a whole may share in the New Humanity of Christ and therefore in the new creation. Thus what is fulfilled intensively in the Church through the Communion of the Spirit is fulfilled in order that it may be fulfilled extensively in all mankind and all creation. As such the Church is to be looked on as the new humanity within the world, the provisional manifestation of the new creation within the old.

This fulfilment intensively in the Church, this participation of the Church in Christ, is the special work of the Holy Spirit, for it is His work to pour out into the Church the life and love of God, and at the same time to create within the Church real reception and participation in the life and love of God in Christ. This union of Christ and His Church in the Spirit, is the mystery hid from the ages but now revealed in the Gospel. But through the Communion of the One Spirit of God the mystery of Christ and His Church presses out toward universal fulness in all creation. In order to understand the operation of the Spirit in this movement of Communion from the particular to the universal, from the nucleus to the fulness, from the one hundred and twenty at Pentecost to all mankind, we have to consider the other primary and no less important factor to which the Communion of the Spirit is correlative, the individual relation of Christ to every member of the Church.

In His Incarnation the Son of God became one particular and individual Man, for that was the way in which He entered into relation with all men in the flesh. Therefore in the new economy of the Covenant determined by the Incarnation the relations of God with all men are to be understood as relations through this one Man, Jesus. That is to say, the relationship of God with every man is acutely individualised through personal and historical relation to Jesus. It belongs to the work of the Spirit to function in correlation with this particular Man, and so to operate in and through encounter between Him and every man. It is not ultimately the individuality of men that makes individual faith and personal decision so important, but the individuality and particularity of Jesus who confronts all men within our humanity. That takes place within the relations of men with men, within all their personal relations and decisions and choices, within the structural relations of their creation, in birth and growth, in family and nation and race, within their speech and communications, and the whole context of their humanity. Within all that Jesus comes as man to man, person to person, and therefore in address and response, in word and spirit, but it is as the Lord become Man, as Saviour become what we are, that He comes, and therefore as proper Man to man, as the Person to person, in Word and Spirit.

Word is the means of personal and human and historical communication through which Christ has ordained that He will be met and known, and through which He has ordained that He and His Gospel will be proclaimed to all men. That encounter through the Word is one to which the risen and ascended Christ has joined the mission of His Spirit, so that through the communication of the Word men may hear not only the words of other men who communicate it, but the Words of the living God, the Words that are Spirit and Life. It is in that encounter that each man hears the Word which proceeds like a sharp two-edged sword out of the mouth of Christ, the sword of the Spirit, uncovering the thoughts and intents of his innermost being, setting him face to face with the last things and with ultimate decision—this is the work of the Spirit convicting of sin, righteousness and judgement; but in that encounter each man is made to stand on his feet before God in Christ, as the man that is loved by God to the uttermost, the man for whom Christ died and rose again, the man who through the love of God poured out upon him by the Spirit is enabled to say "He loved me and gave Himself for me" and so in Christ to say "Abba, Father". It is in that encounter that each man may through the Spirit share in the faith and obedience of Christ, and himself live the life of faith and obedience to Him.

It is because Christ is Himself "the One and the Many", the One who includes the Many, and the Many who includes each one, that He encounters men always and only in this two-fold way, within the corporate community of the Many, and within the life of each man. It is in that togetherness that the Word is communicated and received in and through the Communion of the Spirit, so that private and corporate communion in the Spirit belong inseparably together and are mutually dependent within the fellowship of the Church. But this obtains only on the ground of the universal Headship of Christ and within the universal range of the Spirit's activity. It is in the light of this three-fold dimension that we are required to understand the operation of the Spirit. In the universal dimension we can hardly speak of it as a "Communion", but in the other two dimensions we can and must speak of it thus: as a corporate Communion, that is a Communion of mutual participation through the Spirit in Christ and His graces, and a personal Communion which each may have with Christ within the corporate Communion. That is the doctrine of the Church as the Communion of Saints, in which each shares with the other and all share together in the life and love of God in Jesus Christ. In that Communion no one can live for himself alone, or believe or worship alone, for he is nothing without his brother for whom Christ died, and has no relation to Christ except in Christ's relation with all for whom He died.

This means that the Church is such a Communion in the Spirit, through whom it participates in Christ who has poured Himself out upon and for all men, that by the irresistible compulsion of the same Spirit the Church is turned outward to all for whom Christ became incarnate and lived and died that they might be gathered into the life of God. Thus the Church cannot live to itself, for by the Communion of the Spirit it is made to transcend itself and find its fulness in the creation in which its own mystery is at work in Christ. The Church does not possess the mystery in and for itself. It shares in it, but the whole of creation shares in it, so that the boundaries of the Church must ever be open toward all men outside and toward the full consummation of the purposes of God for all things. Thus the range of the Communion of the Spirit cannot be limited and bound to the Church, but through the universal range of the Spirit the Church is catholicised or universalised and made to reach out to the fulness of Him who fills all in all.

On the other hand, it is through the Communion of the Spirit that the Church finds itself in tension with the world, for in the world the Word of God is as yet resisted, and the Spirit of God is abroad convicting of sin, righteousness and judgement. Thus by sharing in the New Humanity of Christ, by sharing in His obedience and love, through the Communion of the Spirit, the Church by being Church condemns the world—that is to say, it calls the world into question, proclaims to it the Gospel which claims the world for God and which therefore resists and judges the will of the world to isolate itself from the love of God. It is thus that the Church finds itself separated from the world, by its participation in the self-sanctification of Christ, although by its participation in the reconciliation of Christ, it is thrust out into the world with the message of reconciliation. That tension reaches down to every member of the Church and is found in the struggle between the flesh and the Spirit. But where that tension is found—this is a favourite theme of these Catechisms—there we are given strange and unavoidable evidence of our participation in the Communion of the Spirit. Hence the very struggle of the flesh against the Spirit and of the Spirit against the flesh, the very tension between the world and the Church and the Church and the world, must be recognised as a God-given token of His favour and presence, and is therefore to be regarded as "a singular comfort".

This tension, however, is provisional. It is indeed a sign of the end, for it indicates that the movement of the Spirit is already reaching out toward victorious triumph and consummation. The Communion of the Spirit is correlative to Union with Christ, but Christ has risen and ascended to the throne of God, waiting till the decisive hour when He will come again to take up His reign, to judge and renew His creation. Thus the correlation of Communion of the Spirit and Union with Christ carries within it the eschatological hope of the Church, and indeed what John Craig called "the end of all flesh". As he saw clearly, here following closely the teaching of St. Paul, that end is bound up with the consummation by the Spirit of "the adoption, to wit, the redemption of the body". The creation fell for man's sake and with man, but it is in and with the adoption of the sons of God that the creation will receive its emancipation and renewal. Then the universal range of Christ and His Spirit will be coincident with the Communion of the Spirit, that is, the sphere wherein all who share in the Spirit share in Christ's Sonship. Today that universal Communion of the Spirit has its provisional and proleptic form in the historical Church, but then the Church attaining to the fulness of Christ will be coincident with the whole Kingdom spanning the new heaven and the new earth.

Part I

THE LARGER CATECHISMS

CALVIN'S CATECHISM 1541

The Catechism of the Church of Geneva
A Formulary for the Instruction of Children in Christianity
in the Form of a Dialogue in which the Minister
interrogates and the Child responds

by John Calvin

The Doctrine of the Apostles and Prophets is
The Foundation of Christ's Church
Eph. 2:20.

WHEN John Calvin was constrained to join William Farel in reforming the Church in Geneva in 1536, he set himself to compose an instrument for popular instruction in the faith, reducing to simpler form the substance of his 1536 *Institute*. This *Instruction in Faith* was first published in French early in 1537, while in the following year a Latin version was issued in Basel under the title *Catechism or Institute of Christian Religion*. This was not a catechism in the form of question and answer but a straightforward exposition of the leading tenets of the Christian faith in brief sections.

In 1541 Calvin returned from Strasburg to Geneva to face once more the task of reformation. It was then that he produced *The Geneva Catechism*, along with the *Ecclesiastical Ordinances*. For this purpose he adapted and enlarged the earlier work of 1537, regrouping the material and arranging it in questions and answers. It was published in French late in 1541 or early in 1542. Its primary object was to recover the catechetical teaching of the ancient Catholic Church, to provide it in a mode suitable for the instructing of children from the ages of ten to fifteen, and for directing the minds of all the faithful to one Christ, that being united in His truth they might grow up together into one Body and one Spirit, and with one mouth proclaim what belongs to the substance of the Faith. Several years later, in 1545, Calvin published an edition of the Catechism in Latin in the hope that it might be used to maintain sacred communion among the Churches and help them to express and proclaim their agreement in the Christian Faith. Very soon it was translated into other languages, and became the basis for the great host of Catechisms that appeared in the sixteenth and seventeenth centuries, especially in England and Scotland.

It was the French edition of 1541 that was translated for use in Scotland, its 373 questions and answers being divided up into sections suitable for use Sunday by Sunday in the regular instruction of the Church. It is a new translation of the French text that is given here.

THE CATECHISM OF THE CHURCH OF GENEVA

It has always been a matter which the Church has held in singular commendation, to see that little children should be instructed in Christian doctrine. That this might be done, not only were schools opened in early times, and people enjoined to teach their families well, but it was also a public practice, to examine children in the churches on articles of faith common to all Christians. That this might be carried out in order, a formulary was used which was called a Catechism. Thereafter the devil rending the Church, and making it a fearful ruin (the marks of which are still visible in most of the world), overthrew this sacred polity, and left nothing behind but certain remnants, which cannot but beget superstition, without any edification. This is 'confirmation', as they call it, in which there is nothing but mimicry, and has no foundation. What we set before you, therefore, is nothing else than the use of things which from ancient times were observed among Christians, and which has never been neglected except when the Church has been wholly corrupted.

THE CATECHISM OF THE CHURCH OF GENEVA

I. FAITH

1. *Minister. What is the chief end of human life?*
Child. To know God.
2. *M. Why do you say that?*
C. Because He created us and placed us in this world to be glorified in us. And it is indeed right that our life, of which He Himself is the beginning, should be devoted to His glory.

3. *M. What is the sovereign good of man?*

C. The same thing.

4. *M. Why do you hold that to be the sovereign good?*

C. Because without it our condition is more miserable than that of brute-beasts.

5. *M. Hence, then, we see that nothing worse can happen to a man than to live without God.*

C. It is so.

6. *M. What is the true and right knowledge of God?*

C. When we know Him in order that we may honour Him.

7. *M. How do we honour Him aright?*

C. We put our reliance entirely on Him, by serving Him in obedience to His will, by calling upon Him in all our need, seeking salvation and every good thing in Him, and acknowledging with heart and mouth that all our good proceeds from Him.

8. *M. To consider these things in order, and explain them more fully—what is the first point?*

C. To rely upon God.

9. *M. How can we do that?*

C. First by knowing Him as almighty and perfectly good.

10. *M. Is this enough?*

C. No.

11. *M. Why?*

C. Because we are unworthy that He should show His power in helping us, or employ His goodness toward us.

12. *M. What more then is required?*

C. That we be certain that He loves us, and desires to be our Father, and Saviour.

13. *M. How do we know that?*

C. By His Word, in which He declares His mercy to us in Christ, and assures us of His love toward us.

14. *M. Then the foundation for true reliance upon God is to know Him in Jesus Christ (John 17:3)?*

C. That is true.

15. *M. What then briefly is the substance of this knowledge?*

C. It is contained in the Confession of Faith used by all Christians. It is commonly called the Apostles' Creed, because it is a summary of the true faith which has always been held in Christ's Church, and was also derived from the pure doctrine of the Apostles.

16. *M. Recite it.*

C. I believe in God the Father Almighty, Maker of heaven and earth; and in Jesus Christ, His only Son, our Lord, who was conceived by the Holy Ghost, born of the Virgin Mary, suffered under Pontius Pilate, was crucified, dead, and buried; He descended into hell; the third day He rose again from the dead; He ascended into heaven, and sitteth on the right hand of God the Father Almighty, from thence He shall come to judge the quick and the dead. I believe in the Holy Ghost; the holy Catholic Church; the communion of saints; the forgiveness of sins; the resurrection of the body; and the life everlasting. Amen.

17. *M. In order to expound this confession in detail, into how many parts do we divide it?*

C. Into four principal parts.

18. *M. What are they?*

C. The first is about God the Father; the second about His Son Jesus Christ, which also includes the whole history of our redemption; the third is about the Holy Spirit; the fourth is about the Church, and the gracious gifts of God conferred on her.

19. *M. Since there is but one God, why do you mention the Father, Son, and Holy Spirit, who are three?*

C. Because in the one essence of God, we have to look on

the Father as the beginning and origin, and the first cause of all things; then the Son, who is Eternal Wisdom; and the Holy Spirit who is His virtue and power shed abroad over all creatures, but still perpetually resident in Himself.

20. *M. You mean then that there is no objection to our understanding that these three persons are distinctly in one Godhead, and that God is not therefore divided?*

C. Just so.

21. *M. Now repeat the first part.*

C. "I believe in God the Father Almighty, Maker of heaven and earth."

22. *M. Why do you call Him Father?*

C. It is with reference to Christ who is His eternal Word, begotten of Him before all time, and being sent into this world was demonstrated and declared to be His Son. But since God is the Father of Jesus Christ, it follows that He is our Father also.

23. *M. In what sense do you mean that He is Almighty?*

C. That does not only mean that He has a power which He does not exercise, but that He disposes all things by His Providence, governs the world by His will, ruling all as it seems good to Him.

24. *M. You mean that the power of God is not idle, but consider rather that His hand is always engaged in working, so that nothing is done except through Him, with His permission and His decree.*

C. It is so.

25. *M. Why do you add that He is Creator of heaven and earth?*

C. Because He has manifested Himself to us by works (Ps. 104; Rom. 1:20) we ought to seek Him in them. Our mind cannot comprehend His essence. But the world is for us like a mirror in which we may contemplate Him in so far as it is expedient for us to know Him.

26. *M. Do you not understand by "heaven and earth" all other creatures?*

C. Yes indeed; under these two words all are included, because they are all heavenly or earthly.

27. *M. But why do you call God a Creator only, seeing that it is much more to uphold and preserve creatures in their state, than to have once created them?*

C. This term does not signify that God brought His works into being at a single stroke, and then left them without a care for them. We ought rather to understand, that as the world was made by God in the beginning, so now it is preserved by Him in its estate, so that the heavens, the earth and all creatures do not continue in their being apart from this power. Besides, seeing that He holds all things in His hand, it follows that the government and lordship over them belongs to Him. Therefore, in that He is Creator of heaven and earth, it is His to rule the whole order of nature by His goodness and power and wisdom. It is He who sends rain and drought, hail, tempest and fair weather, fruitfulness and barrenness, health and sickness. In short, all things are under His command, to serve Him as it seems good to Him.

28. *M. But what about wicked men and devils? Are they also subject to Him?*

C. Although He does not guide them by His Holy Spirit, nevertheless He curbs them by His power, so that they cannot budge unless He permits them. He even constrains them to execute His will, although it is against their own intention and purpose.

29. *M. What good do you derive from the knowledge of this fact?*

C. Very much. It would go ill with us if devils and wicked men had power to do anything in spite of the will of God. Moreover we could never be at rest in our minds if we were exposed to them in danger, but when we know that they are curbed by the will of God, so that they can do nothing without His permission, then we may rest and breathe again, for God has promised to protect and defend us.

30. *M. Let us now come to the second part.*

C. "And in Jesus Christ His only Son our Lord", etc.

31. *M. What briefly does it comprehend?*

C. That we acknowledge the Son of God as our Saviour, and the means by which He has redeemed us from death, and acquired salvation.

32. *M. What is the meaning of the name Jesus which you give to Him?*

C. It means Saviour, and was given to Him by the angel at the command of God (Matt. 1:21).

33. *M. Is this of more importance than if men had given it?*

C. Oh, yes. For since God wills that He be called so, He must be so in truth.

34. *M. What, next, is meant by the name Christ?*

C. By this title His office is still better expressed—for it signifies that He was anointed by the Father to be ordained King, Priest, and Prophet.

35. *M. How do you know that?*

C. Because according to the Scripture, anointing is used for these three things. Also, because they are attributed to Him many times.

36. *M. But with what kind of oil was He anointed?*

C. Not with visible oil as was used for ancient kings, priests, and prophets, but this anointing was by the grace of the Holy Spirit, who is the reality signified by that outward anointing made in time past (Isa. 61:1, Ps. 45:7).

37. *M. But what is this Kingdom of which you speak?*

C. It is spiritual, and consists in the Word and Spirit of God, and includes righteousness and life.

38. *M. What of the priesthood?*

C. It is the office and prerogative of presenting Himself before God to obtain grace and favour, and appease His wrath in offering a sacrifice which is acceptable to Him.

39. *M. In what sense do you call Christ a Prophet?*

C. Because on coming down into the world (Isa. 7:14) He was the sovereign messenger and ambassador of God His Father, to give a full exposition of God's will toward the world and so put an end to all prophecies and revelations (Heb. 1:2).

40. *M. But do you derive any benefit from this?*

C. All this is for our good. For Jesus Christ has received all these gifts in order that He may communicate them to us, and that all of us may receive out of His fullness.

41. *M. Expound this to me more fully.*

C. He received the Holy Spirit in full perfection with all His graces, that He may lavish them upon us and distribute them, each according to the measure and portion which the Father knows to be expedient (Eph. 4:7). Thus we may draw from Him as from a fountain all the spiritual blessings we possess.

42. *M. What does His Kingdom minister to us?*

C. By it, we are set at liberty in our conscience and are filled with His spiritual riches in order to live in righteousness and holiness, and we are also armed with power to overcome the devil, the flesh, and the world—the enemies of our souls.

43. *M. What about His Priesthood?*

C. First, by means of it He is the Mediator who reconciles us to God His Father; and secondly, through Him we have access to present ourselves to God, and offer Him ourselves in sacrifice with all that belongs to us. And in this way we are companions of His Priesthood.

44. *M. There remains His Prophetic Office.*

C. Since this office was given to the Lord Jesus to be the Master and Teacher of His own, its end is to bring us the true knowledge of the Father and of His Truth, so that we may be scholars in the household of God.

45. *M. You would conclude, then, that the title of Christ includes three offices which God has given to His Son, in order to communicate virtue and fruit to His faithful people?*

C. That is so.

46. *M. Why do you call Him the only Son of God, seeing that God calls us all His children?*

C. We are the children of God not by nature, but only by adoption and by grace, in that God wills to regard us as such (Eph. 1:5). But the Lord Jesus who was begotten of the substance of His Father, and is of one essence with Him, is rightly called the only Son of God (John 1:14; Heb. 1:2) for there is no other who is God's Son by nature.

47. *M. You mean to say, then, that this honour is proper to Him alone, and belongs to Him by nature, but it is communicated to us through a gratuitous gift, in that we are His members.*

C. That is so. Hence in regard to this communication He is called elsewhere "the First-born among many brethren" (Rom. 8:29; Col. 1:15).

48. *M. How is He "our Lord"?*

C. Because He was appointed by the Father to have us under His government, to administer the Kingdom and the Lordship of God in heaven and on earth, and to be the Head of men and believers (Eph. 5:23; Col. 1:18).

49. *M. What is meant by what follows?*

C. It declares how the Son of God was anointed by the Father to be our Saviour. That is to say, He assumed human flesh, and accomplished all things necessary to our salvation, as enunciated here.

50. *M. What do you mean by the two clauses, "Conceived of the Holy Ghost, born of the Virgin Mary"?*

C. That He was formed in the womb of the Virgin Mary,

of her proper substance, to be the seed of David, as had been foretold (Ps. 132:11), and yet that this was wrought by the miraculous operation of the Holy Spirit, without the co-operation of a man (Matt. 1:18; Luke 1:35).

51. *M. Was it then required that He should put on our very flesh?*

C. Yes, because it was necessary that the disobedience committed by man against God should be redressed in human nature. And moreover He could not otherwise be our Mediator to reconcile us to God His Father (1 Tim. 2:5; Heb. 4:15).

52. *M. You say that Christ had to become man, to fulfil the office of Saviour, as in our very person.*

C. Yes, indeed. For we must recover in Him all that we lack in ourselves, and this cannot be done in any other way.

53. *M. But why was that effected by the Holy Spirit, and not by the work of man according to the order of nature?*

C. As the seed of man is in itself corrupt, it was necessary that the power of the Holy Spirit should intervene in this conception, in order to preserve our Lord from all corruption, and to fill Him with holiness.

54. *M. Thus we are shown that He who is to sanctify others was free from every stain, and from His mother's womb He was consecrated to God in purity from the very beginning, in order that He may not be subject to the universal corruption of the human race.*

C. So I understand it.

55. *M. Why do you go immediately from His birth to His death, passing over the whole history of His life?*

C. Because nothing is said here about what belongs properly to the substance of our redemption.

56. *M. Why is it not said simply and in a word that He died while Pontius Pilate is spoken of, under whom He suffered?*

C. That is not only to make us certain of the history, but is also meant to signify that His death involved condemnation.

57. *M. How is that?*

C. He died to suffer the punishment due to us, and thus to deliver us from it. However, because we were guilty before the judgement of God as evil-doers, in order to represent us in person He was pleased to appear before the tribunal of an earthly judge, and to be condemned by his mouth, that we might be acquitted before the throne of the celestial Judge.

58. *M. But Pilate pronounced Him innocent, and therefore did not condemn Him as if He were worthy of death (Matt. 27:24; Luke 23:14).*

C. Both were involved. He was justified by the testimony of the judge, to show that He did not suffer for His own unworthiness but for ours and yet He was solemnly condemned by the sentence of the same judge, to show that He is truly our surety, receiving condemnation for us in order to acquit us from it.

59. *M. That is well said, for if He had been a sinner He could not have suffered death for others; and yet in order that His condemnation might be our deliverance, He had to be reckoned among transgressors (Is. 53:12).*

C. I understand so.

60. *M. Is there any greater importance in His having been crucified than if He had been put to death in another way?*

C. Yes, as Paul also shows us when he says that He hanged on a tree to take our curse upon Himself and acquit us of it (Gal. 3:13). For that kind of death was accursed of God (Deut. 21:23).

61. *M. What? Is it not to dishonour the Lord Jesus, to say He was subjected to the curse, and that before God?*

C. By no means, for in taking it upon Himself He abolished it, by His power, yet in such a way that He did not cease to be blessed throughout in order that He might fill us with His blessing.

62. *M. Explain the rest.*

C. Since death was the curse on man as a result of sin, Jesus Christ has endured it, and in enduring it overcame it. And to show that He underwent a real death, He chose to be placed in the tomb like other men.

63. *M. But nothing seems to redound to us from this victory, since we do not cease to die.*

C. That is no obstacle. The death of believers is nothing else than a way of entering into a better life.

64. *M. Hence it follows that we ought no longer to dread death as if it were a fearful thing, but we should willingly follow Jesus Christ our Head and Captain, who precedes us, not in order to let us perish, but in order to save us.*

C. That is so.

65. *M. What is the meaning of the additional clause: "He descended into hell"?*

C. That He not only suffered natural death, which is the separation of the body from the soul, but also that His soul was pierced with amazing anguish, which St. Peter calls the pains of death (Acts 2:24).

66. *M. Why and how did that happen to Him?*

C. Because He presented Himself to God in order to make satisfaction in the name of sinners, it was necessary that He should suffer fearful distress of conscience, as if He had been forsaken by God, and even as if God had become hostile to Him. It was in this extremity that He cried, "My God, my God, why hast thou forsaken me?" (Matt. 27:46; Mark 15:34).

67. *M. Was His Father then opposed to Him?*

C. No. But He had to be afflicted in this way in fulfilment of what had been foretold by Isaiah, that "he was smitten by the hand of God for our sins and wounded for our transgressions" (Isa. 53:5; 1 Pet. 2:24).

68. *M. But since He is God Himself, how could He be in such dread, as if He were forsaken by God?*

C. We must hold that it was according to His human nature that He was in that extremity: and that in order to allow this, His Deity held itself back a little, as if concealed, that is, did not show its power.

69. *M. How is it possible that Jesus Christ, who is the salvation of the world, should have been under such damnation?*

C. He was not to remain under it. For though He experienced the horror we have spoken of, He was by no means oppressed by it. On the contrary, He battled with the power of hell, to break and destroy it.

70. *M. Thus we see the difference between the torment which He suffered and that which sinners experience when God punishes them in His wrath. For what He suffered for a time in Himself is perpetual in the others, and what was only a needle to sting Him is to them a sword to deliver a mortal wound.*

C. It is so, for Jesus Christ, even in the midst of such distress, did not cease to hope in God. But sinners whom God condemns rush into despair, defy, and even blaspheme Him.

71. *M. May we not gather from this what fruit we receive from the death of Jesus Christ?*

C. Yes, indeed. And, first, we see that it is a sacrifice by which He has made satisfaction for us before the judgement of God, and so has appeased the wrath of God and reconciled us to Him. Secondly, that His blood is the laver by which our souls are cleansed from all stains. Finally, that by this death our sins are effaced, so as never to be remembered before God, and thus the debt which was against us is abolished.

72. *M. Do we not have any other benefit from it?*

C. Yes, we do. If we are true members of Christ, our old man is crucified, our flesh is mortified, so that evil desires no longer reign in us.

73. *M. Expound the next article.*

C. This is: "On the third day He rose again from the dead." By this He declared Himself the conqueror of death and sin, for by His resurrection He swallowed up death, broke the fetters of the devil, and destroyed all his power (1 Pet. 3:22).

74. *M. In how many ways does this resurrection benefit us?*

C. First, by it righteousness was fully acquired for us. Secondly, it is also a sure pledge to us that we shall rise again one day in immortal glory (1 Cor. 15:20-23).

Thirdly, if we truly participate in His resurrection, even now we are raised in newness of life, to serve God and to live a holy life according to His pleasure (Rom. 6:4).

75. *M. Continue.*

C. "He ascended into heaven."

76. *M. Did He ascend in such a way that He is no longer on earth?*

C. Yes. For after He had performed all that He was enjoined by the Father, and was required for our salvation, there was no need for Him to remain longer on earth.

77. *M. What benefit do we obtain from this ascension?*

C. The benefit is twofold. For inasmuch as Jesus Christ entered heaven in our name, as He had descended for our sake, He has given us an entry, and assured us that the door, previously shut because of sin, is now open for us (Rom. 6:8-11). Secondly, He appears before the face of the Father as our Intercessor and Advocate (Heb. 7:25).

78. *M. But did Christ in going to heaven withdraw from us, in such a way that He has now ceased to be with us?*

C. No. On the contrary, He has promised that He will be with us to the end (Matt. 28:20).

79. *M. Is it in bodily presence that He remains with us?*

C. No, for it is one thing to speak of His body which was taken up into heaven, and another to speak of His power, which is spread abroad everywhere (Luke 24:51; Acts 2:33).

80. *M. How do you understand that He "sitteth on the right hand of the Father"?*

C. It means that He has received the dominion of heaven and earth, so that He reigns and rules over all (Matt. 28:18).

81. *M. But what is meant by "right hand", and by "sitteth"?*

C. It is a similitude taken from earthly princes, who are wont to place on their right hand those whom they make their lieutenants to govern in their name.

82. *M. You do not mean anything more then than Paul when he says that Christ has been appointed Head of the Church, and raised above all principality, has secured a Name which is above every name (Eph. 1:22; 4:15; Phil. 2:9).*

C. That is so.

83. *M. Continue.*

C. "From thence He will come to judge the quick and the dead." That is to say, He will appear again from heaven in judgement, as He was seen to ascend (Acts 1:11).

84. *M. As the judgement is not to be before the end of the world, how do you say that some men will then be alive, and thus will be dead, seeing it is appointed to all men once to die? (Heb. 9:27, 28).*

C. Paul answers this question when he says, that those who then survive will suddenly be changed so that their corruption will be abolished, and their bodies will put on incorruption (1 Cor. 15:52; 1 Thess. 4:17).

85. *M. You understand then that this change will be for them like a death, for it will abolish their first nature, and raise them up in a new state.*

C. That is it.

86. *M. Does the fact that Christ is to come again to judge the world bring us any consolation?*

C. Yes, indeed. For we are certain that He will appear only for our salvation.

87. *M. We should not then fear the last judgement, and have a horror of it?*

C. No, since we are not to come before any other Judge than He who is our Advocate, and who has taken our cause in hand to defend us.

88. *M. Let us come now to the third part.*

C. This is faith in the Holy Spirit.

89. *M. What do we gain by it?*

C. The knowledge that as God has redeemed and saved us by Jesus Christ, He will also make us partakers of this redemption and salvation, through His Holy Spirit.

90. *M. How?*

C. As the blood of Christ is our cleansing, the Holy Spirit must sprinkle our consciences with it that they may be cleansed (1 Pet. 1:19).

91. *M. This requires a clearer explanation.*

C. I mean that the Holy Spirit, while He dwells in our hearts, makes us feel the virtue of our Lord Jesus (Rom. 5:5). For He enlightens us to know His benefits; He seals and imprints them in our souls, and makes room for them in us (Eph. 1:13). He regenerates us and makes us new creatures, so that through Him we receive all the blessings and gifts which are offered to us in Jesus Christ.

92. *M. What follows?*

C. The fourth part, where it is said that we believe in the Catholic Church.

93. *M. What is the Catholic Church?*

C. The community of the faithful which God has ordained and elected to eternal life.

M. Is it necessary to believe this article?

94. C. Yes, indeed, unless we want to make the death of Christ of none effect, and all that has already been said. The fruit that proceeds from it is the Church.

95. *M. You mean then that up to this point we have spoken of the cause and foundation of salvation, how God has received us in love through the mediation of Jesus, and has confirmed this grace in us through His Holy Spirit. But now the effect and fulfilment of all this is explained in order to give us greater certainty.*

C. It is so.

96. *M. In what sense do you call the Church holy?*

C. All whom God has chosen He justifies, and reforms to holiness and innocence, that His glory may be reflected in them (Rom. 8:30). And so Jesus Christ sanctified the Church which He redeemed, that it might be glorious and without blemish (Eph. 5:25-27).

97. *M. What is meant by the word Catholic or Universal?*

C. It is meant to signify, that as there is only one Head of the faithful, so they must all be united in one body, so that there are not several churches but one only, which is extended throughout the whole world (Eph. 4:15; 1 Cor. 12:12 and 27).

98. *M. And what is the meaning of what follows concerning the communion of saints?*

C. That is added to express more clearly the unity which exists among the members of the Church. Moreover by this we are given to understand, that all the benefits that the Lord gives to the Church, are for the good and salvation of every Church, because they all have communion together.

99. *M. But is this holiness which you attribute to the Church already perfect?*

C. Not as long as she battles in this world, for elements of imperfection always remain and will never be entirely removed, until she is united completely to Jesus Christ her Head, by whom she is sanctified.

100. *M. Can this Church be known in any other way than by believing in her?*

C. There is indeed the visible Church of God, for the recognition of which He has certain signs, but here we speak properly of the fellowship of those whom He has elected to salvation which cannot be seen plainly by the eye.

101. *M. What comes next?*

C. I believe in "the forgiveness of sins".

102. *M. What do you understand by this word "forgiveness"?*

C. That God by His pure goodness forgives and pardons the sins of believers, so that they are not brought to account before His judgement, in order to be punished.

103. *M. Hence it follows that it is not at all through our own satisfaction that we desire to have God's pardon?*

C. That is true; for the Lord Jesus has made payment and born the punishment. We on our part could not make any recompence to God, but may only receive pardon for all our misdeeds through the pure generosity of God.

104. *M. Why do you insert this article after the Church?*

C. Because no man obtains pardon for his sins without being previously incorporated into the people of God, persevering in unity and communion with the Body of Christ in such a way as to be a true member of the Church.

105. *M. And so outside the Church there is nothing but damnation and death?*

C. Certainly, for all those who separate themselves from the community of the faithful to form a sect on its own, have no hope of salvation so long as they are in schism.

106. *M. What follows?*

C. I believe in "the resurrection of the flesh and the life everlasting".

107. *M. Why is this article inserted?*

C. To show us that our happiness is not situated on the earth. This serves a two-fold end. We are to learn to pass through this world as though it were a foreign country, treating lightly all earthly things and declining to set our hearts on them.

Secondly, we are not to lose courage, no matter how much we fail to perceive as yet the fruit of the grace which the Lord has wrought for us in Jesus Christ, but wait patiently until the time of revelation.

108. *M. How will this resurrection take place?*

C. Those who were formerly dead will resume their bodies, but with another quality; that is, they will no longer be subject to death or corruption, even although their substance will remain the same. Those who will survive God will miraculously raise up through a sudden change, as it is said (1 Cor. 15:52).

109. *M. Will this resurrection not be common to the evil and the good?*

C. Yes indeed, but not in the same way. Some will rise to salvation and joy, others to condemnation and death (John 5:29; Matt. 25:46).

110. *M. Why then is eternal life only spoken of here, and hell not at all?*

C. Because nothing is set down in this summary that does not tend to the consolation of faithful consciences. It relates to us only the benefits which God performs for His servants. Accordingly no mention is made of the wicked, who are excluded from His Kingdom.

111. *M. Since we have the foundation on which faith is laid, we should be quite able to gather from it what true faith is.*

C. Yes, indeed. It is a sure and steadfast knowledge of the love of God toward us, according as He declares in His gospel that He is our Father and Saviour (through the mediation of Jesus Christ).

112. *M. Can we have this by ourselves, or does it come from God?*

C. Scripture teaches that it is the singular gift of the Holy Spirit, and experience also demonstrates it.

113. *M. How so?*

C. Our mind is too weak to comprehend the spiritual wisdom of God which is revealed to us by faith, and our hearts are too prone either to defiance or to a perverse confidence in ourselves or creaturely things. But the Holy Spirit enlightens us to make us capable of understanding what would otherwise be incomprehensible to us, and fortifies us in certitude, sealing and imprinting the promises of salvation on our hearts.

114. *M. What good comes to us from this faith, when we have it?*

C. It justifies us before God, and makes us obtain eternal life.

115. *M. How so? Is not man justified by good works in a holy life and in conformity to God?*

C. If any one be found so perfect, he might well be deemed righteous, but since we are all poor sinners, we must look elsewhere for a worthiness in which to make answer before the judgement of God.

116. *M. But are all our works so reprobate that they cannot merit grace before God?*

C. First, all that we do of ourselves, by our own nature, is vicious, and therefore cannot please God. He condemns them all.

117. *M. You say then that before God has received us in His grace, we can do nothing but sin, just as a bad tree cannot but produce bad fruit?* (Matt. 7:17).

C. It is so. For even if our works appear beautiful outwardly, yet they are evil, since the heart, to which God looks, is perverted.

118. *M. Hence you conclude, that we cannot by our merits anticipate God, and so induce Him to be kind to us, but on the contrary that we do nothing but provoke Him to be against us?*

C. Yes. And therefore I say: merely through His goodness,

without any regard to our works, He is pleased to accept us freely in Jesus Christ, imputing His righteousness to us, and does not impute our sins to us (Tit. 3:5-7).

119. *M. What do you mean then by saying that a man is justified by faith?*

C. That in believing the promises of the gospel and in receiving them in true affiance of the heart, we enter into this righteousness.

120. *M. You mean then that as God offers righteousness to us by the gospel, so it is by faith that we receive it?*

C. Yes.

121. *M. But after God has once received us, are the works which we do by His grace, not pleasing to Him?*

C. Yes they are, in that He generously accepts them, not however in virtue of their own worthiness.

122. *M. How is that? Are they not accepted as worthy, seeing that they proceed from the Holy Spirit?*

C. No. For there is always some weakness in them, the weakness of our flesh, through which they are defiled.

123. *M. By what means, then, are they made acceptable?*

C. It is by faith. That is to say, that a person is assured in his conscience that God will not examine him harshly, but covering his defects and impurities by the purity of Jesus Christ, He will regard him as perfect.

124. *M. But can we say from this that a Christian man is justified by works after God has called him, or that through them he merits the love of God, and so obtains eternal life?*

C. No. On the contrary, it is said that no man living will be justified in His sight (Ps. 143:2). Therefore we have to pray that He will not enter into judgement with us, nor call us to account.

125. *M. You do not mean therefore that the good works of believers are useless?*

C. No. For God promises to reward them fully, both in

this world and in Paradise. But this comes from His gratuitous love toward us: moreover He buries all our faults, so as never to remember them.

126. *M. But can we believe that we are justified, without doing good works?*

C. That is impossible. For to believe in Jesus Christ is to receive Him as He has given Himself to us. He promises not only to deliver us from death and to restore us to favour with God His Father, through the merit of His innocence, but also to regenerate us by His Spirit, that we may be enabled to live in holiness.

127. *M. Faith, then, not only does not make us careless of good works, but is the root from which they are produced.*

C. It is so, and for this reason the doctrine of the Gospel is comprehended in these two points, faith and repentance.

128. *M. What is repentance?*

C. Dissatisfaction with and a hatred of evil and a love of good proceeding from the fear of God, and inducing us to mortify our flesh, so that we may be governed and led by the Holy Spirit, in the service of God.

129. *M. But this second point we have mentioned concerning the Christian life.*

C. Yes, and we said that the true and legitimate service of God is to obey His will.

130. *M. Why?*

C. Because He will not be served according to our own imagination, but in the way that pleases Him.

II. THE LAW

131. *M. What rule has He given us by which we may direct our life?*

C. His law.

132. *M. What does it contain?*

C. It is divided into two parts: the first contains four commandments, the other six. Thus there are ten in all.

133. *M. Who made this division?*

C. God Himself, who delivered it to Moses written on two tables, and declared that it was reduced into ten words (Exod. 32:15; 34:29; Deut. 4:13; 10:1).

134. *M. What is the content of the first table?*

C. The Way of the true worship of God.

135. *M. And the second?*

C. How we are to live with our neighbours, and what we owe them.

136. *M. Repeat the first commandment.*

C. Hear, O Israel, I am the Lord thy God, who brought thee out of the land of Egypt, out of the house of bondage: thou shalt have no other gods before Me (Exod. 20:2, 3; Deut. 5:6, 7).

137. *M. Explain the meaning.*

C. At first He makes a kind of preface for the whole law. For in calling Himself the Eternal and the Creator of the world, He claims authority to command. Then He declares that He is our God, in order that we may esteem His doctrine. For if He is our Saviour, that is good reason why we should be an obedient people to Him.

138. *M. But is not that which He says after the deliverance from the land of Egypt, addressed particularly to the people of Israel?*

C. Yes, it does refer to the physical deliverance of Israel, but it also applies to us all in a general way, in that He has delivered our souls from the spiritual captivity of sin, and the tyranny of the devil.

139. *M. Why does He mention this at the beginning of His law?*

C. To remind us how much we are bound to obey His good

pleasure, and what ingratitude it would be on our part if we do the contrary.

140. *M. And what does He require briefly in this first commandment?*

C. That we reserve for Him alone the honour that belongs to Him, and do not transfer it elsewhere.

141. *M. What is the honour due to Him?*

C. To adore Him alone, to call upon Him, to have our affiance in Him, and all similar things due to His majesty.

142. *M. Why is it said "Before my face"?*

C. Since He who sees and knows all is the Judge of the secret thoughts of men, it means that He wants to be worshipped as God, not only by outward confession, but also in pure trust and affection of heart.

143. *M. Turn to the second Commandment.*

C. Thou shalt not make unto thee a graven image, nor any form that is in heaven above, or on the earth beneath, or in the water under the earth. Thou shalt not do honour to them.

144. *M. Does He entirely forbid us to make any image?*

C. No, but He forbids us to make any image with which to represent God, or to worship Him.

145. *M. Why is it unlawful to represent God visibly?*

C. Because there is no resemblance between Him who is eternal Spirit and incomprehensible, and corporal, dead, corruptible and visible matter (Deut. 4:15; Isa. 40:7; Rom. 1:23; Acts 17:24, 25).

146. *M. You think then that it does dishonour to His majesty to represent Him in this way?*

C. Yes.

147. *M. What kind of worship is here condemned?*

C. When we come before an image intending to pray, or bow our knee before it; or make any other sign of reverence, as if God were there showing Himself to us.

148. *M. This does not mean that all sculpture or painting is universally forbidden, but only all images used in the service of God, or in worshipping Him in visible things, or indeed for any abuse of them in idolatry of any kind whatsoever.*

C. That is so.

149. *M. Now to what end shall we refer this commandment?*

C. With the first commandment, God declared that He alone, and no one beside Him, should be worshipped: so now He shows us the correct form of worship, in order that He may draw us away from all superstitions, and carnal ceremonies.

150. *M. Let us proceed.*

C. He adds a warning that He is the Eternal, our God, strong and jealous, visiting the iniquity of the fathers upon the children of them who hate Him, to the third and fourth generation.

151. *M. Why does He make mention of His might?*

C. To indicate that He has power to maintain His glory.

152. *M. What is meant by jealousy?*

C. That He cannot allow an associate. For as He has given Himself to us out of His infinite goodness, so He would have us to be entirely His. And this is the chastity of our souls, to be consecrated and dedicated to Him. On the other hand it is a spiritual whoredom for us to turn away from Him to any superstition.

153. *M. How is this to be understood, that He punishes the sin of the fathers on their children?*

C. To give us greater fear of Him. He says not only that He will inflict punishment on those who offend Him, but that their offspring also will be cursed after them.

154. *M. But is it not contrary to the justice of God to punish someone for others?*

C. If we consider the condition of the human race, the question is answered. For by nature we are all cursed, and we cannot complain of God when He leaves us in this condition. Moreover as He manifests His grace and love toward His servants in blessing their children, so this is a testimony to His punishment of the wicked, when He leaves their seed accursed.

155. *M. What more does He say?*

C. To incite us by gentleness, He says that He will have mercy on all who love Him and observe His commands, to a thousand generations.

156. *M. Does He mean that the obedience of a faithful man will save the whole of his race, even if they are still wicked?*

C. No, but that He will extend His goodness toward the faithful to such an extent, that in love for them He will make Himself known to their children, not only to prosper them according to the flesh, but to sanctify them by His Spirit, that He might make them obedient to His will.

157. *M. But this is not always so.*

C. No. For as the Lord reserves for Himself the freedom to show mercy to the children of the ungodly, so on the other hand He retains the power to elect or reject in the generation of the faithful as it seems good to Him (Rom. 9:15-22). However, He does this in such a way that men may acknowledge that this promise is not vain or fallacious (Rom. 2:6-10).

158. *M. Why does He mention here a thousand generations, and in regard to punishment mention only three or four?*

C. To signify that it is His nature to exercise kindness and gentleness much more than strictness or severity, as He testifies, when He says that He is ready to show mercy, but slow to anger (Ex. 34:6, 7; Ps. 103:8).

159. *M. Let us come to the third commandment.*

C. Thou shalt not take the name of the Lord thy God in vain.

160. *M. What does this mean?*

C. He forbids us to abuse the name of God, not only in perjury, but also in superfluous and idle swearing.

161. *M. Can the name of God be used lawfully in oaths?*

C. Yes, when they are necessary, i.e. in order to uphold the truth, when it requires it, and in maintaining love and concord among us.

162. *M. Does He reprove no other oaths, than those which are a dishonour to God?*

C. In this one case He gives us a general instruction never to utter the name of God except with fear and humility in order to glorify it. For since it is holy and honourable, we ought to guard against taking the Name of God in such a way that we appear to hold it in contempt, or give others occasion to vilify it.

163. *M. How is this to be done?*

C. By never thinking or speaking of God and His works without honour and reverence.

164. *M. What follows?*

C. A warning, that He will not hold him guiltless, who takes His name in vain.

165. *M. Since elsewhere He gives a general warning that He will punish all transgressors, what is the advantage of this warning?*

C. He wants to declare how highly He regards the glory of His name, explicitly mentioning that He will not suffer anyone to despise it, so that we may be all the more careful to hold it in reverence.

166. *M. Let us come to the fourth commandment.*

C. Remember the Sabbath day, to keep it holy. Six days shalt thou labour, and do all thy work: But the seventh is the Sabbath of the Lord thy God: in it thou shalt not do any work, thou, nor thy son, nor thy daughter, thy man-servant, nor thy maid-servant, nor thy cattle, nor thy stranger that is within thy gates: For in six days the Lord made heaven and earth, the sea, and all that in them is, and rested the seventh day: wherefore the Lord blessed the Sabbath day, and hallowed it.

167. *M. Does He order us to labour six days a week that we may rest on the seventh?*

C. Not precisely, but in allowing us to labour for six days, He excepts the seventh, on which it is not right to be engaged in work.

168. *M. Does He thus forbid us all work one day a week?*

C. This commandment has a particular reason, for the observance of rest is part of the ceremonies of the ancient Law, which was abolished at the coming of Jesus Christ.

169. *M. Do you mean that this commandment properly belongs to the Jews, and that it was given for the time of the Old Testament?*

C. I do, in so far as it is ceremonial.

170. *M. How is that? Is there anything else in it besides the ceremony?*

C. It was given for three reasons.

171. *M. What are they?*

C. To represent spiritual rest, in aid of ecclesiastical polity, and for the relief of servants.

172. *M. What is this spiritual rest?*

C. It is to cease from our own works, that the Lord may work in us.

173. *M. How is that done?*

C. By mortifying our flesh, that is, renouncing our own nature, so that God may govern us by His Spirit.

174. *M. Is this to be done only one day a week?*

C. This is to be done continually. After we have once begun, we must continue all our life.

175. *M. Why, then, is a certain day appointed to represent this?*

C. It is not required that the representation should be altogether identical with the truth, but it is sufficient that there should be some resemblance.

176. *M. But why is the seventh day appointed rather than any other day?*

C. The number seven implies perfection in Scripture. Thus it is suited to denote perpetuity. It reminds us also that our spiritual rest is only begun in this life, and will not be perfect until we depart from this world.

177. *M. But what is meant when our Lord asserts that we must rest as He did?*

C. After having created all His works in six days, He dedicated the seventh to the contemplation of His works. And in order better to induce us to do this, He set before us His own example. For nothing is so desirable as to be conformed to Him.

178. *M. Must we meditate continually on the works of God, or is it sufficient on one day out of seven?*

C. We must do it every hour, but because of our weakness, one day is specially appointed. And this is the polity of which I spoke.

179. *M. What order, then, is to be observed on that day?*

C. That the people meet to hear the doctrine of God, to engage in common prayer, and bear witness to their faith and religion.

180. *M. What do you mean by saying that this commandment is also given to provide for the relief of servants?*

C. To give some relaxation to those who are under the power of others. And likewise, this tends to maintain a common polity. For everyone accustoms himself to labour for the rest of the time, when there is one day for rest.

181. *M. Let us now see how this commandment addresses itself to us.*

C. As for the ceremony, it was abolished, for we have the accomplishment of it in Jesus Christ.

182. *M. How?*

C. Our old man is crucified, through the power of His death, and through His resurrection we are raised up to newness of life (Rom. 6:6).

183. *M. What else is there here for us?*

C. That we observe the order constituted in the Church, to hear the Word of God, to engage in public prayers and in the Sacraments, and that we do not contravene the spiritual order among the faithful.

184. *M. And does the figure give us any further benefit?*

C. Yes, indeed. It should lead us to the truth, namely, that being true members of Christ, we should cease from our own works, and put ourselves under His government.

185. *M. Let us come to the second table.*

C. It begins, "Honour thy father and thy mother".

186. *M. What do you mean by "honour"?*

C. That children be humble and obedient toward their parents, doing them honour and reverence, helping them and being at their command, as they are bound.

187. *M. Proceed further.*

C. God adds a promise to the commandment, "That thy days may be prolonged on the land which the Lord thy God will give thee."

188. *M. What does that mean?*

C. That God will give long life to those who honour their father and mother as they ought.

189. *M. Seeing this life is so full of misery, why does God promise man as a favour that he will live long?*

C. However miserable it may be, life on earth is a blessing from God to the faithful, if only for this reason, that in it God testifies to His fatherly love in supporting them in it.

190. *M. Does it follow conversely, that the man who dies prematurely is cursed of God?*

C. By no means. Rather does it sometimes happen that the

M

Lord withdraws from this world more quickly those whom He loves most.

191. *M. In so doing, how does He fulfil His promise?*

C. All that God promises us in earthly blessings, we must receive under this condition, viz. that it is expedient for our spiritual salvation. For it would be poor indeed if that did not have precedence.

192. *M. What of those who are rebellious against their father and mother?*

C. Not only will God punish them at the last judgement, but here also God will exercise judgement on their bodies, it may be by letting them die before their time, or ignominiously, or in some other way.

193. *M. Does He not speak expressly of the land of Canaan in this promise?*

C. Yes, so far as the children of Israel are concerned, but the term ought to have a more general meaning for us. For seeing that the earth is the Lord's, whatever be the country we inhabit, He assigns it to us for our habitation (Ps. 24:1; 89:12; 115:16).

194. *M. Is that all there is to the commandment?*

C. Though father and mother only are mentioned, nevertheless all superiors are intended, as the reason is the same.

195. *M. What is the reason?*

C. That God has given them pre-eminence; for there is no authority whether of parents, or princes, or of any others who are over us, but what God has ordained (Rom. 13:1).

196. *M. Repeat the sixth commandment.*

C. Thou shalt not kill.

197. *M. Does it forbid nothing but murder?*

C. Yes, indeed. For seeing it is God who speaks, He gives us law not only for outward deeds, but primarily for the affections of our heart.

198. *M. You mean then that there is some kind of inward murder which God forbids to us?*

C. I do: hatred and rancour, and desire to do evil to our neighbour.

199. *M. Is it sufficient for us not to hate or to bear ill will?*

C. No, for in condemning hatred God signifies that He requires us to love our neighbours and seek their salvation, and all this with true affection and without simulation.

200. *M. State the seventh commandment.*

C. Thou shalt not commit adultery.

201. *M. What is the essence of this?*

C. That all fornication is cursed by God, and therefore we must abstain from it if we do not want to provoke His anger against us.

202. *M. Does it not require anything else?*

C. We must always regard the nature of the Lawgiver, who does not halt at the outward act, but requires the affection of the heart.

203. *M. What more then does it mean?*

C. Since our bodies and our souls are temples of the Holy Spirit (1 Cor. 3:16; 6:15; 2 Cor. 6:16), we must preserve them in uprightness. And so we must be chaste not only in deed, but also in desire, word and gesture. Accordingly no part of us is to be polluted by unchastity.

204. *M. Let us come to the eighth commandment.*

C. Thou shalt not steal.

205. *M. Is it only meant to prohibit the thefts which are punished by justice, or does it extend further?*

C. It refers to all evil traffic and unscrupulous means of acquiring our neighbour's goods, whether by violence, or fraud, or in any other kind of way that God has not allowed.

206. *M. Is it enough to abstain from evil deeds, or is covetousness also included here?*

C. We must ever return to this, that the Lawgiver is spiritual, that He does not speak simply of outward thefts, but all schemes, wishes and plans to enrich ourselves at the expense of our neighbour.

207. *M. What are we to do then?*

C. We must do our duty in preserving for every man his own.

208. *M. What is the ninth commandment?*

C. Thou shalt not bear false witness against thy neighbour.

209. *M. Does it forbid perjury in court, or any kind of lying against our neighbour?*

C. In mentioning this one case it gives a general instruction, that we are not to speak evil of our neighbour falsely, nor by our slanders and lies are we to do him harm in his possessions, or in his reputation.

210. *M. But why does He expressly mention public perjury?*

C. That He may give us a greater abhorrence of this vice of evil speaking and slander, telling us that if a man accustom himself to slandering and defaming his neighbour, he will soon descend to perjury in court.

211. *M. Does He only forbid evil speaking, or does He also include evil thinking?*

C. Both of them, for the reason already stated. For whatever it is wrong to do before men, it is wrong to wish before God.

212. *M. Then summarise its meaning.*

C. He enjoins us not to be inclined to misjudge and defame our neighbours, but rather to esteem them highly, as far as the truth will permit, and to preserve their good reputation in our speech.

213. *M. Let us come to the last commandment.*

C. Thou shalt not covet thy neighbour's house, thou shalt not covet thy neighbour's wife, nor his man-servant, nor his maid-servant, nor his ox, nor his ass, nor any thing that is thy neighbour's.

214. *M. Seeing that the whole law is spiritual, as you have so often said before, and the other commandments are not only to order outward acts, but also the affections of the heart, what more is added here?*

C. The Lord wished by the other commandments to rule our affections and will, but here He imposes a law also on our thoughts which though charged with covetousness and desire, yet stop short of an active intention.

215. *M. Do you mean that the least temptation that enters into the thought of a believer is sin, even though he resists it and does not consent to it?*

C. It is certain that all evil thoughts proceed from the infirmity of our flesh, even though we do not consent to them. But I say that this commandment speaks of concupiscence which tickles and pierces the heart of man, without bringing him to a deliberate purpose.

216. *M. You say then that the evil affections which involve a definite act of will or resolution are already condemned, but now the Lord requires of us such integrity, that no wicked desire may enter our hearts, to solicit and incite them to evil.*

C. That is right.

217. *M. Can we not now give a short summary of the whole law?*

C. We can, reducing it to two articles—the first of which is that we are to love God with all our heart, and with all our soul, and with all our strength; the second that we love our neighbours as ourselves.

218. *M. What is meant by the love of God?*

C. To love Him as God is to have and hold Him as Lord, Saviour and Father, and this requires reverence, honour, faith, and obedience along with love.

219. *M. What does "with all our heart" signify, and "with all our soul, and all our strength"?*

C. Such a zeal and such a vehemence, that there is in us no desire, no will, no intention and no thought, contrary to this love.

220. *M. What is the meaning of the second article?*

C. As we are by nature so prone to love ourselves, that this affection overcomes all others, so love to our neighbour should be so predominant in our hearts, as to direct and govern us, and be the rule of all our thoughts and actions.

221. *M. What do you understand by "our neighbours"?*

C. Not only parents and friends, or those acquainted with us, but also those who are unknown to us, and even enemies.

222. *M. But what connection do they have with us?*

C. That which God has placed among all men on the earth, and is so inviolable, that it cannot be abolished by the malice of any man.

223. *M. You say, then, that if any man hate us, the blame is his own, and yet according to the order of God, he does not cease to be our neighbour, and we are to regard him as such?*

C. It is so.

224. *M. Seeing that the law of God comprises the form of worshipping Him aright, should not the Christian man live according to its command?*

C. Yes indeed. But there is some infirmity in us, so that no man acquits himself perfectly in it.

225. *M. Why then does the Lord require a perfection which is beyond our ability?*

C. He requires nothing which we are not bound to perform. Nevertheless, provided we take care to conform our life to what we are told here, although we are very far from reaching perfection, the Lord does not impute our faults to us.

226. *M. Do you speak of all men in general, or of believers only?*

C. He who is not yet regenerated by the Spirit of God cannot begin to do the least of the commandments. Moreover, even if a person could be found who had fulfilled some part of the law, he would not acquit himself before God, for our Lord pronounces that all those who have not fulfilled all the things contained in it, will be accursed (Deut. 27:26; Gal. 3:10).

227. *M. Hence we must conclude that the law has a two-fold office, in accordance with the fact that there are two classes of men.*

C. Yes, in regard to unbelievers it seems but to convict and make them inexcusable before God (Rom. 3:3). And this is what Paul says, that it is the ministry of death and condemnation (2 Cor. 3:6, 9). In regard to believers, it has a very different use.

228. *M. What?*

C. First, in that it shows them that they cannot justify themselves by their works, it humbles them and disposes them to seek their salvation in Jesus Christ (Rom. 5:18-21). Secondly, inasmuch as it requires of them much more than they are able to perform, it admonishes them to pray unto the Lord, that He may give them strength and power (Gal. 4:6), and at the same time reminds them of their perpetual guilt, that they may not presume to be proud. Thirdly it is a kind of bridle, by which they are kept in the fear of God.

229. *M. We say then that although during this mortal life we will never fulfil the Law, such perfection is not required of us in vain, for it shows us the mark at which we ought to aim, that each of us, according to the grace God has bestowed on him, may strive continually to press toward it, and to advance day by day.*

C. That is as I understand it.

230. *M. Do we not have a perfect rule of goodness in the Law?*

C. Yes, and therefore God demands nothing from us, but to follow it; and, on the other hand, repudiates and rejects all that a man undertakes to do beyond what it contains. The only sacrifice He requires is obedience (1 Sam. 15:22; Jer. 7:21-23).

231. *M. What is the purpose then of all the admonitions, reproofs, commandments, and exhortations made both by Prophets and Apostles?*

C. They are nothing else than declarations of the Law, leading us into obedience to it rather than turning us away from it.

232. *M. But nothing is said about particular vocations?*

C. When it is said that we are to render to every one his due, we may well infer what the duty of each is in his own vocation. Moreover as we have already said, this is expounded for us in the whole of Scripture, for what the Lord has set down in this summary, He treats of there, and with much fuller teaching.

III. PRAYER

233. *M. Since we have spoken sufficiently of the service of God, which is the second part of His worship, let us now speak of the third part.*

C. We said it was the invocation of God in all our needs.

234. *M. Do you think that He alone is to be invoked?*

C. Yes, for He requires this as the worship proper to His Deity.

235. *M. If it is so, in what way is it legitimate for us to ask the aid of men?*

C. There is a great difference between these two things. For we call upon God to protest that we expect no good but from Him, and that we have no refuge elsewhere, and yet we ask the assistance of men, as far as He permits, and has given them the power and means of helping us.

236. *M. You mean that when we seek the succour of men, there is nothing to prevent our calling upon God alone, seeing that we do*

not put our reliance on them, and do not seek their aid except in so far as God has ordained them to be ministers and dispensers of His blessings, in order to assist us.

C. That is true. And indeed, every benefit that comes to us we should take as coming from God Himself, as in truth it is He who sends it to us by their hands.

237. *M. Nevertheless, should we not give thanks to men for the kindness which they do to us?*

C. Certainly, if only for the reason that God honours them by communicating His blessings to us through their hands, for in this way He lays us under obligation to Him, and wishes us to be mindful of them.

238. *M. Can we not conclude from this that it is wrong to invoke angels, and saints who have departed from this world?*

C. Yes, indeed; for God has not assigned to saints this office of aiding and assisting us. And in regard to angels, though He employs their ministry for our salvation, nevertheless He does not wish us to invoke them, nor to address ourselves to them.

239. *M. You say, then, that all that conflicts with the order instituted by the Lord, contravenes His will?*

C. Yes, for it is a sure sign of infidelity if we are not contented with what the Lord gives to us. Moreover, if instead of having a refuge in God alone, in obedience to His command, we have recourse to them, putting something of our reliance on them, we fall into idolatry, seeing we transfer to them that which God has reserved for Himself.

240. *M. Let us now speak of the way of prayer to God. Is it sufficient to pray with the tongue, or does prayer require also the spirit and the heart?*

C. The tongue is not always necessary, but there must be understanding and affection.

241. *M. How will you prove that?*

C. Since God is Spirit, He always requires the heart, and

especially in prayer, in which we enter into communication with Him, wherefore He promises to be near to those only who call upon Him in truth (Ps. 145:18). On the other hand, He curses all who pray to Him in hypocrisy, and without affection (Isa. 29:13, 14).

242. *M. All prayers, then, made only with the mouth are vain?*

C. Not only vain, but also displeasing to God.

243. *M. What kind of affection should we have in prayer?*

C. First, that we feel our misery and poverty, and that this feeling should beget sorrow and anguish in us. Secondly, that we have an earnest desire to obtain grace from God. This desire will also kindle our hearts, and engender in us an ardent longing to pray.

244. *M. Does this derive from our nature, or from the grace of God?*

C. Here God must come to our aid, for we are too dull, but the Spirit of God helps us with groanings that cannot be uttered, and forms in our hearts the affection and zeal that God requires, as Paul says (Rom. 8:26; Gal. 4:6).

245. *M. Does this mean that we have not to incite and urge ourselves to pray?*

C. By no means. On the contrary, when we do not feel such a disposition within us we should beseech the Lord to put it into us, so as to make us capable and fit to pray as we ought.

246. *M. You do not, however, mean that the tongue is quite useless in prayer?*

C. Not at all, for sometimes it helps the mind, sustaining and keeping it from being drawn away from God so easily. Besides, since more than all the other members it was formed to the glory of God, it is very reasonable that it should be employed by all means for this purpose. Moreover, the zeal of the heart by its own ardour and vehemence often constrains the tongue to speak quite spontaneously.

247. *M. If so, what about prayer in an unknown tongue?*

C. It is a mockery of God, and a perverse hypocrisy (1 Cor. 14:14).

248. *M. But when we pray to God, is it a venture in which we do not know whether we will succeed or not? Or ought we to be certain that our praying will be heard?*

C. The ground of our prayers should always be, that they will be received by God, and that we shall obtain what we request as far as it is expedient for us. And therefore St. Paul says that true prayer comes from faith (Rom. 10:14). For if we have no reliance upon the goodness of God, it will be impossible for us to call upon Him in truth.

249. *M. And what of those who doubt, not knowing if God hears or not?*

C. Their prayers are utterly void, since they have no promise, for He says that whatever we shall ask, believing, we shall receive (Matt. 21:22; Mark 11:24).

250. *M. It remains to learn how and in whose name we can have the boldness to present ourselves before God, seeing that we are so unworthy in ourselves.*

C. First we have the promises on which we must rest, without considering our worthiness (Ps. 50:15; 91:3; 145:18; Isa. 30:15; 65:24; Jer. 29:12; Joel 3:5). Secondly, if we are children of God, He induces and urges us by His Holy Spirit to betake ourselves to Him familiarly, as to our Father (Matt. 9:2, 22; etc.). And lest we, who are poor worms of the earth, and miserable sinners, should be afraid to appear before His glorious majesty, He gives us our Lord Jesus Christ as a Mediator (1 Tim. 2:5; Heb. 4:16; 1 John 2:1), that through Him we may have access and have no doubt of finding grace.

251. *M. Do you understand that we are to call upon God only, in the Name of Jesus Christ?*

C. I understand so, for we have an express commandment

about this. And in it we are promised that by His intercession our requests will be heard (John 14:13).

252. *M. It is not, then, temerity or foolish presumption on our part, if we presume to address God personally, seeing that we have Jesus Christ for our Advocate, and if we set Him before us, that God may for His sake be gracious to us and accept us?*

C. No, for we pray as it were by His mouth, since He gives us entrance and audience, and intercedes for us (Rom. 8:34).

253. *M. Let us now speak of the substance of our prayers. Can we ask for all that comes into our mind, or is there a certain rule to be observed about it?*

C. If we followed our own fantasy, our prayers would be very badly ordered. We are so ignorant that we cannot judge what it is good to ask: moreover, all our desires are so intemperate that it is necessary that we should not give them a loose rein.

254. *M. What is to be done, then?*

C. That God Himself should instruct us, according to what He knows to be expedient; that we do nothing but follow Him, as if He were leading us by the hand.

255. *M. What instructions has He given?*

C. He has given us ample instructions throughout Scripture; but that we may address ourselves the better to a definite end, He has given us a form in which He has briefly comprehended everything that is legitimate and expedient for us to pray for.

256. *M. Repeat it.*

C. Our Lord Jesus Christ, being asked by His Disciples to teach them how to pray, answered that they should pray thus (Matt. 6:9-13; Luke 11:1-4):

"Our Father, which art in heaven, hallowed be thy name. Thy kingdom come. Thy will be done in earth, as it is in heaven. Give us this day our daily bread. And forgive us our debts, as we forgive our debtors. And lead us not into temptation; but deliver us from evil: For thine is the kingdom, and the power, and the glory, for ever. Amen."

257. *M. To make it easier to understand, tell me how many sentences it contains.*

C. Six, of which the first three concern the glory of God alone, without any reference to ourselves; the other three are for us, and concern our blessing and profit.

258. *M. Are we then to ask God for anything from which no benefit redounds to us?*

C. It is true that God, by His infinite goodness, so arranges and orders things, that nothing tends to the glory of His Name, without being also salutary to us. Therefore, when His Name is sanctified, He turns it to our sanctification; when His Kingdom comes, we are, in a way, sharers in it. But in desiring and asking all these things, we ought to have regard only for His glory, without thinking of ourselves, or seeking our own profit.

259. *M. According to what you say, the first three of these requests are expedient for us, and yet they ought not to be made with any other intention than of desiring that God may be glorified.*

C. It is so. And similarly, although the last three requests are appointed as prayers for what is expedient to us, yet even in them we ought to seek the glory of God, so that it may be the end of all our desires.

260. *M. Let us come to the exposition. And before we go any further, why is God called our Father, rather than some other name?*

C. Since it is essential that our consciences have a steadfast assurance, when we pray, our God gives Himself a name, which suggests only gentleness and kindness, in order to take away from us all doubt and anxiety, and to give us boldness in coming to Him personally.

261. *M. Shall we then dare to go to God familiarly, as a child to his father?*

C. Yes, in fact with greater assurance of obtaining what we ask. For if we, being evil, cannot refuse our children bread and meat, when they ask, how much less will our heavenly Father, who is not only good, but sovereign goodness itself (Matt. 7:11)?

262. *M. Can we not prove from this very Name, what has been said, viz. that prayer should be grounded on the intercession of Jesus Christ?*

C. Yes, certainly. For God does not acknowledge us as His children, except in so far as we are members of His Son.

263. *M. Why do you not call God your God, but call Him our Father together?*

C. Each believer may indeed call Him his own Father, but in this formula Jesus Christ instructs us to pray together, to remind us that in our prayers we are to exercise charity towards our neighbours, and not only to care for ourselves.

264. *M. What is meant by the clause "who art in heaven"?*

C. It is just the same as if I were to call Him exalted, mighty, incomprehensible.

265. *M. To what end, and for what reason?*

C. That when we call upon Him, we may learn to lift up our thoughts on high, and not to have any carnal or earthly thoughts of Him, not to measure Him by our apprehension, nor to subject Him to our will, but to adore His glorious Majesty in humility. It teaches us also to have more reliance on Him, since He is Governor and Master of all.

266. *M. Now expound the first petition.*

C. The Name of God is His renown, with which He is celebrated among men. We pray then that His glory may be exalted above all, and in all things.

267. *M. Do you think that His glory can increase or decrease?*

C. Not in itself. But this means that it may be manifested, as it ought to be, that all the works which God performs may appear glorious, as indeed they are, so that He Himself may be glorified in every way.

268. *M. What do you understand by the Kingdom of God in the second petition?*

C. It consists principally of two things: that He leads His own, and governs them by His Spirit, and on the other hand casts down and confounds the reprobate who refuse to subject themselves to His rule, and so makes it clear that there is no power which can resist His power.

269. *M. In what sense do you pray that this Kingdom may come?*

C. That day by day the Lord may increase the numbers of the faithful, that day by day He may increasingly bestow His graces upon them, until He has filled them completely; moreover, that He cause His truth to shine more and more and manifest His justice, so that Satan and the powers of darkness may be put to confusion, and all iniquity be destroyed and abolished.

270. *M. Is that not taking place today?*

C. Yes indeed—in part, but we pray that it may continually increase and advance, until at last it comes to its perfection in the day of Judgement, in which God alone will be exalted, and every creature will be humbled before His Majesty, and He will be all in all (1 Cor. 15:28).

271. *M. What do you mean by asking that the will of God may be done?*

C. That all creatures may be brought under obedience to Him, and so that everything may be done according to His good will.

272. *M. Do you mean that nothing can be done contrary to His will?*

C. We ask not only that He may bring all things to pass, as He has determined in His counsel, but also that, putting down all rebellion, He may bring all wills to conform to His own.

273. *M. In so doing, do we not renounce our own wills?*

C. We do, not only that He may overthrow our desires, which are at variance with His own good will, bringing them all to nought, but also that He may create in us new spirits and new hearts, so that we may will nothing of ourselves, but rather that His Spirit may will in us, and bring us into full agreement with Him.

274. *M. Why do you add "on earth as it is in heaven"?*

C. Since His heavenly creatures or His angels have it as their only object to obey Him, promptly without any opposition, we desire that the same thing may be done on earth, that is, that all men may yield themselves in voluntary obedience.

275. *M. Let us come to the second part. What mean you by "the daily bread" you ask for?*

C. In general, everything that we need for our body, not only food and clothing, but all that God knows to be expedient for us, that we may be able to eat our bread in peace.

276. *M. But why do you ask God to give you your food, when He orders us to win it, by working with our hands?*

C. Though He commands us to work for our living, nevertheless it is not our labour, industry, and diligence, that provide us with food, but the blessing of God alone, which makes the labour of our hands to prosper. Moreover we ought to understand that it is not meat that nourishes us, although we have it owing to His command, but the power of the Lord alone who uses it as His instrument (Deut. 8:3, 17).

277. *M. Why do you call it yours, when you ask God to give it to you?*

C. Because by the kindness of God it becomes ours, though it is by no means due to us. We are also reminded by this not to desire the bread of others, but only that which we acquire by legitimate means, according to the ordinance of God.

278. *M. Why do you say "daily" and "this day"?*

C. That we may learn to be content, and not to covet more than our need requires.

279. *M. Since this prayer is common to all, how can the rich, who have an abundance of good things, provided for a long time, ask for bread each day?*

C. The rich, as well as the poor, should understand that none of the things profit them, unless the Lord grant them the use of them, and by His grace make it profitable to them. Thus in having we have nothing, unless He gives it to us.

280. *M. What does the fifth petition contain?*

C. That is pleases God to pardon our sins.

281. *M. Is any man living so righteous, that He does not need to make this petition?*

C. No, for the Lord Jesus gave this form of prayer to His Apostles for His Church. Wherefore he who would exempt himself from this, must renounce the community of Christians. And indeed Scripture testifies to us that even the most perfect man seeking to justify himself before God in a single matter, will be found guilty in a thousand (Job 9:3). Thus the only refuge we may have is in His mercy.

282. *M. How do you think that such remission is granted to us?*

C. As the words Jesus Christ used declare: because our sins are debts, making us liable to eternal death, we pray that God will pardon us out of His sheer kindness.

283. *M. You mean, then, that it is by the gratuitous goodness of God that we obtain remission of sins?*

C. Yes, for we can offer no satisfaction for the smallest sin we commit, if God does not exercise His sheer kindness toward us in forgiving us them all.

284. *M. What gain and profit do we receive, when God pardons our sins?*

C. We are acceptable to Him, just as if we were righteous

N

and innocent, and our consciences are assured of His paternal love, from which comes salvation and life.

285. *M. When you pray that He may forgive us as we forgive our debtors, do you mean that in pardoning men we merit pardon from God?*

C. By no means, for then pardon would not be by grace, and would not be founded, as it ought to be, on the satisfaction which Jesus Christ made for us in His death. But since by forgetting the injuries done to ourselves, we follow His gentleness and clemency, and so demonstrate that we are His children, God has given us this as a sign in confirmation that we are His children. On the other hand, He indicates to us that we cannot expect anything at His judgement but utter severity and extreme rigour, if we are not ready to pardon and show mercy to others who are guilty toward us.

286. *M. Do you think, then, God refuses to have as His children those who cannot forget the offences committed against them, so that they cannot hope to be partakers of His grace?*

C. Yes. And He intends that all men may know that with what measure they mete to their neighbours, it shall be measured to them

287. *M. What follows?*

C. "Lead us not into temptation, but deliver us from evil."

288. *M. Do you treat this as one petition?*

C. Yes, for the second part is an explanation of the first part.

289. *M. What is the substance of it?*

C. That God does not allow us to fall into evil, or permit us to be overcome by the devil, and the lustful desires of our flesh, which strive against us (Rom. 7:23), but He gives us strength to resist, sustains us by His hand, takes us into His safe keeping, to defend and lead us.

290. *M. How is this done?*

C. When He governs us by His Spirit, to make us love the

good, and hate the evil, follow justice, and flee from sin. By the power of His Spirit, we may overcome the devil, sin and the flesh.

291. *M. Do we stand in need of this?*

C. Yes, for the devil continually watches for us, like a roaring lion ready to devour us (1 Peter 5:8). We are so feeble and frail that he would immediately overcome us, if God did not fortify us, that we might be victorious over him.

292. *M. What does the word "temptation" signify?*

C. The wiles and assaults of the devil, which he uses to attack us, seeing that our natural judgement is prone to be deceived and to deceive us, and our will is always ready to addict itself to evil rather than to good.

293. *M. But why do you pray God not to lead you into evil, when this is the proper office of Satan the devil?*

C. As God by His mercy preserves the faithful, and does not permit the devil to seduce them, or sin to overcome them, so those whom He means to punish He not only abandons, and deprives of His grace, but also yields to the devil to be subjected to his tyranny, blinds them and delivers them over to a reprobate mind.

294. *M. What is intended by the addition, "For thine is the kingdom, and the power, and the glory, for ever"?*

C. To remind us again that our prayers are altogether grounded on the power and goodness of God, and not on ourselves, for we are not worthy to open our mouth in prayer; and also that we may learn to close all our prayers in His praise.

295. *M. Is it lawful to ask anything else, not mentioned here?*

C. Although we are free to use other words, and another form and manner, yet no prayer will ever please God which does not correspond to this as the only rule of right prayer.

IV. THE WORD AND SACRAMENTS

296. *M. It is time to come to the fourth part of the worship we are to render to God.*

C. We said that this consists in acknowledging with the heart and confirming with the mouth that God is the author of all good, that thereby we may glorify Him.

297. *M. Has He given us any rule for this?*

C. All the praises and thanksgivings contained in Scripture ought to be our rule and guide.

298. *M. Is there nothing regarding this in the Lord's Prayer?*

C. Yes there is, for when we pray that His name may be hallowed, we pray that He may be glorified in all His works, as indeed He is—that He may be praised for His justice when He punishes, for His mercy when He pardons, and for His faithfulness when He fulfils His promises; in short, that there is nothing in which His glory does not shine forth. This is to ascribe to Him the praise for all blessing.

299. *M. What shall we infer from all that we have said?*

C. What truth itself tells us, and was stated at the outset, viz. that this is eternal life to know one true God the Father, and Jesus Christ whom He has sent (John 17:3)—to know Him, I say, in order that we may worship Him aright, that He may be not only our Master, but also our Father and Saviour, and we be in turn His children and servants, and a people dedicated to His glory.

300. *M. How can we attain to such blessedness?*

C. For this end God has left us His holy Word, which is, as it were, an entry into His heavenly Kingdom.

301. *M. Where do you find this Word?*

C. It is comprised for us in the Holy Scriptures.

302. *M. How are we to use it in order to profit by it?*

C. By receiving it with the full consent of our conscience,

as truth come down from heaven, submitting ourselves to it in right obedience, loving it with a true affection by having it imprinted in our hearts, we may follow it entirely and conform ourselves to it.

303. *M. Is all this within our own power?*

C. None of it; but God works them in us in this way by His Holy Spirit.

304. *M. But are we not to take trouble and be diligent, and zealously strive by hearing and reading its teaching, as it is declared to us?*

C. Yes, indeed: first each one of us in particular ought to study it: and above all, we are frequently to attend the sermons in which this Word is expounded in the Assembly of the Christians.

305. *M. Do you mean that it is not enough for people to read it privately at home, without altogether hearing its teaching in common?*

C. That is just what I mean, while God provides the way for it.

306. *M. Why do you say that?*

C. Because Jesus Christ has established this order in His Church (Eph. 4:11), and He has declared this to be the only means of edifying and preserving it. Thus we must keep ourselves to it and not be wiser than our Master.

307. *M. Is it necessary, then, that there should be pastors?*

C. Yes; and that we should hear them, receiving the teaching of the Lord in humility by their mouth. Therefore whoever despises them and refuses to hear them, rejects Jesus Christ, and separates himself from the fellowship of the faithful (Matt. 10:40; Luke 10:16).

308. *M. But is it enough to have been instructed by them once, or ought he to continue to do this?*

C. It is little to have begun, unless you go on and persevere.

We must continue to be disciples of Christ right to the end. But He has ordained the ministers of the Church to teach in His Name.

309. *M. Is there no other means than the Word by which God communicates Himself to us?*

C. To the preaching of His Word He has conjoined the Sacraments.

310. *M. What is a Sacrament?*

C. An outward attestation of the grace of God which, by a visible sign, represents spiritual things to imprint the promises of God more firmly in our hearts, and to make us more sure of them.

311. *M. What? Does a visible and natural sign have this power to assure the conscience?*

C. No, not of itself, but in so far as it is ordained of God for this end.

312. *M. Seeing it is the proper office of the Holy Spirit to seal the promises of God in our hearts, how do you attribute this to the Sacraments?*

C. There is a great difference between the one and the other. The Spirit of God in very truth is the only One who can touch and move our hearts, enlighten our minds, and assure our consciences; so that all this ought to be judged as His own work, that praise may be ascribed to Him alone. Nevertheless, the Lord Himself makes use of the Sacraments as inferior instruments according as it seems good to Him, without in any way detracting from the power of His Spirit.

313. *M. You think, then, that the efficacy of the Sacraments does not consist in the outward element, but proceeds entirely from the Spirit of God?*

C. Yes; for the Lord is pleased to work by these instruments which He has instituted: without detracting from His own power.

314. *M. And what moves God to do that?*

C. For the alleviation of our weakness. If we were spiritual by nature, like the angels, we could behold God and His graces. But as we are bound up with our bodies, it is needful for us that God should make use of figures to represent to us spiritual and heavenly things, for otherwise we could not comprehend them. At the same time, it is expedient for us to have all our senses exercised in His holy promises, in order to confirm us in them.

315. *M. Since God has introduced the Sacraments to meet our need, it would be arrogance and presumption to think that we could dispense with them.*

C. Certainly: hence he who voluntarily abstains from using them thinks that he has no need of them, condemns Jesus Christ, rejects His grace, and quenches His Holy Spirit.

316. *M. But what assurance of grace can the Sacraments give, seeing that good and bad both receive them?*

C. Although the unbelievers and the wicked make of none effect the grace offered to them through the Sacraments, yet it does not follow that the proper nature of the Sacraments is also made of none effect.

317. *M. How, then, and when do the Sacraments produce this effect?*

C. When we receive them in faith, seeking Jesus Christ alone and His grace in them.

318. *M. Why do you say that we must seek Jesus Christ in them?*

C. I mean that we are not to be taken up with the earthly sign so as to seek our salvation in it, nor are we to imagine that it has a peculiar power enclosed within it. On the contrary, we are to employ the sign as a help, to lead us directly to the Lord Jesus, that we may find in Him our salvation and all our well-being.

319. *M. Seeing that faith is required, why do you say that they are given to confirm us in faith, to assure us of the promises of God?*

C. It is not sufficient for faith once to be generated in us. It must be nourished and sustained, that it may grow day by day and be increased within us. To nourish, strengthen, and increase it, God gives us the Sacraments. This is what Paul indicates when he says that they are used to seal the promises of God in our hearts (Rom. 4:11).

320. *M. But is it not a sign of unbelief when the promises of God are not firm enough for us, without support?*

C. It is a sign of the smallness and weakness of faith, and such is indeed the faith of the children of God, who do not, however, cease to be faithful, although their faith is still imperfect. As long as we live in this world some elements of unfaithfulness remain in our flesh, and therefore we must always advance and grow in faith.

321. *M. How many Sacraments are there in the Christian Church?*

C. There are only two Sacraments common to all which the Lord Jesus has instituted for the whole company of the faithful.

322. *M. What are they?*

C. Baptism and the Holy Supper.

323. *M. What likeness and difference is there between them?*

C. Baptism is for us a kind of entrance into the Church of God, for it testifies that instead of our being strangers to Him, God receives us as members of His family. The Supper testifies that God as a good Father carefully feeds and refreshes the members of His household.

324. *M. That the meaning may be more clear to us, let us treat of them separately. First, what is the meaning of Baptism?*

C. It consists of two parts. The Lord represents to us in it, first, the forgiveness of our sins (Eph. 5:26, 27) and, secondly, our regeneration or spiritual renewal (Rom 6:4).

325. *M. What resemblance has water with these things in order to represent them?*

C. The forgiveness of sins is a kind of washing, by which our souls are cleansed from their defilements, just as the stains of the body are washed away by water.

326. *M. What about the other part?*

C. The beginning of our regeneration and its end is our becoming new creatures, through the Spirit of God. Therefore the water is poured on the head as a sign of death, but in such a way that our resurrection is also represented, for instead of being drowned in water, what happens to us is only for a moment.

327. *M. You do not mean that the water is a washing of the soul.*

C. By no means, for that pertains to the blood of Jesus Christ alone, which was shed in order to wipe away all our stains and render us pure and unpolluted before God (1 John 1:7; 1 Peter 1:19). This is fulfilled in us when our consciences are sprinkled by the Holy Spirit. But by the Sacrament that is sealed to us.

328. *M. Do you think that the water is only a figure for us?*

C. It is such a figure that the reality is conjoined with it, for God does not promise us anything in vain. Accordingly it is certain that in Baptism the forgiveness of sins is offered to us and we receive it.

329. *M. Is this grace fulfilled indiscriminately in all?*

C. No, for some make it of no effect by their perversity. Nevertheless, the Sacrament loses nothing of its nature, although none but believers feel its efficacy.

330. *M. From what does regeneration get its power?*

C. From the death and resurrection of Christ. His death has had this effect, that through it our old Adam is crucified, and our evil nature is, as it were, buried, so that it no longer has the strength to rule over us. And the renewal of our life, in obedience to the righteousness of God, derives from the resurrection of Christ.

331. *M. How is this grace applied to us in Baptism?*

C. In it we are clothed with Jesus Christ, and receive His Spirit, provided that we do not make ourselves unworthy of the promises given to us in it.

332. *M. What is the proper use of Baptism on our part?*

C. It consists in faith and in repentance. That is, assurance that we have our spiritual purity in Christ, and in feeling within us, and declaring to our neighbours by our works, that His Spirit dwells in us to mortify our natural desires and bring us to follow the Will of God.

333. *M. If this is required, how is it that we baptise little infants?*

C. It is not said that faith and repentance should always precede the reception of the Sacrament, but they are only required from those who are capable of them. It is sufficient, then, if infants produce and manifest the fruit of their Baptism after they come to the age of discretion.

334. *M. Can you show that there is nothing inconsistent in this?*

C. Circumcision was also a Sacrament of repentance, as Moses and the prophets declare (Deut. 10:16; 30:6; Jer. 4:4); and was a Sacrament of faith, as St. Paul says (Rom. 4:11, 12). And yet God has not excluded little children from it.

335. *M. But can you show that they are now admitted to Baptism for the same reason as in the case of circumcision?*

C. Yes, for the promises which God anciently gave to His people of Israel are now extended to the whole world.

336. *M. But does it follow from this that we are to use the sign also?*

C. That becomes evident when everything is considered.

Jesus Christ has not made us partakers of His grace, which formerly had been bestowed on the people of Israel, in order to diminish it in us, or make it more obscure, but rather to manifest it and to bestow it upon us in increased abundance.

337. *M. Do you reckon that if we denied Baptism to little infants, the grace of God would then be diminished by the coming of Christ?*

C. Yes; for the sign of the bounty and mercy of God toward our children, which they had in ancient times, would be wanting in our case, the very sign which ministers so greatly to our consolation, and to confirm the promise already given in the Command.

338. *M. You mean then that since God in ancient times declared Himself to be the Saviour of little infants, and wanted to have this promise sealed on their bodies by an external Sacrament, it is right that confirmation of it should not be less after the advent of Christ, since the same promise remains and indeed is more clearly attested by the Word and ratified in action.*

C. Yes. And besides, since it is quite evident that the power and the substance of Baptism pertain to little children, to deny them the sign, which is inferior to the substance, would be to do them injury.

339. *M. On what conditions should we baptise little children?*

C. As a sign and testimony that they are heirs of God's blessing promised to the seed of the faithful, that when they come of age they are to acknowledge the truth of their Baptism, in order to derive benefit from it.

340. *M. Let us speak of the Supper. And, first, what is its signification?*

C. Our Lord instituted it to assure us that by the communication of His body and blood, our souls are nourished, in the hope of eternal life.

341. *M. But why does the Lord represent His body by the bread and His blood by the wine?*

C. To signify that as it is the particular virtue of bread to nourish our bodies, to refresh and sustain us in this mortal life, so it pertains to His body to act toward our souls, i.e. in nourishing and quickening them spiritually. Likewise as wine strengthens, refreshes, and rejoices a man physically, so His blood is our joy, our refreshing and our spiritual strength.

342. *M. Do you mean that we must truly communicate in the body and blood of the Lord?*

C. I understand so. But since the whole affiance of our salvation rests in the obedience which He has rendered to God, His Father, in order that it may be imputed to us as if it were ours, we must possess Him: for His blessings are not ours, unless He gives Himself to us first.

343. *M. But did He not give Himself to us when He exposed Himself to death, to reconcile us to God His Father, and deliver us from damnation?*

C. That is true; but it is not enough for us unless we receive Him, in order that we may feel in ourselves the fruit and the efficacy of His death and passion.

344. *M. Is not the way to receive Him by faith?*

C. Yes. Not only in believing that He died and rose again, in order to deliver us from eternal death, and acquire life for us, but also that He dwells in us, and is conjoined with us in a union as the Head with the members, that by virtue of this conjunction He may make us partakers of all His grace.

345. *M. Does this communion take place apart from the Supper alone?*

C. Yes, indeed, we have it through the Gospel, as St Paul declares (1 Cor. 1:9): in that the Lord Jesus Christ promises us in it, that we are flesh of His flesh and bone of His bone (Eph. 5:30), that He is that living bread which came down from heaven to nourish our souls (John 6:51), and that we are one with Him, as He is one with the Father (John 17:21).

346. *M. What is the blessing that we have in the Sacrament, and what more does it minister to us?*

C. This communion is more abundantly confirmed in us, ratified as it were, for although Jesus Christ is truly communicated to us both by Baptism and by the Gospel, nevertheless this is only in part, and not fully.

347. *M. What then fully do we have through the sign of the bread?*

C. That the body of the Lord Jesus which was once offered to reconcile us to God, is now given to us, to certify to us that we have part in this reconciliation.

348. *M. What do we have in the sign of wine?*

C. That the Lord Jesus, who once shed His blood in payment and satisfaction for our offences, gives it to us to drink, that we may have no doubt at all of receiving its fruit.

349. *M. According to your replies, the Supper takes us back to the death and passion of Jesus Christ, that we may communicate in its virtue?*

C. Yes, for then the unique and perpetual sacrifice was offered for our redemption. Therefore there remains for us nought but to enjoy it.

350. *M. The Supper, then, was not instituted in order to offer up the body of Jesus the Son to His Father?*

C. No, for this office pertains to none but Him alone, since He is the eternal Priest (Heb. 5:5). But He commands us only to receive His body, not to offer it (Matt. 26:26).

351. *M. Why is there a double sign?*

C. Our Lord has appointed it for the sake of our weakness, in order to teach us that He is not only food to our souls, but drink also, so that we may seek our nourishment wholly and entirely in Him, and not elsewhere.

352. *M. Should all men equally use the second sign, that is the chalice?*

C. Yes, this is according to the commandment of Jesus Christ, against which nothing is to be attempted.

353. *M. Do we have in the Supper simply the testimony of the things already mentioned, or are they truly given to us in it?*

C. Seeing that Jesus Christ is the Truth, there can be no doubt that the promises which He made at the Supper, are actually fulfilled in it, and that what He figures in it is made true. Thus in accordance with what He promises and represents in the Sacrament, I do not doubt that He makes us partakers of His very substance, in order to unite us with Himself in one life.

354. *M. But how can this be, when the body of Jesus Christ is in heaven, and we are pilgrims on this earth?*

C. By the incomprehensible power of His Spirit, who conjoins things separated by distance.

355. *M. You do not think, then, either that the body is enclosed in the bread, or the blood in the chalice?*

C. No. On the contrary, in order to have the reality of the Sacraments, we must lift up our hearts on high to heaven, where Jesus Christ is in the glory of His Father, from whence we expect Him in our redemption, and do not seek Him in these corruptible elements.

356. *M. You understand, then, that there are two things in this Sacrament, material bread and wine, which we see by the eye, handle by the hands, and perceive by the taste, and Jesus Christ by whom our souls are inwardly nourished?*

C. Yes, but in such a way that we have in it also a testimony and a kind of pledge for the resurrection of our bodies, in that they are made partakers in the sign of life.

357. *M. What is the right use of this Sacrament?*

C. That which St. Paul declares, namely that a man examine himself before he approach to it (1 Cor. 11:28).

358. *M. In what is he to examine himself?*

C. Whether he is a true member of Jesus Christ.

359. *M. By what sign can he know this?*

C. If he has a true faith and repentance, if he loves his neighbour in true charity, and is not tainted by hatred or rancour or discord.

360. *M. But is it necessary to have perfect faith and charity?*

C. Both should be entire and unfeigned, but to have such a perfection, from which nothing is wanting, will not be found among men. Moreover the Supper would have been instituted in vain if no one could receive it unless he were entirely perfect.

361. *M. Imperfection, then, does not prevent us from approaching it.*

C. On the contrary, the Supper would be of no use to us, if we were not imperfect. It is an aid and support for our weakness.

362. *M. Do these two Sacraments not serve any other end?*

C. Yes, they do. They are also signs and marks of our profession. That is to say, by them we declare that we are of the people of God, and make confession of our Christianity.

363. *M. How ought we to judge a man who never wishes to use it?*

C. He could not be regarded as a Christian, for in so doing he refuses to confess himself as such, and tacitly, as it were, disavows Jesus Christ.

364. *M. Is it sufficient to receive each once?*

C. Baptism is only ordered to be received once, and may not lawfully be repeated. But this is not so with the Supper.

365. *M. What is the reason for that?*

C. By Baptism God introduces and receives us into His

Church. After He has received us, He signifies by the Supper that He wishes continually to nourish us.

366. *M. To whom does it belong truly to baptise and administer the Supper?*

C. To those who are publicly charged to teach in the Church. For the preaching of the Word and the distribution of the Sacraments are things conjoined.

367. *M. Is there any certain proof for this?*

C. Yes, indeed. Our Lord specially charged His Apostles to baptise as well as to preach (Matt. 28:19). In regard to the Supper, He ordered all to follow His example. Moreover He performed the office of a minister in order to give it to others.

368. *M. But ought pastors, who are appointed to dispense the Sacraments, to admit without discretion all who present themselves there?*

C. In regard to Baptism, as it is administered today only to infants, there is no need for discrimination; but in the Supper the minister ought to take heed not to give it to a man whom he recognizes to be entirely unworthy.

369. *M. Why so?*

C. Because it would pollute and dishonour the Sacrament.

370. *M. But our Lord admitted Judas to the Supper, impious though he was?*

C. His iniquity was still hidden, and although our Lord knew it, yet it was not evident to all.

371. *M. What then is to be done with hypocrites?*

C. The minister cannot exclude them as unworthy, but must wait until God has revealed their iniquity.

372. *M. But what if he knows or has been warned that someone is unworthy?*

C. That would not be sufficient to exclude him, unless there were a legitimate investigation and decision of the Church.

373. *M. Then there ought to be some order and polity regarding this.*

C. Yes, if the Church is to be well ordered. Some persons must be appointed to watch out for the offences that may be committed. And they, with the authority of the Church, should refuse communion to those who are quite unfit, and to whom communion cannot be given without dishonouring God and scandalising the faithful.

THE HEIDELBERG CATECHISM, 1563

THE Heidelberg Catechism was first published in 1563 under the title *Catechism or Christian Instruction, as conducted in the Churches and Schools of the Electoral Palatinate.* It was composed in German by Zacharias Ursinus and Casper Olevianus, both Professors at the University of Heidelberg, and issued under the authority of Frederick III and with a preface by his hand, for the use of the Church in the Palatinate. While the influence of Calvin and Peter Martyr is apparent throughout it, the exposition brings together both Lutheran and Reformed teaching and as such has exercised a powerful mediating influence.

One of the outstanding features of the Catechism relates to the fact that it was published as an integral part of the Church Ordinances, being given its place between the formulary for Holy Baptism and that for Holy Communion. This means that faith and order, doctrine and worship, were intentionally held together in unity, with the result that if the Catechism supplies the norm for the life and liturgy of the Church, it is no less true that its doctrinal instruction cannot be divorced from the daily worship of the Community.

A Latin translation of the Catechism was published also in 1563, with the title *Catechism of Christian Religion*. It was this edition that was several times translated into English. One of these, accompanied by notes, was issued by the authority of the King for the use of the Church of Scotland in 1591, and another was "appointed to be printed for use of the Kirk of Edinburgh" in 1615. *The Palatine Catechism*, as it came to be called, was much beloved in Scotland and came to be bound up with copies of the *Book of Common Order* and the *Psalm*

Book, while the Latin translation was widely used in the Grammar Schools and Colleges. Its examination and approval without alteration by the Synod of Dort in 1618 greatly enhanced its authority.

It is a revised translation of the original German text that is offered here.

THE HEIDELBERG CATECHISM

Question 1. What is your only comfort in life and in death?

Answer. That I, with body and soul, both in life and in death, am not my own, but belong to my faithful Saviour Jesus Christ, who with His precious blood has fully satisfied for all my sins, and redeemed me from all the power of the devil; and so preserves me that without the will of my Father in heaven not a hair can fall from my head: indeed, all things must minister to my salvation. Therefore, by His Holy Spirit He also assures me of everlasting life, and makes me willing and ready in heart henceforth to live unto Him.

Q.2. How many things do you need to know, that you may live and die in this comfort and blessing?

A. Three things: *First,* how great is my sin and misery. *Second,* how I am redeemed from all my sins and misery. *Third,* how I am to be grateful to God for such redemption.

I

The Misery of Man

Q.3. Where do you learn of your misery?

A. In the Law of God.

Q.4. What does the Law of God require of us?

A. This Christ teaches us briefly in Matt. 22: *Thou shalt love the Lord thy God with all thy heart, and with all thy soul, and with all thy mind, and with all thy strength. This is the first and great commandment; and the second is like unto it: Thou shalt love thy neighbour as thyself. On these two commandments hang all the law and the prophets.*

Q.5. Can you keep all this perfectly?

A. No; for by nature I am prone to hate God and my neighbour.

Q.6. Did God then create man evil and perverse like this?

A. No, but God created man good, and according to His own image—that is, in true righteousness and holiness, that he might know God his Creator aright, love Him with his heart, and live with Him in eternal blessedness, to praise and glorify Him.

Q.7. Where, then, does this corrupt nature of man come from?

A. From the fall and disobedience of our first parents, Adam and Eve, in Paradise, whereby our nature became so poisoned that we are all conceived and born in sin.

Q.8. But are we so corrupt that we are altogether incapable of any good, and prone to all evil?

A. Yes, unless we are born again through the Spirit of God.

Q.9. Does not God, then, deal unjustly with man by requiring of him in His law what he cannot perform?

A. No; for God so created man that he could perform it. But man, through the instigation of the devil, by wilful disobedience deprived himself and all his posterity of these gifts.

Q.10. Will God allow such disobedience and defection to go unpunished?

A. Not at all, but He is fearfully angry both with our innate and our actual sins, and will punish them in righteous judgement in time and in eternity, as He has declared: *Cursed is every one that continueth not in all things which are written in the book of the law, to do them.*

Q.11. Is, then, God not also merciful?

A. God is indeed merciful, but He is also just. Therefore His righteousness requires that sin, which is committed against the sovereign majesty of God, be also punished with complete, that is, with everlasting punishment of body and soul.

II

THE REDEMPTION OF MAN

Q.12. Since, then, by the righteous judgement of God we have deserved temporal and eternal punishment, how may we face this punishment, and be restored to grace?

A. God wills that His righteousness be satisfied; therefore we must make full payment to His righteousness, either by ourselves or by another.

Q.13. But can we make this satisfaction by ourselves?

A. Not at all. Rather do we increase our guilt daily.

Q.14. Can any mere creature make payment for us?

A. No, for, first, God will not punish in any other creature that of which man has made himself guilty. Secondly, no mere creature can bear the burden of God's eternal wrath against sin, and redeem others from it.

Q.15. Then, what kind of mediator and redeemer must we seek?

A. One who is a true and righteous man, and yet more powerful than all creatures, that is, one who is at the same time true God.

Q.16. Why must He be a true and righteous Man?

A. Because the righteousness of God requires that the same human nature which has sinned should make payment for sin; but no man, who is himself a sinner, could pay for others.

Q.17. Why must He at the same time be true God?

A. That by the power of His Godhead He might bear, in His manhood, the burden of God's wrath, and recover and restore to us righteousness and life.

Q.18. But who is that Mediator, who is at the same time true God and a true, righteous Man?

A. Our Lord Jesus Christ, who is given unto us for complete redemption and righteousness.

Q.19. How do you know this?

A. From the Holy Gospel, which God Himself revealed in the beginning in Paradise, afterwards proclaimed by the holy Patriarchs and Prophets, and foreshadowed by the sacrifices and other ceremonies of the law, and finally fulfilled by His well-beloved Son.

Q.20. Are all men, then, restored by Christ, as they perished by Adam?

A. No, but only those who through true faith are incorporated into Him, and receive all His benefits.

Q.21. What is true faith?

A. It is not only a certain knowledge whereby I hold for truth all that God has revealed to us in His Word, but also a hearty trust which the Holy Ghost works in me through the Gospel, that not only to others, but to me also, forgiveness of sins, everlasting righteousness and blessedness, are given by God, out of pure grace, for the sake of Christ's merits alone.

Q.22. What then is it necessary for a Christian to believe?

A. All that is promised us in the Gospel, which the articles of our catholic, undoubted Christian faith teach us in summary form.

Q.23. What are these Articles?

A. *I believe in God the Father Almighty, Maker of heaven and earth. And in Jesus Christ, His only-begotten Son, our Lord; who was conceived by the Holy Ghost, born of the Virgin Mary; suffered under Pontius Pilate, was crucified, dead, and buried; He descended into Hell; the third day He rose from the dead; He ascended into Heaven, and sitteth at the right hand of God the Father Almighty; from thence He shall come to judge the quick and the dead.*

I believe in the Holy Ghost; the holy Catholic Church; the communion of saints; the forgiveness of sins; the resurrection of the body, and the life everlasting.

Q.24. How are these Articles divided?

A. Into three parts: The first is of *God the Father* and our *creation*; the second, of *God the Son* and our *redemption*; the third, of *God the Holy Ghost* and our *sanctification*.

Q.25. Since there is only one Divine Being, why do you speak of three, Father, Son, and Holy Spirit?

A. Because God has so revealed Himself in His Word that these three distinct Persons are the one, true, eternal God.

GOD THE FATHER

Q.26. What do you believe when you say: I believe in God the Father Almighty, Maker of Heaven and Earth?

A. That the eternal Father of our Lord Jesus Christ, who created out of nothing the heaven and the earth, with all things in them, who also upholds and governs the same by His eternal counsel and providence, is for the sake of Christ His Son my God and my Father, in whom I so trust that I do not doubt that He will provide me with all things necessary for body and soul; and further, that whatever evil He sends upon me in this miserable life, He will turn to my good; for He is able to do it, as Almighty God, and He is willing to do it, as a faithful Father.

Q.27. What do you understand by the Providence of God?

A. The almighty and present power of God, whereby He still upholds, as it were by His hand, and governs heaven and earth, with all creatures, so that herbs and grass, rain and drought, fruitful and unfruitful years, meat and drink, health and sickness, riches and poverty, and all things, come upon us not by chance, but by His fatherly hand.

Q.28. What benefit do we derive from the knowledge of God's creation and providence?

A. That we ought to be patient in all adversity, thankful in prosperity, and for the future have great confidence in our faithful God and Father, assured that no creature shall separate us from His love, since all creatures are so in His hand that without His will they cannot even stir or move.

GOD THE SON

Q.29. Why is the Son of God called Jesus, that is, Saviour?

A. Because He saves us from our sins, and because salvation is to be sought or found in no other.

Q.30. Do they, then, believe in the only Saviour Jesus who seek their blessing and salvation from saints, or themselves, or any other source?

A. No, for although they make boast of Him, yet in act they deny Jesus who alone brings blessing and salvation. For either Jesus is not a complete Saviour, or they who by true faith receive this Saviour must have in Him all that is necessary for their salvation.

Q.31. Why is He called Christ, that is, Anointed?

A. Because He is ordained of God the Father, and anointed with the Holy Spirit to be our chief Prophet and Teacher, who fully reveals to us the secret counsel and will of God concerning our redemption; to be our only High Priest, who by the one sacrifice of His body has redeemed us, and continually makes intercession for us with the Father; and to be our eternal King, who governs us by His Word and Spirit, and defends and maintains us in the redemption obtained for us.

Q.32. But why are you called a Christian?

A. Because by faith I am a member of Christ, and thus a partaker of His anointing, in order that I also may confess His name, may present myself a living sacrifice of thanksgiving to Him, and may with a free conscience fight against sin and the devil in this life, and hereafter, in eternity, rule with Him over all creatures.

Q.33. Why is He called God's only-begotten Son, since we also are God's Children?

A. Because Christ alone is the eternal natural Son of God, but we are adopted to be children of God through grace for His sake.

Q.34. Why do you call Him our Lord?

A. Because, not with gold or silver, but with His precious blood, He has redeemed and purchased us, body and soul, from sin and from all the power of the devil, to be His own.

Q.35. What is the meaning of Conceived by the Holy Ghost, born of the Virgin Mary?

A. That the eternal Son of God, who is and remains true and eternal God, took upon Him true human nature from the flesh and blood of the Virgin Mary, through the operation of the Holy Spirit, so that He also might be the true seed of David, like unto His brethren in all things, sin excepted.

Q.36. What benefit do you receive from the holy conception and birth of Christ?

A. That He is our Mediator, and with His innocence and perfect holiness He covers, before God's face, my sin wherein I was conceived.

Q.37. What do you understand by the word Suffered?

A. That all the time of His life on earth, but especially at the end of it, He bore, in body and soul, the wrath of God against the sin of the whole human race, in order that by His passion, as by the only atoning sacrifice, He might redeem our body and soul from everlasting damnation, and obtain for us God's grace, righteousness, and eternal life.

Q.38. Why did He suffer under Pontius Pilate, the judge?

A. That He, being innocent, might be condemned by the temporal judge, and thereby set us free from the severe judgement of God which ought to fall upon us.

Q.39. Is there anything more in His having been crucified than if He had died some other death?

A. Yes, for by this I am sure that He took on Himself the curse which lay upon me, because the death of the Cross was cursed by God.

Q.40. Why did Christ have to suffer death?

A. Because, on the ground of God's righteousness and truth, reparation for our sins could be made no other way than through the death of the Son of God.

Q.41. Why was He buried?

A. To show thereby that He was really dead.

Q.42. Since, then, Christ died for us, why must we also die?

A. Our death is not a reparation for our sin, but only a dying to sins and entering into eternal life.

Q.43. What further benefit do we receive from the sacrifice and death of Christ on the Cross?

A. That by his power our old man is with Him crucified, slain, and buried; so that the evil lusts of the flesh may no more reign in us, but that we may offer ourselves unto Him a sacrifice of thanksgiving.

Q.44. Why is it added: He descended into Hell?

A. That in the greatest assaults of evil upon me, I may be assured that Christ my Lord, by His unspeakable anguish, pains, and terrors which He suffered also in His soul on the Cross and before, has redeemed me from the anguish and torment of hell.

Q.45. What benefit do we receive from the resurrection of Christ?

A. First, by His resurrection He has overcome death, that He might make us partakers of the righteousness which He has obtained for us by His death. Secondly, we too are now by His power raised up to a new life. Thirdly, the resurrection of Christ is to us a sure pledge of our blessed resurrection.

Q.46. How do you understand the words, He ascended into Heaven?

A. That before the eyes of His disciples, Christ was taken up from the earth into heaven, and remains there for our good, until He comes again to judge the living and the dead.

Q.47. Is not Christ with us, then, unto the end of the world, as He has promised us?

A. Christ is true Man and true God. According to His human nature, He is now not on earth, but according to His Godhead, majesty, grace, and Spirit, He is never absent from us.

Q.48. But are not the two natures in Christ separated from one another in this way, if the Manhood is not wherever the Godhead is?

A. By no means. For since the Godhead is incomprehensible and everywhere present, it must follow that it is indeed beyond the bounds of the Manhood which it has assumed, and yet is none the less within it as well, and remains personally united to it.

Q.49. What benefit do we receive from Christ's ascension into Heaven?

A. First, that He is our Advocate in Heaven before the face of His Father. Secondly, that we have our flesh in Heaven, as a sure pledge that He, as the Head, will also take us, His members, up to Himself. Thirdly, that He sends down to us His Spirit, as a counter-pledge by whose power we seek what is above, where Christ sits on the right hand of God, and not what is on earth.

Q.50. Why is it added, And sitteth at the right hand of God?

A. Because Christ ascended into Heaven for this end, that He might show Himself there as Head of His Christian Church, through whom the Father governs all things.

Q.51. What benefit do we receive from this glory of Christ, our Head?

A. First, that by His Holy Spirit He pours out heavenly gifts into us, His members; then, that by His power He protects and preserves us against all enemies.

Q.52. What comfort is it to you that Christ shall come again to judge the quick and the dead?

A. That in all afflictions and persecution, with uplifted head, I may wait for the Judge from Heaven who has already offered Himself to the judgement of God for me, and has taken away from me all curse; who will cast all His and my enemies into everlasting condemnation, but shall take me with all His chosen ones to Himself, into heavenly joy and glory.

God the Holy Ghost

Q.53. What do you believe concerning the Holy Ghost?

A. First, that He is co-eternal God with the Father and the Son. Secondly, that He is also given to me, makes me by a true faith partaker of Christ and all His benefits, comforts me, and shall abide with me forever.

Q.54. What do you believe concerning the Holy Catholic Church?

A. That out of the whole human race, from the beginning of the world to its end, the Son of God, by His Spirit and Word, gathers, protects, and preserves for Himself in the unity of the true faith and unto everlasting life, a chosen community; and that I am, and forever shall remain, a living member of the same.

Q.55. What do you understand by the communion of saints?

A. First, that believers, all and every one, as His members have fellowship in the Lord Christ, and in all His treasures and gifts. Secondly, that each one must know that he is bound to use his gifts, readily and cheerfully, for the benefit and salvation of the other members.

Q.56. What do you believe concerning the forgiveness of sins?

A. That God, for the sake of Christ's satisfaction, will no more remember my sins, or the sinful nature with which I have to struggle all my life long, but graciously imparts to me the righteousness of Christ, that I may nevermore come into condemnation.

Q.57. What comfort do you derive from the resurrection of the body?

A. That not only shall my soul, after this life, be immediately taken up to Christ its Head, but also that this flesh of mine, raised by the power of Christ, shall again be united with my soul, and shall be made conformable to the glorious body of Christ.

Q.58. What comfort do you have from the article on the life everlasting?

A. That, since I now feel in my heart the beginning of eternal joy, I shall possess after this life complete blessedness such as eye has not seen, nor ear heard, and which has not entered into the heart of man, therein to praise God for ever.

Q.59. But what does it help you now that you believe all this?

A. That in Christ I am righteous before God, and an heir of eternal life.

Q.60. How are you righteous before God?

A. Only through true faith in Jesus Christ; wherefore although my conscience already accuses me that I have grievously sinned against all the commandments of God, and have not kept any one of them, and that I am still ever prone to all evil, yet God, without any merit of my own, out of sheer grace, grants and imputes to me the perfect satisfaction, righteousness, and holiness of Christ, as if I had never committed nor had a single sin, and had myself accomplished all the obedience which Christ has fulfilled for me, if only I receive such a benefit with a believing heart.

Q.61. Why do you say that you are righteous by faith alone?

A. Not because I please God on account of the worthiness of my faith; but because the satisfaction, righteousness, and holiness of Christ alone is my righteousness before God, and because I can receive it and make it my own in no other way than by faith alone.

Q.62. But why cannot our good works contribute in whole or part to our righteousness before God?

A. Because the righteousness which can stand before the judgement of God must be perfect throughout, and wholly conformable to the Law, whereas even our best works in this life are all imperfect and defiled with sins.

Q.63. Do then our good works merit nothing, even when it is God's will to reward them in this and in the future life?

A. The reward derives not from merit, but from grace.

Q.64. But does not this teaching make people careless and profane?

A. No, for it is impossible that those who are ingrafted into Christ through true faith should not bring forth fruits of thankfulness.

THE HOLY SACRAMENTS

Q.65. Since, then, faith alone made us partakers of Christ and all His benefits, where does such faith come from?

A. The Holy Spirit works it in our hearts by the preaching of the holy Gospel, and confirms it by the use of the holy Sacraments.

Q.66. What are the Sacraments?

A. The Sacraments are visible, holy signs and seals, ordained by God in order that He, by their use, may the more fully declare and seal to us the promise of the Gospel, namely, that He grants us out of free grace the forgiveness of sins and everlasting life, for the sake of the one sacrifice of Christ accomplished on the Cross.

Q.67. Are both these, then, the Word and the Sacraments,

designed to direct our faith to the sacrifice of Jesus Christ on the Cross as the only ground of our salvation?

A. Yes, indeed, for the Holy Spirit teaches in the Gospel, and establishes by the holy Sacraments, that our whole salvation stands in the one sacrifice of Christ offered for us on the Cross.

Q.68. How many Sacraments has Christ ordained in the New Testament?

A. Two: holy Baptism and the holy Supper.

HOLY BAPTISM

Q.69. How are you put in mind and confirmed in holy Baptism that the one sacrifice of Christ on the Cross avails for you?

A. Thus: that Christ has ordained this outward washing with water, and has thereby promised that I am washed with His blood and Spirit from the uncleanness of my soul, that is, from all my sins, as surely as I am washed outwardly with water which is normally used to remove the impurity of the body.

Q.70. What does it mean to be washed with the blood and Spirit of Christ?

A. It means to have the forgiveness of sins from God, through grace, for the sake of Christ's blood, which He has shed for us in His sacrifice on the Cross; and also to be renewed by the Holy Ghost, and sanctified to be a member of Christ, so that we may more and more die unto sin, and lead a life blessed by God and without blame.

Q.71. Where has Christ promised that we are as certainly washed with His blood and Spirit as with the water of Baptism?

A. In the institution of Baptism, which runs thus: *Go ye, therefore, and teach all nations, baptising them in the name of the Father, and of the Son, and of the Holy Ghost. He that believeth and is baptised, shall be saved; but he that believeth not, shall be damned.* This promise is also repeated where the Scripture calls

P

Baptism the washing of regeneration and the washing away of sins.

Q.72. Is, then, the outward washing of water itself the washing away of sins?

A. No, for the blood of Jesus Christ alone and the Holy Spirit cleanse us from all sin.

Q.73. Why, then, does the Holy Spirit call Baptism the washing of regeneration and the washing away of sins?

A. God speaks thus not without great cause: namely, not only to teach us thereby that just as the impurity of the body is taken away by water, so our sins also are taken away by the blood and Spirit of Christ; but much more, that by this divine pledge and true sign He may assure us that we are as really washed from our sins spiritually as our bodies are washed with water physically.

Q.74. Are infants also to be baptised?

A. Yes; for since they, as well as their elders, belong to God's covenant and His community, and both redemption from sin in the blood of Christ and the Holy Spirit, who works faith, are promised to them no less than to adults, they are also by Baptism, as a sign of the covenant, to be incorporated into the Christian Church, and distinguished from the children of unbelievers, as was done in the Old Testament through Circumcision, in place of which Baptism is ordained in the New Testament.

THE HOLY SUPPER OF JESUS CHRIST

Q.75. How are you put in mind and confirmed in the Holy Supper that you have communion in the one sacrifice of Christ on the Cross and all His benefits?

A. Thus, that Christ has commanded me and all believers to eat of this broken bread, and to drink of this cup, in remembrance of Him, and has thereby promised: First, that His body was offered and broken on the Cross for me, and His blood was shed for me, as surely as I see with my eyes the bread of the Lord broken for me, and the cup communicated to me; and, second, that He Himself with His crucified body and shed blood feeds and nourishes my soul with food and drink to everlasting life, as surely as I receive from the hand of the minister, and physically partake of the bread and cup of the Lord, which are given me as true and certain signs of the body and blood of Christ.

Q.76. What does it mean to eat the crucified body and drink the shed blood of Christ?

A. It is not only to embrace with a believing heart the whole passion and death of Christ, and thereby to obtain the forgiveness of sins and everlasting life, but in addition to be so united more and more to His blessed body by the Holy Spirit, who dwells both in Christ and in us, that although He is in heaven, and we on the earth, we are nevertheless flesh of His flesh and bone of His bone, and ever live and are governed by one Spirit, as the members of the body are by one soul.

Q.77. Where has Christ promised that He will give believers His body and blood to eat and drink, as surely as they eat of this broken bread and drink of this cup?

A. In the institution of the Supper, which runs thus: *The Lord Jesus, the same night in which he was betrayed, took bread; and when he had given thanks, he brake it, and said: Take, eat, this is my body, which is broken for you; this do in remembrance of me. After the same manner also he took the cup, when he had supped, saying: This cup is the New Testament in my blood; this do ye as often as ye drink it, in remembrance of me. For as often as ye eat this bread, and drink this cup, ye do show the Lord's death till he come.*

And this promise is repeated also by St. Paul, where he says: *The cup of blessing which we bless, is it not the communion of the blood of Christ? The bread which we break, is it not the*

communion of the body of Christ? For we, being many, are one
bread, and one body; for we are all partakers of that one bread.

Q.78. *Do, then, the bread and wine become the very body and*
blood of Christ?

A. No, but as the water in Baptism is not changed into the
blood of Christ, nor becomes the washing away of sins itself,
but only a true divine sign and confirmation of it, so also in
the Lord's Supper the sacred bread does not become the body
of Christ itself, although in accordance with the nature and
usage of sacraments it is called the body of Christ.

Q.79. *Why, then, does Christ call the bread His body, and the*
cup His blood or the New Testament in His blood, and St. Paul
call it the communion of the body and blood of Christ?

A. Christ does not speak in this way without great cause:
namely, not only to teach us thereby that as bread and wine
sustain this temporal life, so also His crucified body and shed
blood are the true meat and drink of our souls unto eternal
life; but much more, by this visible sign and pledge to assure
us that we are as really partakers of His true body and blood,
through the working of the Holy Spirit, as we receive by the
mouth of the body these holy signs in remembrance of Him;
and that all His sufferings and obedience are as certainly our
own as if we had ourselves suffered and made satisfaction in
our own persons.

Q.80. *What difference is there between the Lord's Supper and*
the Popish Mass?

A. The Lord's Supper testifies to us that we have complete
forgiveness of all our sins through the one sacrifice of Jesus
Christ, which He Himself has once accomplished on the Cross;
and that through the Holy Spirit we are incorporated into
Christ, who with His true body is now in heaven at the right
hand of the Father, and is to be there worshipped. But the Mass
teaches that the living and the dead do not have forgiveness

of sins through the sufferings of Christ unless Christ is still daily offered for them by the priests; and that Christ is bodily under the appearance of bread and wine, and is therefore to be worshipped in them. And so the Mass at bottom is nothing else than a denial of the one sacrifice and passion of Jesus Christ and an accursed idolatry.

Q.81. Who should come to the Table of the Lord?

A. Those who are displeased with themselves for their sins, and yet trust that these are forgiven them, and that their remaining infirmity is covered by the passion and death of Christ, who also desire more and more to strengthen their faith and amend their life. But the impenitent and hypocrites eat and drink judgement to themselves.

Q.82. Then should those also be admitted to this Supper who show themselves to be, by their confession and life, unbelievers and ungodly men?

A. No; for in this way the covenant of God is profaned, and His wrath is provoked against the whole congregation. Therefore the Christian Church is obliged, according to the ordinance of Christ and His Apostles, by the office of the keys to exclude such people until they amend their lives.

Q.83. What is the Office of the Keys?

A. The preaching of the holy Gospel and Christian discipline, through both of which the Kingdom of Heaven is opened to believers and shut against unbelievers.

Q.84. How is the Kingdom of Heaven opened and shut by the preaching of the holy Gospel?

A. In this way, when according to the command of Christ, it is proclaimed and openly testified to believers, one and all, that as often as they receive the promise of the Gospel with true faith, all their sins are truly forgiven by God for the sake of Christ's merits; and on the contrary, to all unbelievers and hypocrites, that the wrath of God and eternal condemnation lie on them so long as they are not converted. It is according to this testimony of the Gospel that God will pass judgement both in this life and in the life to come.

Q.85. How is the Kingdom of Heaven opened and shut by Christian discipline?

A. In this way, when according to the command of Christ, those who under the Christian name show themselves un-Christian either in doctrine or life, and after repeated brotherly admonition refuse to turn from their errors or evil ways, they are brought before the Church, or those ordained by the Church for this, and if they do not change as a result of their admonition, then through their exclusion from the holy Sacraments they are shut out of the Christian Community, and by God Himself from the Kingdom of Christ, but if they promise and show real amendment, they are received again as members of Christ and the Church.

III

THANKFULNESS

Q.86. Since, then, we are redeemed from our misery by grace through Christ, without any merit of ours, why should we do good works?

A. Because since Christ has redeemed us by His blood, He renews us also by His Holy Spirit according to His own image, that with our whole life we may show ourselves thankful to God for His goodness, and that He may be glorified through us; and further, that we ourselves on our part may be assured of our faith by its fruits, and by our godly life may win our neighbours also to Christ.

Q.87. Can they, then, not be saved who do not turn to God from their unthankful, impenitent life?

A. By no means; for, as the Scripture says, no unchaste

person, idolater, adulterer, thief, covetous man, drunkard, slanderer, robber, or any such like, shall inherit the Kingdom of God.

Q.88. In how many things does true repentance or conversion consist?

A. In two things: the mortification of the old man, and the resurrection of the new.

Q.89. What is the mortification of the old man?

A. To be heartily sorry for sin, and more and more to hate and turn from it.

Q.90. What is the resurrection of the new man?

A. Heartfelt joy in God through Christ, and a passionate love to live according to the will of God in all good works.

Q.91. But what works are good?

A. Those only which are done from true faith, according to the law of God, for His glory, and not those based on our own opinion or the commandments of men.

Q.92. What is the law of God?

A. God spake all these words, saying:

FIRST COMMANDMENT

I am the Lord thy God, which have brought thee out of the land of Egypt, and out of the house of bondage. Thou shalt have no other gods before me.

SECOND COMMANDMENT

Thou shalt not make unto thee any graven image, or any likeness of any thing that is in heaven above, or that is in the earth beneath, or that is in the water under the earth; thou shalt not bow down thyself to them, nor serve them. For I the Lord thy God am a jealous God, visiting the iniquity of the fathers upon the children unto the third and fourth generation of them that hate me; and showing mercy unto thousands of them that love me and keep my commandments.

THIRD COMMANDMENT

Thou shalt not take the name of the Lord thy God in vain; for the Lord will not hold him guiltless that taketh his name in vain.

FOURTH COMMANDMENT

Remember the Sabbath day to keep it holy. Six days shalt thou labour, and do all thy work: but the seventh day is the Sabbath of the Lord thy God; in it thou shalt not do any work, thou, nor thy son, nor thy daughter, thy man-servant, nor thy maid-servant, nor thy cattle, nor the stranger that is within thy gates. For in six days the Lord made heaven and earth, the sea, and all that in them is, and rested the seventh day; wherefore the Lord blessed the Sabbath day, and hallowed it.

FIFTH COMMANDMENT

Honour thy father and thy mother; that thy days may be long upon the land which the Lord thy God giveth thee.

SIXTH COMMANDMENT

Thou shalt not kill.

SEVENTH COMMANDMENT

Thou shalt not commit adultery.

EIGHTH COMMANDMENT

Thou shalt not steal.

NINTH COMMANDMENT

Thou shalt not bear false witness against thy neighbour.

TENTH COMMANDMENT

Thou shalt not covet thy neighbour's house; thou shalt not covet thy neighbour's wife, nor his man-servant, nor his maid-servant, nor his ox, nor his ass, nor any thing that is thy neighbour's.

Q.93. How are these commandments divided?

A. Into two tables: the first of which teaches us, in four commandments, how we ought to act toward God; the second, in six commandments, what we owe to our neighbour.

Q.94. What does the Lord require in the first commandment?

A. That, on peril of my soul's salvation and happiness, I must avoid and flee all idolatry, sorcery, enchantments, invocation of saints or of other creatures, and rightly acknowledge the only true God, trust in Him alone, with all humility and patience expect all good from Him alone, and love, fear, and worship Him with my whole heart, so as to renounce all creatures rather than do the least thing against His will.

Q.95. What is idolatry?

A. It is to conceive or have something else on which to place one's trust, instead of the one true God who has revealed Himself in His Word, or side by side with Him.

Q.96. What does God require in the second commandment?

A. That we are in no way to make any representation of God, nor to worship Him in any other way than He has commanded in His Word.

Q.97. Then is one not to make any image at all?

A. God cannot and may not be imaged in any way, although creatures may well be imaged, yet God forbids us to make or keep any likeness of them in order to worship them, or to serve Him by means of them.

Q.98. But may not pictures be tolerated in Churches as books for the laity?

A. No, for we must not be wiser than God, who will not have His people instructed by means of dumb idols, but by the living proclamation of His Word.

Q.99. What is required in the third commandment?

A. That we must not profane or abuse the name of God by cursing, or by false oaths, or by unnecessary swearing. Not even by our silence and connivance are we to be partakers of such horrible sins. In short, we must never use the holy name of God except with fear and reverence, so that He may be rightly confessed and invoked by us, and be glorified in all our words and works.

Q.100. Is it then so great a sin to take the name of God in vain by cursing and swearing, so that God is angry with those also who do not help to hinder and forbid it as much as they can?

A. Yes indeed; for no sin is greater or provokes God's wrath more than the defaming of His name. Therefore He even commanded it to be punished with death.

Q.101. But may we not swear by the name of God in a godly way?

A. Yes; when the authorities require it of their subjects, or when it is required to maintain and promote fidelity and truth, to the glory of God and the welfare of our neighbour. For such swearing is grounded in God's Word, and therefore was rightly used by the saints in the Old and New Testament.

Q.102. May we swear by the saints or other creatures?

A. No; for a lawful oath is a calling upon God, as the only searcher of hearts, to bear witness to the truth, and to punish me if I swear falsely. No creature is due such honour as that.

Q.103. What does God require in the fourth commandment?

A. First, that the ministry of the Gospel and schools be maintained; and that I, especially on the day of rest, diligently go to God's Church, to learn the Word of God, to use the holy Sacraments, to call publicly upon the Lord, and to give Christian alms. Secondly, that all the days of my life I rest from my evil works, allow the Lord to work in me by His Spirit, and thus begin in this life the everlasting Sabbath.

Q.104. What does God require in the fifth commandment?

A. That I must show all honour, love, and faithfulness to my father and mother, and to all in authority over me, submit myself with due obedience to all good instruction and punishment, and also to have patience with their faults, since it is God's will to govern us by their hand.

Q.105. What does God require in the sixth commandment?

A. That neither by thought, nor by word, nor by gesture, much less by deed, am I to revile, hate, insult, or kill my neighbour, whether by myself or by another; but lay aside all desire of revenge. Moreover, I am not to harm myself, nor wilfully to run into any danger. The magistrate is therefore armed with the sword, in order to restrain murder.

Q.106. But this commandment speaks only of killing.

A. In forbidding murder, however, God means to teach us that He abhors the root of murder, namely, envy, hatred, anger, and desire or revenge and before Him all this is hidden murder.

Q.107. Is it, then, sufficient if we do not kill our neighbour in any such way?

A. No; for in that God condemns envy, hatred, and anger, He requires us to love our neighbour as ourselves, to show patience, peace, meekness, mercy, and friendliness towards him, and, so far as we can, to prevent his hurt; also, to do good even to our enemies.

Q.108. What does the seventh commandment teach us?

A. That all unchastity is accursed of God; and that we should therefore detest it from the heart, and live chastely and modestly, whether in holy wedlock or in single life.

Q.109. Does God in this commandment forbid nothing more than adultery, and such gross sins?

A. Since our body and soul are both a temple of the Holy Spirit, it is His will that we keep both pure and holy. Therefore He forbids all unchaste actions, gestures, words, thoughts, desires, and whatever may entice men to them.

Q.110. What does God forbid in the eighth commandment?

A. He forbids not only the theft and robbery which the magistrate punishes, for God calls theft also all wicked tricks and devices by which we seek to appropriate our neighbour's goods, whether by force or under the guise of right, such as unjust weights, ells, measures, wares, coins, usury, or any means forbidden by God. To this belongs also all covetousness, and all useless waste of God's gifts.

Q.111. But what does God require of you in this commandment?

A. That I further my neighbour's advantage where I can and may, deal with him as I would have others deal with me, and work faithfully that I may be able to help the indigent in their need.

Q.112. What is required in the ninth commandment?

A. That I bear false witness against no one; twist no one's words; be no backbiter and slanderer; join in condemning no one unheard and rashly; but that I avoid, on pain of God's heavy wrath, all lying and deceit, as the devil's own works; in acts of litigation and in all other affairs, love, honestly speak and confess the truth; and, so far as I can, defend and promote my neighbour's honour and right.

Q.113. What is required in the tenth commandment?

A. That even the least inclination or thought against any of God's commandments should never enter into our heart; but that with our whole heart we are continually to hate all sin, and to take pleasure in all righteousness.

Q.114. Can those who are converted to God keep these commandments perfectly?

A. No, for even the holiest of all, while in this life, have only a small beginning of this obedience. Nevertheless they begin to live with earnest purpose not only according to some, but according to all of God's commandments.

Q.115. Why, then, does God have the ten commandments proclaimed to us so strictly if no one can keep them in this life?

A. First, that all our life long we may learn more and more to know our sinful nature, and so more eagerly seek forgiveness of sins and righteousness in Christ; secondly, that we may continually apply ourselves and ask God for the grace of the Holy Spirit, that we may more and more be renewed in the image of God, until we attain the goal of full perfection after this life.

Prayer

Q.116. Why is prayer necessary for Christians?

A. Because it is the principal element in the thankfulness which God requires of us, and because God will give His grace and Holy Spirit only to those who ask Him with heart-felt longing and without ceasing, and who thank Him for them.

Q.117. What belongs to such a prayer that pleases God and is heard by Him?

A. First, that from the heart we call upon the one true God alone who has revealed Himself to us in His Word, for all that He has commanded us to ask of Him; secondly, that we know our need and misery thoroughly, humbling ourselves before the face of His divine Majesty; thirdly, that we are established upon this unshakeable fact, that, in spite of our unworthiness, for the sake of Christ our Lord, He will undoubtedly hear our prayer, as He has promised us in His Word.

Q.118. What has God commanded us to ask Him?

A. All things necessary for soul and body, which Christ the Lord has comprised in the prayer which He Himself taught us.

Q.119. What is the Lord's Prayer?

A. Our Father who art in heaven: Hallowed be thy name. Thy kingdom come. Thy will be done in earth, as it is in heaven. Give us this day our daily bread. And forgive us our debts, as we forgive our debtors. And lead us not into temptation, but deliver us from evil: For thine is the kingdom, and the power, and the glory, forever. Amen.

Q.120. Why has Christ commanded us to address God as Our Father?

A. That right at the beginning of our prayer He may awaken in us that childlike reverence and trust toward God which ought to be the ground of our prayer, namely, that God has become our Father through Christ, and will much less deny us what we ask of Him in faith than our fathers refuse us earthly things.

Q.121. Why is there added, who art in heaven?

A. That we may have no earthly thought of the heavenly Majesty of God, and may expect from His almighty power all things necessary for body and soul.

Q.122. What is the first petition?

A. *Hallowed be thy name*. That is: Give us first of all to know Thee aright, and to hallow, magnify, and praise Thee in all Thy works, in which shine forth Thy almighty power, wisdom, goodness, righteousness, mercy, and truth. Grant also that we may so order our whole life, in thought, word and work, that Thy name may not be blasphemed on our account, but honoured and praised.

Q.123. What is the second petition?

A. *Thy kingdom come*. That is: So govern us by Thy Word and Spirit that we may more and more submit ourselves to Thee; preserve and increase Thy Church; destroy the works of the devil, every power that exalts itself against Thee, and all wicked counsels devised against Thy holy Word, until the fullness of Thy Kingdom arrives, in which Thou shalt be all in all.

Q.124. What is the third petition?

A. Thy will be done in earth as it is in heaven. That is: Grant that we and all men may renounce our own will, and without gainsaying, may obey Thy will, which alone is good; and so may everyone discharge his office and calling as willingly and faithfully as the angels do in heaven.

Q.125. What is the fourth petition?

A. Give us this day our daily bread. That is: Be pleased to provide for all our bodily need, that thereby we may acknowledge that Thou art the only source of all good, and that without Thy blessing neither our care and work nor Thy gifts can prosper us, and so may we withdraw our trust from all creatures, and place it in Thee alone.

Q.126. What is the fifth petition?

A. And forgive us our debts as we forgive our debtors. That is: Be pleased, for the sake of Christ's blood, not to impute to us, miserable sinners, all our misdeeds, and the evil which still persists in clinging to us; as we also find this witness of Thy grace in us, that it is our entire resolve heartily to forgive our neighbour.

Q.127. What is the sixth petition?

A. And lead us not into temptation, but deliver us from evil. That is: Since we are so weak in ourselves that we cannot stand a moment, and since our declared enemies, the devil, the world, and our own flesh, do not cease to assault us, be Thou pleased to uphold and strengthen us by the power of Thy Holy Spirit, that we may stand firm against them, and not succumb in this spiritual conflict, until at last we obtain complete victory.

Q.128. How do you close this Prayer?

A. For thine is the kingdom, and the power, and the glory, for ever. That is: All this we ask of Thee, because as our King, having power over all things, Thou art willing and able to give us all good, and that thereby not we but Thy holy name may be glorified for ever.

Q.129. *What is the meaning of the word Amen?*

A. *Amen* means: That is indeed true and certain. For my prayer is much more certainly heard of God than I feel in my heart that I desire such things of Him.

CRAIG'S CATECHISM, 1581

A Short Sum of the Whole Catechism
Wherein the Question is put and answered in few Words
for the greater Ease of the Common People and Children

Gathered by M. John Craig,
Minister of God's Word to the King's Majesty

"*This is life eternal to know thee the only true God,*
and Jesus Christ whom thou hast sent."
John 17:3

THE Catechism of John Craig was the first Scottish Catechism to come into widespread use in the Kirk. John Craig was a Dominican theologian who was converted to the Reformed Faith through reading Calvin's *Institutes* while Rector of the Dominican Convent in Bologna. He returned to Scotland in 1561, becoming for a while the colleague of John Knox, before going to Aberdeen in 1571. From 1579 to 1594 Craig was chaplain to the King and minister of the Church of Holyroodhouse.

The Catechism that bears his name was published in 1581, and dedicated to "the professors of Christ's Evangel at New Aberdeen". In his preface Craig urged "this short sum" to be read often and diligently in the homes of the people, that through such continual exercise they might profit more and more in the principal points of salvation. In describing his work Craig wrote, "I have studied to be plain, simple, short, and profitable, not looking so much to the desire and satisfaction of the learned as to the instruction and help of the ignorant."

Q

In a prefatory note "to the Reader" Craig drew attention to the fact that he had not adduced the authority of "the Scriptures or fathers" in confirmation of his teaching, since his purpose was not to instruct the profane atheists and apostates, but to put the brethren in memory of that doctrine which they daily hear confirmed (in our ordinary teaching) by the Scriptures and consent of the godly fathers". For further confirmation of the Biblical nature of this doctrine, readers were directed to Calvin's *Institutes*.

Craig's Catechism was always published along with the so-called *Negative Confession* of 1581 which he drew up at the request of the King, and which was accepted by the General Assembly and later incorporated into the National Covenant.

The version given here represents simply a modernisation of the original text.

CRAIG'S CATECHISM

THE CONTENTS

1. The Creation of man, and his first state of innocence, without death and misery.

2. The miserable fall of man from God and his former state under the bondage of sin, death, and all other kinds of misery.

3. The calling of man again to repentance, and his third state in Jesus Christ, and how he should honour his Redeemer in four ways.

4. The first part of God's honour is Faith, and here the Belief and Faith is declared.

5. The second part of God's honour is obedience, and here the law is declared, and how it differs from the Gospel.

6. The third part of God's honour is prayer, which is declared in general, with an exposition of the Lord's Prayer.

7. The fourth part of God's honour is thanksgiving, where the causes, the rule, and other circumstances of thanks are declared.

8. The ordinary instruments of salvation are these, the Word, the Sacraments, and Ministry of men, which are particularly declared.

9. The first cause of our Salvation, is God's eternal election, and here the progress of the same, and the two ends of all flesh are declared.

[10. A short and general confession of the true Christian faith and religion, according to God's Word, subscribed by the King's Majesty, and his household, etc.]

1. The Creation and First State of Mankind

Q. *Who made man and woman?*

A. The eternal God out of His goodness.

Q. *Of what did He make them?*

A. Of an earthly body, and a heavenly spirit.

Q. *In whose image did He make them?*

A. In His own image.

Q. *What is the image of God?*

A. Perfect uprightness in body and soul.

Q. *To what end were they made?*

A. To acknowledge and serve their Maker.

Q. *How should they have served Him?*

A. According to His holy will.

Q. *How did they know His will?*

A. By His Works, Word, and Sacraments.

Q. *What liberty had they to obey His will?*

A. They had free will to obey and disobey.

Q. *What profit had they by their obedience?*

A. They were blessed and happy in body and soul.

Q. *Was this felicity given to them only?*

A. No, but it was given to them, and their posterity.

Q. *On what condition was it given?*

A. On condition of their obedience to God.

Q. *Why was so small a commandment given?*

A. To show God's gentleness, and to try man's obedience.

Q. *What advantage is there in knowing of his lost felicity?*

A. Hereby we know God's goodness, and our ingratitude.

Q. *But we cannot return to this state.*

A. We come to a better state in Christ.

Q. *What are we to learn from this discourse?*

A. That the Church was first planted, blessed, and made happy, through obedience to God's Word.

2. The Fall of Man from God and his Second State

Q. What brought them down from that blessed state?

A. Satan, and their own inconstancy.

Q. How were they brought to that inconstancy?

A. Through familiar conference with Satan against the Word.

Q. What did Satan first want from them?

A. Distrust and contempt of God's Word.

Q. Why did he begin at their faith?

A. Because he knew it was their life.

Q. How could they consent to their own perdition?

A. They were deceived by the craft of Satan.

Q. What was the craft of Satan here?

A. He persuaded them that good was evil, and evil was good.

Q. How could they be persuaded, when they had the image of God?

A. They had the image, but not the gift of constancy.

Q. What things did they lose through their fall?

A. The favour and image of God, with the use of the creatures.

Q. What succeeded the loss of the favour and image of God?

A. The wrath of God, and original sin.

Q. What is original sin?

A. The corruption of our whole nature.

Q. How does this sin come to us?

A. By natural propagation from our first parents.

Q. What are the fruits of this sin?

A. All other sins which we commit.

Q. What is the punishment of this sin?

A. Death of body and soul, with all other miseries.

Q. What else followed upon this sin?

A. A curse upon the creatures, and our banishment from the use of them.

Q. But very wicked people use them abundantly.

A. That is with the testimony of an evil conscience.

Q. Were these punishments too great for eating the forbidden fruit?

A. Their sins were not simply the eating of the fruit.

Q. Then what properly was their sin?

A. Infidelity, pride, and open rebellion to God.

Q. How can that be proved?

A. They consented to Satan's lies, distrusted God's Word, and sought to be equal with God.

Q. Why are we punished for their sin?

A. We are punished for our own sin, because we are all in them, standing and falling with them.

Q. In what state is all their posterity?

A. Under the same bondage of sin?

Q. What natural freedom do we have?

A. We have freedom to sin, and offend our God.

Q. Do we not have power to serve and please God?

A. None at all, till we are called and sanctified.

Q. Have we lost our minds and wills?

A. No, but we have lost a right mind, and a right will.

Q. May natural men do many good deeds?

A. Yet they cannot please God without faith.

Q. Why did God allow this fall of man?

A. For the declaration of His mercy and justice.

Q. Explain that.

A. By His mercy the chosen are delivered, and the rest punished by His justice.

3. Man's Restoration, and his Third State

Q. Who called our parents to repentance?

A. God only in His infinite mercy.

Q. What did they do when He called them?

A. They hid and excused themselves.

Q. *But it was foolishness to fly from God?*

A. Such is the foolishness of all their posterity.

Q. *How were they converted to God?*

A. By the almighty power of God's Spirit.

Q. *How did the Spirit work their conversion?*

A. He printed the promise of mercy in their hearts.

Q. *What was their promise of mercy?*

A. Victory in the seed of the woman against the Serpent.

Q. *What is the seed of the woman?*

A. Jesus Christ, God and Man.

Q. *How was His posterity converted to God?*

A. By the same Spirit and promise.

Q. *May we understand and receive the promise by ourselves?*

A. No more than blind and dead men can see and walk.

Q. *What more is required for our conversion to God?*

A. He must enlighten our minds, and mollify our hearts, that we may understand, receive, and retain His promise.

Q. *But Adam knew his sin and God's voice.*

A. Yet that knowledge did not bring him to repentance.

Q. *What was the cause of that?*

A. The feeling of mercy was not yet given to him.

Q. *What then are knowledge, calling, accusation, and conviction?*

A. A way of desperation, if mercy is not apprehended.

Q. *What if mercy is offered and apprehended?*

A. Then these things are the beginning of our repentance.

Q. *How did Adam and his posterity receive the promise?*

A. Only through their own lively faith in Christ.

Q. *What was their faith?*

A. A sure confidence in God's mercy through Christ to come.

Q. *Who wrought this faith in them above nature?*

A. God's Spirit through the preaching of the promise.

Q. What is this promise called in the Scripture?

A. The Gospel or Glad Tidings of salvation.

Q. Then the Gospel was preached in Paradise?

A. No doubt, and also the law.

Q. What need was there for them both?

A. By the law they were accused and humbled, and through the Gospel comforted and delivered.

Q. What then were the law and the Gospel?

A. Instruments of God's Spirit for the salvation of man.

Q. In what did their salvation consist?

A. In the remission of their sin, and the reparation of God's image in them.

Q. What followed upon the repairing of that image?

A. A continual battle both within and without.

Q. From whence does this battle proceed?

A. From the two contrary images in mankind.

Q. What are these images?

A. The image of God, and the image of the Serpent.

Q. What will be the end of this battle?

A. Victory to the seed of the woman, and destruction to the seed of the Serpent in mankind.

Q. Was all Adam's posterity delivered and restored?

A. No, but only those who believed the promise.

Q. To what end were these delivered?

A. To acknowledge and serve their God.

Q. In what did their service chiefly consist?

A. In the exercise of faith and repentance.

Q. What rule did He give them for this purpose?

A. His most holy Word and Scriptures.

Q. What was contained in the Word given to them?

A. The Law, the Gospel, and the Sacraments.

Q. What did the law do for them?

A. It revealed their sin, and the right way to know and serve God.

Q. What did the Gospel do?

A. It offered to them mercy in Christ.

Q. What did the Sacraments do for them?

A. They helped their faith in the promises of God.

Q. Was this order kept in the Old Testament?

A. No doubt, as Moses and the Prophets bear witness.

Q. What should we gather from this discourse?

A. That the Church was ever grounded upon the Word of God.

Q. What follows upon the corruption of the Word?

A. The corruption of the true religion, and the Church at all times.

Q. Was the faith and religion of the fathers different from our faith?

A. Not in substance but in certain circumstances.

Q. What is the substance?

A. The covenant of Jesus Christ.

Q. Why do we call it the Old Testament?

A. Because of the obscure shadows and figures joined to the doctrine and religion.

Q. What profit came to the fathers at all times through faith?

A. By this way alone they were blessed and happy.

Q. In what did the unhappiness of men consist?

A. In false knowledge of the true God.

Q. Are we in the same state?

A. No doubt, as our Master testifies.

Q. When do we know God aright?

A. When we give to Him the honour due to Him.

Q. What are the chief elements in this honour due to Him?

A. Faith, obedience, prayer, and thanks, with their fruits.

4. THE FIRST PART OF GOD'S HONOUR

Q. Why is faith given the first place?

A. Because it is the mother of all the rest.

Q. What does faith work in us?

A. It moves us to put our whole confidence in God.

Q. How may we be moved to do this?

A. By the knowledge of His power and goodness.

Q. But we are unworthy and guilty?

A. Therefore we apprehend His promise in Christ.

Q. What are the principal things in His promise?

A. They are contained in our Belief, called the Creed of the Apostles.

Q. Repeat the Belief or Creed of the Apostles.

A. I believe in God the Father Almighty, Maker of heaven and earth. And In Jesus Christ His only Son our Lord, who was conceived by the Holy Ghost, born of the virgin Mary, suffered under Pontius Pilate, was crucified, dead, and buried. He descended into hell.

He rose again the third day from the dead. He ascended into heaven, and sitteth at the right hand of God the Father Almighty. From thence He shall come to judge the quick and the dead.

I believe in the Holy Ghost.

The holy Church Universal, the Communion of Saints: the forgiveness of sins, the resurrection of the body, and the life everlasting.

Q. Why is it called the Creed of the Apostles?

A. Because it agrees with their doctrine and time.

Q. Into how many parts is it divided?

A. Into four principal parts.

Q. What are we taught in the first part?

A. The right knowledge of God the Father.

Q. *What are we taught in the second part?*

A. The right knowledge of God the Son.

Q. *What are we taught in the third part?*

A. The right knowledge of God the Holy Spirit.

Q. *What are we taught in the fourth part?*

A. The right knowledge of the Church, and gifts given to it.

Q. *How many Gods are there?*

A. Only one eternal God, Maker of all things.

Q. *Why then do we name God thrice here?*

A. Because there are three distinct persons in the Godhead.

Q. *Why is the Father put in the first place?*

A. Because He is the fountain of all things.

Q. *Why is the Son put in the second place?*

A. Because He is the eternal wisdom of the Father, begotten before all beginnings.

Q. *Why is the Spirit put in the third place?*

A. Because He is the power proceeding from the Father and the Son.

Q. *Why is the Church put in the fourth place?*

A. Because it is the good work of these three Persons.

THE FIRST PART OF OUR BELIEF

Q. *Why is it said particularly, I believe?*

A. Because every one should live by his own faith.

Q. *Should every one know what he believes?*

A. Otherwise he does not have true faith.

Q. *Are we bound to confess our faith openly?*

A. Yes, no doubt, when time and place require.

Q. *Is it enough to believe that there is a God?*

A. No, but we must know who the true God is.

Q. *How can we know that?*

A. By His promise and works done for our comfort.

Q. *What does He promise to us?*

A. To be our loving Father and Saviour.

Q. *What does this promise require of us?*

A. A full trust and confidence in Him.

Q. *What then moves us to believe in God?*

A. A sense and feeling of His fatherly love.

Q. *Why do we call Him Father?*

A. Because of Christ, and of ourselves.

Q. *Explain that?*

A. He is Christ's Father by nature, and ours by grace through Him.

Q. *Why then are we called the sons of wrath?*

A. Because of our natural state through sin.

Q. *When are we assured that we are His sons?*

A. When we believe in His fatherly love.

Q. *Why do we mention here His power?*

A. To assure that He can and will save us.

Q. *What power do we mean here?*

A. The power which disposes all things.

Q. *What should the knowledge of this work in us?*

A. Humility, confidence, and boldness.

Q. *Why do we begin with His fatherly love and power?*

A. Because they are the chief grounds of our faith.

Q. *Expound that more plainly?*

A. By these two, we are persuaded of all the rest of His promises.

Q. *What is meant here by heaven and earth?*

A. All the creatures in heaven and earth.

Q. *Of what did He make these creatures?*

A. He made them all out of nothing by His Word.

Q. *Why did He do that?*

A. To show His infinite power.

Q. *Why then did He occupy six days?*

A. That we might be able better to consider Him in His works.

Q. Why are they put in our belief?

A. To bear witness to us of their Creator.

Q. What do they testify of Him?

A. That He is infinite in power, in wisdom, and goodness.

Q. What other things do they specially teach us?

A. His fatherly care and providence for us.

Q. Who rules and keeps all things made?

A. The same eternal God, who made them.

Q. Who makes all these fearful alterations in nature?

A. The hand of God, either for our comfort or punishment.

Q. Who rules Satan and all his instruments?

A. Our God also, by His almighty power and providence.

Q. What comfort do we have from this?

A. This comfort, that nothing can hurt us, without our Father's good will.

Q. What if Satan and his instruments should have freedom over us?

A. We should then be in a most miserable state.

Q. What should this fatherly care produce in us?

A. Thanks for all things that come to us.

Q. What other things should it produce?

A. Boldness in our vocation against all impediments.

Q. Who rules sin which is not of God?

A. He alone rules all the actions and defections that come to pass in heaven and earth.

Q. Why do we believe that?

A. Because He is God Almighty above His creatures.

Q. But sin is not a creature?

A. But He would not be Almighty, if He did not rule over it.

Q. Is God partaker of sin when he rules over it?

A. No, for He works His own good work by it.

Q. *Are the wicked excused through their good works?*

A. No, for they work their own evil work.

Q. *Why are they not excused, since God's will concurs with them?*

A. They mean one thing and God another.

Q. *What do they mean in their actions?*

A. A contempt of God, and hurt of His creatures.

Q. *What does God mean in using them, and their sin?*

A. The trial of His own, or the punishment of sin.

Q. *What should we learn by this discourse?*

A. To fear the Lord our God alone.

Q. *What shall we judge of them that use familiarity with Satan?*

A. They deny this first article of our belief.

Q. *May we not conjure Satan to reveal secrets?*

A. No, for he is the author of lies.

Q. *But he often speaks the truth.*

A. That is to get the greater credit in his lies.

Q. *May we not remove witchcraft with witchcraft?*

A. No, for that is to seek help from Satan.

THE SECOND PART OF OUR BELIEF

Q. *What do we learn in the second part?*

A. The truth and justice of God in our redemption.

Q. *Who is our Redeemer and who redeemed us?*

A. Jesus Christ, who redeemed us by His death.

Q. *What kind of person is He?*

A. Perfect God and perfect man.

Q. *Why was He both God and man?*

A. That He might be a suitable Mediator for us.

Q. *Why was this Name Jesus or Saviour given only by God?*

A. To assure us the better of our salvation by Him.

Q. *Is there any virtue in this Name?*

A. No, but the virtue is in the Person.

Q. Why was He called Christ, or anointed?

A. He was anointed King, Priest, and Prophet for us.

Q. What purpose do these titles serve?

A. Hereby is expressed His office, and how He saved us.

Q. Expound that more plainly?

A. He saved us by His Kingdom, Priesthood, and Prophetic Office.

Q. How can this be proved?

A. By the anointing of kings, priests, and prophets, who were figures of His anointing.

Q. Was Christ anointed with material oil?

A. No, but He was anointed with the gift of the Spirit without measure.

Q. What kind of Kingdom does He have?

A. It is Spiritual, pertaining chiefly to our souls.

Q. In what does His Kingdom consist?

A. In God's Word and His Holy Spirit.

Q. What do we get by the Word and Spirit?

A. Righteousness and life everlasting.

Q. What is His Priesthood?

A. An office appointed for the satisfaction of God's wrath.

Q. How did He satisfy God's wrath for us?

A. By His obedience, prayer, and everlasting sacrifice.

Q. Why is He called our only Prophet?

A. He ever was, is, and shall be the only Teacher of the Church.

Q. What then were the Prophets and the Apostles?

A. All these were His disciples and servants.

Q. Why were all these honourable offices given to Him?

A. That He might deliver us from sin.

Q. Expound that particularly in regard to these three offices.

A. By His kingly power we are free from sin, death, and hell.

Q. *But we may easily fall into sin again?*

A. Yet by the same power we shall rise, and gain the victory.

Q. *The battle is very hard?*

A. We do not fight in our own strength.

Q. *What is our armour and strength?*

A. The power and Spirit of Christ in us.

Q. *What profit comes to us through His Priesthood?*

A. Through it He is our Mediator, and we are priests also.

Q. *How are we made priests?*

A. By Him we have freedom to enter in before God, and offer up ourselves and all that we have.

Q. *What kind of sacrifice is this?*

A. A sacrifice of thanksgiving only.

Q. *May we not offer Christ again for our sins?*

A. No, for Christ cannot die again.

Q. *What profit have we from His Prophetic Office?*

A. Through it we know most plainly His Father's will.

Q. *What other profit do we have?*

A. All revelations and prophesies are finished.

Q. *But some things are not yet fulfilled?*

A. That is true, but we speak of things pertaining to His first coming.

Q. *Why was He called God's only Son?*

A. Because He is His only Son by nature.

Q. *Yet He is called the First-begotten among many brethren?*

A. That is in regard to His fellowship with us.

Q. *Why is He called our Lord?*

A. Because He bears rule over us, and is Head of men and Angels.

Q. *Why was He conceived by the Holy Spirit?*

A. That He might be without sin, and so sanctify us.

Q. What if He had been a sinner?

A. Then He could not have delivered us.

Q. Was He only made free from sin?

A. No, but He was also filled with the Holy Spirit without measure.

Q. Why was the fulness of the Spirit given to Him?

A. That He might bestow the Spirit upon us.

Q. Why was He made man like unto us?

A. That He might die for us in our own nature.

Q. What follows upon His incarnation?

A. That life and righteousness are placed in our flesh.

Q. May not this life be lost, as it was in Adam?

A. No, for our flesh is joined personally with the Fountain of life.

Q. Then all men are sure of this life?

A. Not so, but only those who are joined with Him spiritually.

Q. What then does our carnal union with Christ avail for us?

A. Nothing, without our spiritual union with Him.

Q. What purpose is served by His mother's virginity?

A. It is a seal of His miraculous conception.

Q. Was He holy through her virginity?

A. No, since her whole nature was corrupted.

Q. Why is she named in our belief?

A. That we may know His tribe and family.

Q. How can that help our faith?

A. Hereby we may know Him to be the promised Saviour.

Q. Of what tribe and house was He promised?

A. Of the tribe of Judah, and the house of David.

Q. How did He redeem us?

A. He suffered death for us willingly, according to God's decree.

Q. Why did He suffer under the form of judgement?

R

A. To assure us better that we are free from God's judgement.

Q. But Pilate the judge pronounced Him innocent?

A. That made greatly for our comfort.

Q. What comfort have we in that?

A. That He died not for His own sins, but for ours.

Q. But the judge meant no such thing?

A. We are not concerned with what he meant, but with what God meant by his wicked judgement.

Q. Why did He suffer upon the Cross?

A. To assure us, that He took our curse upon Himself.

Q. What assurance have we of this?

A. Because that kind of death was accursed of God.

Q. Was He also cursed of God?

A. No, but He sustained our curse.

Q. Was He guilty before God?

A. No, but He sustained the person of guilty men.

Q. What comfort have we in this?

A. He removed our curse, and gave to us His blessing.

Q. In what part did He suffer?

A. In both body and soul.

Q. Why?

A. Because we were lost both in body and soul.

Q. What did He suffer in His soul?

A. A fearful wrath and angry face of God.

Q. What pain was that?

A. The anguish of death, and pain of hell.

Q. How do we know that?

A. By His praying, sweating, and strong crying with tears.

Q. How did He sustain these pains?

A. Through faith, patience, and prayer to His Father.

Q. How do the damned sustain these pains in hell?

A. With despair and continual blasphemy.

Q. When did Christ descend to hell?

A. When he sustained these fearful pains upon the Cross.

Q. Why did God punish an innocent man so grievously?

A. Because He took upon Himself the burden of our sins.

Q. Was God content with His satisfaction?

A. Without doubt, for He of His mercy appointed it.

Q. Was His death also necessary for our redemption?

A. Otherwise the decrees and the figures in the law would not have been fulfilled.

Q. If He died for us why do we die?

A. Our death is not now a punishment for our sins.

Q. What other thing can it be?

A. It is made (through His death) a ready passage to a better life.

Q. What should we learn by all these fearful pains?

A. To know the terrible wrath of God against sin, and how dearly we are bought.

Q. What comfort do we have by these sufferings of Christ our Redeemer?

A. This, that the faithful members of Christ shall never suffer them.

Q. But we were oppressed by the curse of the law?

A. It is true, but Christ took it upon Himself and gave us the blessing.

Q. What profit do we get especially by His death?

A. It is a sufficient and everlasting sacrifice for our sins.

Q. What does this sacrifice work perpetually?

A. It removes all evil things, and restores all good things.

Q. Is there any priest and sacrifice for sin now?

A. None at all, for Christ has satisfied once for all.

Q. But there are still many spots in our nature?

A. Therefore Christ's blood perpetually washes them away.

Q. The memory and mark of our sins may make us afraid.

A. All punishments due for them, were taken away by the suffering of Christ.

Q. But we find sin still working in us?

A. The death of Christ kills its tyranny.

Q. Does it always remain in us to the end?

A. But through faith it is not imputed to the members of Christ.

Q. Why was He buried?

A. To make us more sure of His death.

Q. What does His burial teach us?

A. Continual mortification of sin.

Q. Why did He rise before us?

A. To assure us of His victory over death for us.

Q. What fruit do we get by His victory?

A. Hereby we are given a sure hope of life eternal. It works newness of life in us here. And it shall raise up our bodies again in the last day.

Q. Why did He ascend into heaven before us?

A. To take possession of our inheritance in our name.

Q. But He said, I shall be with you to the end?

A. He spoke that of His spiritual presence.

Q. What does He do here for us now?

A. He makes continual intercession for us.

Q. What kind of intercession is it?

A. It is the continual mitigation of His Father's wrath for us, through the virtue of His death.

Q. Is He our only Intercessor and Mediator?

A. Without doubt, since He alone died for us.

Q. What does His sitting at the right hand mean?

A. The power He has in heaven and earth.

Q. What comfort do we have in His power and authority?

A. That we are in safety under His protection.

Q. Why will He come again?

A. To put a final end to our redemption.

Q. What will that end be?

A. Eternal joy or misery to every man.

Q. Is not that done in every man's death?

A. No, for the bodies remain still unrewarded.

Q. Will there not be a middle state of men?

A. No, but all will be brought to these two ends.

Q. Why is that, since some are better and some are worse?

A. All those will be judged evil, who are not the members of Christ.

Q. But how can the quick be judged before they die?

A. Their sudden change will be instead of death for them.

Q. But all flesh should return to the dust?

A. Ordinarily it is done so, but this is a special case.

Q. What comfort do we have in the person of the Judge?

A. Our Saviour, Advocate, and Mediator only shall be our Judge.

Q. What should meditation upon this Article work in us?

A. The contempt of all other pleasures, and a delight in heavenly things.

Q. Who will be saved in that day?

A. All who are here made the members of the Church.

Q. Who makes us members of Christ?

A. God's Holy Spirit alone working in our hearts.

THE THIRD PART OF OUR BELIEF

Q. Who is the Holy Spirit?

A. He is God, equal with the Father, and the Son.

Q. From whence does He proceed?

A. From the Father and the Son.

Q. What is His general office?

A. He puts in execution all things that are decreed by God's secret counsel.

Q. What does He do in the order of nature?

A. He keeps all things in their natural state.

Q. Where then do all these alterations come from?

A. From the same Spirit, working diversely in nature.

Q. Is then the Spirit but nature?

A. No. He is God, ruling and keeping nature.

Q. What does He do in the worldly kingdoms?

A. He raises them up and casts them down at His pleasure.

Q. Why are these things attributed to Him?

A. Because He is the power and hand of God.

Q. What does He do in the Kingdom of Christ?

A. He gathers all God's elect to Christ.

Q. Why is He called Holy?

A. Because He is the Fountain of holiness, and makes us holy.

Q. When and how does He do this?

A. When by His mighty power He separates us from our natural corruption and dedicates us to godliness.

Q. What is this natural corruption?

A. A blindness of mind, hardness of heart, and contempt of God.

Q. How does He dedicate us to godliness?

A. He enlightens our minds, mollifies our hearts, and strengthens us.

Q. What then is all flesh without the Spirit of God?

A. Blind and dead in all heavenly things.

Q. What other names has He in the Scriptures?

A. He is called the Spirit of faith, regeneration, strength, and comfort.

Q. Why are these names given to the Holy Spirit?

A. Because He works all these things in us.

Q. What are these graces called?

A. Sanctification, regeneration, or new birth and spirit.

Q. *What is our corrupted state called?*

A. The old man, old Adam, flesh and blood.

Q. *What follows upon our sanctification?*

A. A continual battle between the spirit and the flesh.

Q. *Who strengthens and keeps us in the battle?*

A. The same Spirit who also gives victory in the end.

Q. *What is this battle to us?*

A. A sure seal of the presence of the Holy Spirit.

Q. *What battle has the old man in himself?*

A. None at all against sin and wickedness.

Q. *In whom then is this battle?*

A. Only in the members of Christ and His Church, through the presence of the Spirit.

THE FOURTH PART OF OUR BELIEF

Q. *What is the Church which we confess here?*

A. The whole company of God's elect called and sanctified.

Q. *Do we believe in His Church?*

A. No. We believe only in our God.

Q. *What do we then believe of His Church?*

A. That it was, is, and shall be to the end of the world.

Q. *Why do we need to believe this?*

A. For our great comfort and the glory of God.

Q. *Explain that plainly?*

A. The love of the Father, the death of Christ, and the power of the Spirit shall ever work in some.

Q. *What follows upon this?*

A. The Glory of God and confusion of Satan with our comfort.

Q. *Why is the Church only known to us by faith?*

A. Because it contains only God's elect, which are only known to Himself.

Q. *When and how may we know them?*

A. When we see the fruits of election and holiness in them.

Q. In what respect is the Church called holy?

A. In respect of our justification and sanctification.

Q. How do these two graces differ?

A. The first is perfect and the second imperfect.

Q. What is the reason for that diversity?

A. The first is in Christ, the second in us.

Q. Are not both these gifts ours?

A. Yes, no doubt, seeing that Christ is ours.

Q. May we not come to a full perfection in this life?

A. No, for the flesh rebels continually against the Spirit.

Q. Why does not the Spirit sanctify us perfectly?

A. Lest we should forget our former captivity, and redemption.

Q. What admonition are we given regarding our state?

A. We should be humble, repent, and be thankful to our God.

Q. Why is the Church called universal?

A. Because it is spread through the whole world.

Q. How many Churches are there in the world?

A. One Church, one Christ: as one Body and the Head.

Q. Is it bound to any particular time, place, or persons?

A. No, for then it would not be universal.

Q. What is the Communion of Saints?

A. The mutual participation in Christ, and His graces among His members.

Q. What follows upon this Communion?

A. A spiritual uniting and Communion among all Christ's members.

Q. On what is this Communion grounded?

A. Upon their union with Christ their Head.

Q. Who makes our union with Christ and with one another?

A. The Holy Spirit by His mighty power.

Q. Is there any salvation without this Communion?

A. None at all, for Christ is the ground of salvation.

Q. May men be joined with Christ, and not with His saints?

A. No, not with the saints, if not with Christ.

Q. What then should be our principal concern?

A. To hold fast our union with Christ our Head.

Q. What follows upon that?

A. Then of necessity we are joined with all His saints, and the Church.

Q. Should we not seek them, and join with them externally also?

A. Without doubt, whenever we see them, or hear of them in particular.

HOW THE CHURCH IS TO BE KNOWN

Q. How may we know this company externally?

A. By the true profession of the Word and holy Sacraments.

Q. What if these tokens are not found among them?

A. Then they are not the Communion of Saints.

Q. May we with safe conscience join ourselves with these?

A. No, for they are not the holy Church of God where these tokens are not.

Q. Then we depart from the Universal Church.

A. No, but we depart from the corruption of men and remain in the holy Universal Church.

Q. Yet they will call themselves the Church.

A. We should look for the true marks of the Church.

Q. May we leave the particular Church where the Word is retained?

A. No, even although many other vices abound there.

Q. But the multitude are wicked and profane?

A. Yet there is a true Church, where the Word truly remains.

Q. *What then is the infallible token of Christ's Church?*

A. The Word truly preached and professed.

Q. *Should we discuss who are saints indeed and who are not?*

A. No, for that appertains to God only and to themselves.

Q. *But in this way we are joined with the wicked in the body?*

A. That cannot hurt us, or profit them.

Q. *How is that?*

A. Because we and they are spiritually separated.

Q. *But they make the Word and the Sacraments unfruitful.*

A. Not to us, but to themselves only.

Q. *Why is remission of sins put here?*

A. Because it is proper to the Church and its members.

Q. *Why is it proper to the Church only?*

A. Because in the Church only is the Spirit of faith and repentance.

Q. *Who forgives sins, by whom, and where?*

A. God only, through Christ and His Church here.

Q. *How often are our sins forgiven us?*

A. Continually even unto our lives' end.

Q. *What need is there of this?*

A. Because sin is never thoroughly abolished here.

Q. *How do we get remission of our sins?*

A. Through the mercy of God, and the merit of Christ.

Q. *Is there any remission of sins after this life?*

A. None at all, although some have taught otherwise.

Q. *Are the sin and the punishment both forgiven?*

A. Yes no doubt, since the one follows upon the other.

Q. *But sometimes the punishment remains after the sin?*

A. The punishment is not a satisfaction for sin.

Q. *What is it then, seeing it comes from sin?*

A. It is a Fatherly correction and a preservative medicine.

Q. *What are we yet to expect at the hand of our God?*

A. The resurrection of our bodies, and life eternal.

Q. With what bodies shall we rise again?

A. With the same bodies in substance, as Christ had when He rose.

Q. But the Apostle says that our bodies will be spiritual?

A. That is in comparison to their present state.

Q. What will be the condition of our bodies then?

A. Free from all corruption and alteration.

Q. Why shall we rise with the same bodies?

A. That they may receive their reward with the souls.

Q. What admonition are we given here?

A. That we should dedicate our bodies to the service of God.

Q. But the wicked will be partakers of the same resurrection?

A. No doubt, but to their great confusion.

Q. Many doubt of this resurrection?

A. But we are sure that He who fulfilled the first promises, can and will perform the rest.

Q. What kind of life is promised to us?

A. Life eternal without any misery.

Q. What is prepared for the wicked?

A. Death eternal without any joy.

Q. Yet they will live eternally?

A. That life will be to live in eternal death.

Q. What admonition are we given here?

A. That we should wait continually for the coming of the Lord.

Q. What other admonition are we given?

A. We should thirst continually for eternal life.

Q. Is it enough to know these things to be true?

A. No. We must know and apply them to ourselves.

Q. What are these Articles which we have declared?

A. The ground and foundation of our faith and religion.

Q. How are we to apply them to ourselves?

A. By our own true and lively faith.

TRUE FAITH, WITH ITS FRUITS

Q. What is true faith?

A. An assured knowledge of God's mercy towards us for Christ's sake, according to His promise.

Q. Have we any natural inclination to this faith?

A. None at all, but rather a natural rebellion.

Q. Who then works these things in us?

A. God's Holy Spirit seals them in our hearts.

Q. How can guilty men be assured of God's mercy?

A. By the truth of His promise made to the penitent.

Q. Yet our guiltiness cannot but fear God's justice?

A. Therefore we set between us and it, the satisfaction of Christ.

THE FIRST FRUIT OF FAITH

Q. What is the first fruit of faith?

A. By it we are made one with Christ our Head.

Q. How is the union made, and when?

A. When we are made flesh of His flesh, and bone of His bone.

Q. Was not this done when He took our flesh?

A. No, for He was only then made flesh of our flesh.

Q. When are we made flesh of His flesh?

A. When we are united with Him spiritually as living members with the Head.

THE SECOND FRUIT OF FAITH

Q. What do we get by this union?

A. We are made partakers of all His graces and merits, and our sins are imputed to Him, and abolished from us.

Q. What follows upon this chiefly?

A. A perfect justification and peace of conscience.

Q. In what does our justification consist?

A. In remission of sins and imputation of justice.

Q. How can God's justice forgive sin without satisfaction?

A. Christ satisfied abundantly the justice of God for us.

Q. Whose justice is imputed to us?

A. The perfect obedience and justice of Christ.

Q. How can another man's justice be made ours?

A. Christ is not another man to us properly.

Q. Why is He not another man to us?

A. Because He is given to us freely by the Father with all His graces, and we are joined with Him.

Q. How is justification offered to us?

A. By the preaching of the Gospel.

Q. How do we receive justification?

A. Only by our own lively faith.

Q. Is not justification offered to us by the Law?

A. Yes, but no man is able to fulfil the Law.

Q. What if a man live in godliness and uprightness?

A. No upright man living can be without faith.

Q. Is our faith perfect in all points?

A. No, for it is joined with manifold imperfections.

Q. How then can it justify us?

A. It is only the instrument of our justification.

Q. What does justify us properly?

A. Jesus Christ only by His perfect justice.

THE THIRD FRUIT OF FAITH

Q. Can our faith be without a godly life?

A. No more than fire without heat.

Q. What is the cause of that?

A. Because Christ sanctifies all whom He justifies.

Q. Do not the good works of the faithful merit eternal life?

A. No, for then Christ would not be our only Saviour.

Q. Yet the good works of the faithful please God?

A. Yes no doubt, but only through faith do they please Him.

Q. Why do they not please God, when they are the works of the Spirit?

A. Because they are defiled with the infirmities of the flesh.

Q. Are then our good works unprofitable?

A. That does not follow, since they please God, and have their reward, both here and there.

Q. Does the Gospel teach us to condemn good works?

A. No, for it requires continual faith and repentance.

REPENTANCE

Q. What is true repentance?

A. It is the hatred of sin and the love of justice.

Q. Where does repentance come from?

A. From the fear of God and the hope of mercy.

Q. How are we brought to this fear of God?

A. Through the preaching of the Law.

Q. How do we come to the hope of mercy?

A. By the preaching of the Gospel.

Q. What does repentance work in us?

A. Continual mortification of our lusts and newness of life.

Q. Who works these two things in us?

A. The Spirit of regeneration through the death and resurrection of Christ.

Q. How long should we continue in repentance?

A. All the days of our lives.

Q. What is this exercise before God?

A. His spiritual service and our chief obedience.

Q. What is the rule of Christian repentance?

A. God's holy Law, which is the rule of all godliness of life.

5. The Second Part of God's Honour is Obedience

Q. Recite the words of the Law (Exod. 20).

A. Hear O Israel: I am the Lord thy God which brought thee out of the land of Egypt, out of the house of bondage.

1. Thou shalt have none other gods before me.

2. Thou shalt not make unto thee any graven image or any likeness of any thing that is in heaven above, or that is in the earth beneath, or that is in the water under the earth: thou shalt not bow down thyself to them, nor serve them: for I the Lord thy God am a jealous God, visiting the iniquity of the fathers upon the children unto the third and fourth generation of them that hate me, and showing mercy unto thousands of them that love me and keep my commandments.

3. Thou shalt not take the name of the Lord thy God in vain; for the Lord will not hold him guiltless that taketh his name in vain.

4. Remember the sabbath day, to keep it holy. Six days shalt thou labour and do all thy work: but the seventh day is the sabbath of the Lord thy God: in it thou shalt not do any work, thou, nor thy son, nor thy daughter, thy manservant, nor thy maidservant, nor thy cattle, nor thy stranger that is within thy gates: for in six days the Lord made heaven and earth, the sea, and all that in them is, and rested the seventh day: therefore the Lord blessed the sabbath day, and hallowed it.

5. Honour thy father and thy mother: that thy days may be long upon the land which the Lord thy God giveth thee.

6. Thou shalt not kill.

7. Thou shalt not commit adultery.

8. Thou shalt not steal.

9. Thou shalt not bear false witness against thy neighbour.

10. Thou shalt not covet thy neighbour's house, thou shalt not covet thy neighbour's wife, nor his manservant, nor his maidservant, nor his ox, nor his ass, nor any thing that is thy neighbour's.

Q. *Who gave this Law first to Moses?*

A. The eternal God, distinct in two Tables.

Q. *What does this Law teach?*

A. It teaches and requires our duty toward God and man.

Q. *Is the Law perfect in all points?*

A. Yes, without doubt, since it came from the fountain of all perfection.

Q. *Does the Law require external obedience only?*

A. No, but it requires all the purity of the spirit.

Q. *What reward and punishment does the Law set forth?*

A. The blessing of God to those who keep this Law, and His curse to those who break it.

Q. *How many commandments are in the first table?*

A. Four, which declare our duty to our God.

Q. *How many are in the second table?*

A. Six, which declare our duty to our neighbour.

Q. *What is contained in every commandment?*

A. One thing is commanded and the contrary forbidden.

Q. *What does the preface of the Law contain?*

A. The reasons why God commands and we obey.

Q. *What are they?*

A. His majesty, power, promise, benefits, our promise to Him.

1. *Thou shalt have none other gods, etc.*

Q. *What is forbidden in this first commandment?*

A. All forging or worshipping of false gods.

Q. *What is a false god?*

A. All things that we put in God's place.

Q. When do we put any thing in God's place?

A. When we give it the honour due to God.

Q. What is the honour due to God?

A. Faith, fear, prayer, thanks, and obedience.

Q. What is commanded here?

A. That we settle ourselves upon one true God alone.

Q. Why is this commandment put first here?

A. Because it is the ground of all the rest.

Q. Why does He say, before me?

A. Because He requires the purity of the heart.

2. *Thou shalt not make unto thee any graven images, etc.*

Q. What is forbidden in the second commandment?

A. That we neither represent nor worship God by any image.

Q. Is every kind of imagery forbidden here?

A. No, but only that whereby God is represented or honoured.

Q. What is forbidden here in general?

A. All corrupting of God's service by the inventions of men.

Q. What is required here?

A. That we worship God according to His Word.

Q. What kind of service does He require of us?

A. Both inward and outward service.

Q. May we not serve Him externally as we please?

A. No, for that kind of service is cursed idolatry.

Q. Does God condemn the external service?

A. Yes, if it does not have the inward service as well.

Q. What is it called without the inward service?

A. The dead or dumb letter.

Q. What is the other service called?

A. The Spirit, which gives life to all external service commanded by God.

S

Q. *Why is this commandment put in the second place?*
A. Because it declares how the true God should be served.
Q. *Why are the promise and the threatening added?*
A. To move us more willingly to give obedience.
Q. *Why is the promise longer than the threatening?*
A. Because God is readier to give mercy than to give judgement.

3. *Thou shalt not take the name, etc.*

Q. *What is forbidden in this third commandment?*
A. All dishonouring and abuse of God's Majesty.
Q. *What is commanded here?*
A. Every kind of honour and reverence due to His Majesty.
Q. *What is meant here by His name?*
A. All the titles and names representing His Majesty.
Q. *What things represent Him?*
A. His Word, Sacraments, and works.
Q. *How should we honour His name?*
A. With heart, mouth, and deed, and with all our power.
Q. *When is this done?*
A. When we think, speak, and work all things to His glory.
Q. *May we swear by His name?*
A. We may, and should for good causes.
Q. *What does the added threat signify?*
A. The great regard He has for His own honour.

4. *Remember the Sabbath day to keep it holy, etc.*

Q. *What does this fourth commandment require?*
A. That we keep the Sabbath holy to the Lord.
Q. *When and how is this done?*
A. When we spend it only in God's service.
Q. *Why is God's example added?*
A. To move us more earnestly to follow Him.

Q. *Is there any holiness in that day above the rest?*

A. No for the holiness is only in the exercise.

Q. *What if the exercise is not kept?*

A. Then it is made the devil's own feast day.

Q. *May we work on all other days?*

A. Yes for God has given us free liberty.

Q. *Why was there one day appointed?*

A. To maintain the true religion in the Church.

Q. *For what other reason was it given?*

A. For the relief of servants and beasts.

Q. *Was it for the Jews a Sacrament of their spiritual rest?*

A. Yes, but that ceremony is taken away by Christ.

Q. *Why was it taken away?*

A. Because we have spiritual rest in Him.

5. *Honour thy father and thy mother, etc.*

Q. *What does this fifth commandment require?*

A. That we honour all those whom God has placed above us.

Q. *What are those persons?*

A. Parents, pastors, magistrates, husbands, and masters.

Q. *What honour should we give them?*

A. Love, fear, obedience, and help in their need.

Q. *In what does the equity of this commandment consist?*

A. In that these persons are put in God's place for our comfort.

Q. *How far should we obey them?*

A. As far as the Word of God commands.

Q. *What if they command anything against the Word?*

A. Then we must obey God rather than men.

Q. *What does the added promise contain?*

A. It contains the opposite, a threat against those who break the commandment.

Q. *But neither of them is absolutely kept?*

A. Therefore the blessing and the curse always remain firm.

Q. Why are this promise and threat specially added?

A. Because these superiors are preservers of our lives and livings.

6. *Thou shalt not kill*

Q. What is forbidden in this sixth commandment?

A. All envy, rancour, and hatred, with their fruits.

Q. What is commanded here?

A. Brotherly love with its fruits and signs.

Q. What is the final end of this commandment?

A. The preservation of our neighbour's life.

7. *Thou shalt not commit adultery*

Q. What is forbidden in the seventh commandment?

A. All filthy lusts in our heart, in word, or deed, or gesture.

Q. What is commanded here?

A. All chastity and means of preserving it.

Q. Is marriage condemned here?

A. No, but rather is hereby established.

Q. What is the end of this commandment?

A. That we keep both our bodies and hearts pure and clean.

8. *Thou shalt not steal*

Q. What is forbidden in the eighth commandment?

A. All wrong and deceitful dealing with our neighbour.

Q. What is commanded here?

A. Equity and justice to every man.

Q. How is this to be done?

A. With mind, heart, mouth, and deed, and with all our power.

Q. What is the end of this commandment?

A. That we seek to let every man have his own.

9. *Thou shalt not bear false witness, etc.*

Q. What is forbidden in the ninth commandment?

A. False reports about our neighbour, and hearing of them.

Q. Is this enough for our discharge?

A. No. The uprightness of the heart is required also.

Q. What is the end of this commandment?

A. That the simple truth remain among us.

10. *Thou shalt not covet, etc.*

Q. What is forbidden in this last commandment?

A. All light and impetuous inclinations to evil.

Q. Were not those inclinations forbidden before?

A. No. Consent to them and their performance only were forbidden.

Q. Then what degrees of sin are forbidden?

A. The lust, the consent, and the deed.

Q. What is this lust?

A. Original infection, the mother of the rest of our sins.

Q. What is commanded here?

A. The perfect love of our neighbour with its fruits.

Q. Who is our neighbour?

A. Every man, friend or foe.

Q. What is the reason for this law?

A. That we are all brethren and bear the image of our God.

THE SUM OF THE LAW

Q. What is the sum and end of these commandments?

A. The perfect love of God and of our neighbour.

Q. When is our love perfect and the law absolutely fulfilled?

A. When our minds and hearts are wholly filled with the love of God and of our neighbour.

Q. Did anyone ever fulfill this law?

A. None at all, except Jesus Christ.

Q. What do they get, then, who seek salvation by the Law?

A. Their own double condemnation.

Q. Why did God give this straight law to mankind?

A. Because it agrees with His nature and our first estate.

Q. But we are changed and made weak through sin.

A. But God has not changed His will and Law.

Q. Is all flesh hereby accursed and damned?

A Yes, but God has given a sufficient remedy in Christ.

Q. Explain how that is possible when the Law curses man.

A. By Faith we escape the curse and receive the blessing of the Law.

THE USE OF THE LAW

Q. What purpose then does the Law serve?

A. It is profitable both to the faithful and unfaithful.

Q. What profit does it bring to the unfaithful?

A. It shows their sin and just condemnation.

Q. But is that not hurtful to them?

A. No, because they are thus sent to Christ.

Q. But many others despair or become worse?

A. That does not come from the law, but from our corrupt nature.

Q. When are they sent to Christ by the Law?

A. When they get a taste of mercy in Christ, after they are humbled by the Law.

Q. Is this the ordinary way of our conversion?

A. Yes no doubt, for Christ saves only the humbled.

Q. What profit do the faithful derive from the Law?

A. It puts them daily in remembrance of their sins.

Q. What good fruit comes from that?

A. Humility and an earnest reliance on Christ.

Q. What other profit do they derive from the Law?

A. It is a bridle for their affections and a rule of all godliness.

Q. If it is a bridle, do they not then hate the Law?

A. No. They hate their own affections and love the Law.

Q. Does this knowledge come from the Law?

A. No. It comes from the Gospel.

THE DIFFERENCE BETWEEN THE LAW AND THE GOSPEL

Q. Where does this difference come from?

A. From the Spirit who is joined with the Gospel, and not with the Law.

Q. What follows from this?

A. The Law commands, but it gives no strength.

Q. What does the Gospel do?

A. It gives freely all that it requires of us.

Q. What other difference is there between them?

A. The Law has no compassion on sinners.

Q. What about the Gospel?

A. It offers mercy only to sinners.

Q. What other difference is there?

A. In the manner of our justification.

Q. What does the Law demand in our justification?

A. Our own perfect obedience.

Q. What does the Gospel demand?

A. Faith only in the obedience of Christ Jesus.

Q. Does the Gospel favour the transgression of the Law?

A. No. It gives strength to obey the Law.

HOW THE LAW AND THE GOSPEL AGREE

Q. Wherein do the Law and the Gospel agree?

A. They are both from God, and set forth the same kind of justice.

Q. What is this justice?

A. The perfect love of God and our neighbour.

Q. What follows from this?

A. That the severe Law pronounces all the faithful just.

Q. How can the Law pronounce them just?

A. Because they have in Christ all that the Law demands.

Q. But they remain transgressors of the Law?

A. That is in themselves, and yet they are just in Christ, and in themselves they love justice.

Q. What then is the state of the faithful here?

A. They are saved in Christ, and yet they still fight against sin.

Q. What battle do we have?

A. We have a battle both within and without.

Q. What battle do we have within?

A. The battle of the flesh against the Spirit.

Q. What battle do we have without?

A. The temptations of Satan, and the world.

Q. What armour do we have?

A. True faith, with fervent prayer to our God.

Q. Is prayer the cause of our victory?

A. No, but it is a means by which God saves us, and in which He is honoured.

6. The Third Part of God's Honour, Prayer in General

Q. What is prayer or calling upon God?

A. It is a humble lifting up of our minds and hearts to God.

Q. Why do we go to God only in our prayers?

A. Because prayer is part of our true worship of Him.

Q. Why then do we seek needful things at the hands of men?

A. Because they are appointed to be stewards to us.

Q. How are we to go to them?

A. As to God's instruments only.

Q. To whom should we give praise?

A. Only to God, to whom all praise belongs.

Q   *May we pray to saints and angels?*

A. No. That is manifest idolatry.

Q. *And are the angels appointed to serve us?*

A. Yes, but we have no commandment to seek them.

Q. *What shall we say of the common custom used in the time of blindness?*

A. We should be content with the order appointed by God.

Q. *How should we pray to our God?*

A. With our minds and hearts, for He is a Spirit.

Q. *What is a prayer without the mind and heart?*

A. It is unprofitable and cursed of God.

Q. *What attitude of mind and affection is required?*

A. First an earnest feeling of our own misery through sin.

Q. *What is required next?*

A. A fervent desire accompanied by faith and hope to receive what we pray for.

Q. *Who moves us to pray fervently?*

A. God's Holy Spirit alone.

Q. *Should this make us cold in prayer?*

A. No, but rather fervent in calling on the Spirit.

Q. *What is the value of prayer with the tongue?*

A. It is a great help, if we pray with the mind as well.

Q. *What is prayer in a strange language?*

A. It is a plain mockery of God.

Q. *Should we be certain that we are heard in our prayer?*

A. Otherwise we pray in vain, and without faith.

Q. *What are the grounds of our assurance?*

A. God's promise, His Spirit in us, and our Mediator.

Q. *In whose Name should we pray?*

A. In the Name of our Lord Jesus Christ.

Q. *How can that be proved?*

A. By God's commandment and promise to hear us in so doing (John 16:23).

Q. What should we ask of God?

A. All things promised or commanded in the Word.

Q. May we not follow our own imagination in our prayer?

A. No, for then our prayer would be but vanity.

Q. Why is that, since all men desire good things?

A. Because we neither know nor desire the things that are best for us.

Q. What then should we do in our prayer?

A. We must learn of God, what, and how we should ask.

Q. How then should we begin our prayer?

A. We should first submit our affections to God's will.

Q. What rule has God given us for this purpose?

A. The Scriptures and chiefly the Lord's Prayer.

Q. Recite the Lord's Prayer (Matt. 6:9).

A. Our Father which art in heaven.

1. Hallowed be thy name. Thy kingdom come. Thy will be done in earth, as it is in heaven.

2. Give us this day our daily bread. And forgive us our trespasses, as we forgive them that trespass against us. And lead us not into temptation, but deliver us from evil. For thine is the kingdom, the power, and the glory, for ever and ever. Amen.

THE DIVISION AND ORDER OF PRAYER

Q. How is this prayer divided?

A. Into a preface and six petitions.

Q. How do the six petitions differ?

A. The first three concern the glory of God only.

Q. With what are the other three concerned?

A. Principally with our comfort.

Q. What should we first seek in our prayer?

A. The glory of our God before all things.

Q. Is not that hard for flesh and blood?

A. Yes, but it is the work of God's Holy Spirit only.

Q. Are we not happy when God is glorified in us?

A. Yes no doubt, but we should have regard only to God's glory.

Q. Do not the other three tend to the same end?

A. Yes, but we are permitted to think of ourselves also.

Q. What is the purpose of the preface?

A. To prepare ourselves to pray aright.

THE PREFACE

Q. Why do we call Him Father?

A. To assure us of His good will.

Q. Why do we call Him our Father in common?

A. Because our prayer should be for our brethren also.

Q. What is meant here by the heaven?

A. God's Majesty, power, and glory.

Q. What purpose do these serve in our prayer?

A. They prepare us to have reverence and hope.

THE FIRST PART

Q. What is meant here by His Name?

A. His due honour, glory, fame, and estimation.

Q. Can His honour either increase or diminish?

A. Not in itself, but only in the hearts of men.

Q. What then do we pray for first here?

A. Our Father's honour and glory in this world.

Q. When and how is this done?

A. When with heart, mouth, and deed, He is extolled above all things.

Q. How are men brought to do this?

A. By the living knowledge of His Majesty.

Q. How can His unsearchable Majesty be known?

A. By His Word, Sacraments, and manifold works.

Q. What should men learn by these names?

A. His infinite power, goodness, mercy, justice, providence, truth, and constancy, etc.

Q. Is it not enough that we ourselves honour His Name?

A. No. We must desire and work for the honour of God's Name amongst all men, according to our power and vocation.

Q. When and where should we do this?

A. In prosperity and adversity, privately and publicly.

Q. What if we find fault with His Word or works?

A. Then we extol our own name, and profane His holy name.

Q. What if we are not moved at the thought of profaning His Name?

A. Then we are not the sons of God.

Q. What is the source of this petition?

A. A vehement affection for our Father's glory.

Q. What is this affection to us?

A. A plain testimony of our adoption.

Q. What do we desire when we pray for His Kingdom?

A. That He might reign more and more in the hearts of His chosen people.

Q. When is this done?

A. When the Spirit reforms and rules our hearts.

Q. What else do we ask for here?

A. That the tyranny of Satan may be beaten down.

Q. What purpose does the third petition serve?

A. Through it the other two are performed.

Q. Explain that more plainly?

A. His name is sanctified, and He reigns when His will is done.

Q. Are not all things compelled to obey His will?

A. Yes, but we speak here of men's voluntary obedience.

Q. How can that be proved?

A. By the comparison here added.

Q. When will these three petitions be perfectly fulfilled?

A. Never in this world, because of our corruption.

Q. Why do we pray for things that will not take place?

A. We always pray for what ought to be, and one day shall be done.

Q. But all these things will come to pass, whether we pray or not?

A. No doubt, but here we declare our good will for our Father's glory.

Q. What should we gather from this?

A. That he is not the child of God, who does not seek this before all things.

Q. Do we not pray here against our own natural wills?

A. Yes indeed. We desire them to be reformed according to God's will.

THE SECOND PART

Q. What do we mean by our daily bread?

A. All things needful for this present life.

Q. But He commands us to labour for it?

A. Our labours are in vain without His blessing.

Q. Why do we call it ours, when it is His gift?

A. Because we ask no more than is given us by lawful means.

Q. Why do we ask for this day only?

A. To teach us to be content with His present provision.

Q. Then must we beg daily at His hand?

A. Our felicity consists in this, to depend upon Him daily.

Q. Do the rich need this daily seeking?

A. Yes no doubt, for riches do not always have the blessing of God.

Q. What do we ask in the other two petitions?

A. The continual comfort of our souls.

Q. Why do we seek the comfort of our bodies first?

A. To assure us the better of our spiritual comfort.

Q. Explain that.

A. If He takes care of our bodies, how much more will He provide for our souls?

Q. What do we seek in this fifth petition?

A. Remission of our sins or spiritual debts.

Q. Why are our sins called debts?

A. Because they incur an everlasting penalty.

Q. Why do we pray for free remission?

A. Because we can by no means offer satisfaction for them.

Q. Is the penalty remitted freely with the sin?

A. Yes, for Christ has offered full satisfaction for us.

Q. Should every man pray thus continually?

A. Yes, for all flesh is subject to sin.

Q. But sometimes men do good things?

A. Yet they sin in the best thing they do.

Q. What benefit do we get by this petition?

A. Only in this way do we and our works please God.

Q. Why is the condition added?

A. To remind us of our duty.

Q. What is our duty?

A. To forgive freely all offences done to us.

Q. Is this the reason why we seek remission?

A. No, but we take it as a sign that we bear the inward seal of God's children.

Q. What is the inward seal of God's children?

A. The image of God who freely forgives.

Q. What does this image work in all His children?

A. Free remission of all offences done to them.

Q. Who are those who will not forgive?

A. Those who do not bear the image of our heavenly Father.

Q. What do we ask in the last petition?

A. Defence against all temptations to evil.

Q. Does every man need this defence?

A. Yes without doubt, for without it no flesh can stand.

Q. Why is that when we have the Spirit?

A. Because the dangers are great and many, within us and without.

Q. How are we preserved from these temptations?

A. By the mighty power of the Spirit working in us.

Q. Does God draw any man into wickedness?

A. No. That is contrary to His nature.

Q. Why then do we ask this of God?

A. Because no man is led into sin without His willing permission.

Q. Who properly speaking leads men into sin?

A. Satan and men's own wicked lusts.

Q. When does God willingly permit men to be led into temptation?

A. When He delivers them unto Satan, and their own lusts.

Q. What moves our good God to do this to men?

A. His justice provoked through their ingratitude.

Q. What does Satan mean in leading men from sin to sin?

A. Malice conceived against both God and man.

Q. Do all kinds of temptation proceed from Satan?

A. No, for God often tempts men as well.

Q. When and how does He do this?

A. When He offers occasions to discover their hearts.

Q. What things are discovered then?

A. Notable gifts of His or monstrous sins of theirs.

Q. Should we desire not to be tried thus?

A. No, for that would not be profitable for us.

Q. What should we learn from these last petitions?

A. To commit both body and soul to God's providence.

Q. *What else should we do?*

A. Pray for the welfare of our brethren.

Q. *May we not change the form of this prayer?*

A. We may change the words, but not the sense.

Q. *But every man may pray particularly for himself?*

A. But he is not to exclude the welfare of his brethren.

Q. *Are all things needful for us contained in this prayer?*

A. Yes, since the wisdom of God gave it.

Q. *At what time especially are we to use prayer?*

A. At all times, but principally in time of trouble.

Q. *What if God delay granting our petitions?*

A. We should continue in prayer with patience and hope.

Q. *What are we to hope for from His long delay?*

A. That He will turn all things to our comfort.

Q. *What does the additional clause mean, For thine is the kingdom, etc.?*

A. It sets forth the cause and ground of our prayer to God.

Q. *What else are we taught here?*

A. That we should conclude our prayers with thanksgiving.

7. THE FOURTH PART OF GOD'S HONOUR: THANKSGIVING

Q. *What is thanksgiving or praising of God?*

A. It is to acknowledge Him as the Author and Fountain of all good things.

Q. *May we not give thanks to angels or saints?*

A. No. That would be manifest idolatry.

Q. *Are we not to be thankful to men?*

A. Yes, but the chief praise belongs to God.

Q. *How are we to praise Him?*

A. With mind, heart, mouth, and works.

Q. *What rules of thanksgiving have we?*

A. The Scripture, and examples of His servants.

Q. For what are we to praise Him?

A. For His infinite benefits, corporal and spiritual.

Q. But we are often in great misery.

A. We should even praise Him for that as well.

Q. Why?

A. Because He turns all things to our comfort.

Q. Through whom should we praise Him?

A. Through Jesus Christ only.

Q. Why through Him only?

A. Because through Christ alone do we receive His graces.

Q. Where should we praise God?

A. Both publicly and privately.

Q. How long should we praise Him?

A. So long as we enjoy His benefits.

Q. How do prayer and thanksgiving differ?

A. Prayer seeks and thanks acknowledges that our prayer is heard or delayed for our comfort.

Q. What other difference is there?

A. Prayer may partly cease for a time, but not thanks.

Q. What is the cause of that?

A. Because we always have benefits from God.

Q. How should we then begin and end our prayer?

A. Evermore with thanksgiving to our God.

Q. Was the sacrifice of praise known to the fathers?

A. Yes, and all that we do in faith, is a sacrifice of thanksgiving.

Q. What may we learn from all that we have spoken?

A. That this is life eternal, to know God through Jesus Christ, and to honour Him aright.

Q. What are these four parts of God's honour?

A. They are the only service of God pleasing to Him.

Q. What are these four parts to us?

A. Infallible seals of our election and salvation.

T

Q. By whom are we kept in this state?

A. By the power of the Holy Spirit.

Q. What instruments does He use for this purpose?

A. The Word, the Sacraments, and the Ministry of men.

8. THE OUTWARD INSTRUMENTS OF OUR SALVATION
The Word of God

Q. Where shall we find the Word?

A. In the Holy Scriptures.

Q. How should we behave towards the Word?

A. We should love, receive, and obey it, as God's eternal truth.

Q. But it comes to us only through men?

A. Nevertheless we should always receive it as sent from God.

Q. Who can assure us of this?

A. The Holy Spirit only, working in our hearts.

Q. How should we use the Word?

A. We should read it, and hear it reverently.

Q. May the common people read the Scriptures?

A. They may, and are commanded to read them.

Q. May they have them in their own language?

A. Certainly, for otherwise they could not get any benefit from them.

Q. Is not private reading sufficient for us?

A. Not if public teaching is available.

Q. How is that to be proved?

A. From the fact that as Ministers are commanded to teach, so are we commanded to hear them.

Q. How far should we obey their doctrine?

A. So far as it agrees with the Word.

Q. How long are we to continue in hearing?

A. As long as we live and teaching is available.

Q. What need is there for this continual hearing?

A. Because we are both ignorant and forgetful.

Q. What shall we say of those who will not hear?

A. They refuse the helping hand of God.

Q. What shall we do when preaching is not available?

A. We should read the Scriptures with all diligence.

Q. What if we cannot read them?

A. We should have recourse to those who can read.

Q. But the Scriptures are obscure and hard.

A. The Holy Spirit will help the willing.

Q. What if we were once well instructed by our Pastors?

A. We must still continue in this school to the end.

Q. Why, if we are already sufficiently instructed?

A. God has established this order in His Church because we need continually to be instructed.

Q. What follows from this?

A. The ministers or pastors are needful for us.

Q. But they are commonly neglected and despised?

A. He who despises them, despises God and his own salvation.

Q. What should this continual exercise produce in us?

A. Increase of faith, and godliness of life.

Q. What if these two things fail to follow?

A. Then our reading and hearing is in vain.

Q. What else is joined with the Word for our comfort?

A. The holy Sacraments of Jesus Christ.

THE SACRAMENTS IN GENERAL

Q. What is a Sacrament?

A. A sensible sign, and seal of God's favour offered and given to us.

Q. To what end are the Sacraments given?

A. To nourish our faith in the promise of God.

Q. How can sensible signs do this?

A. They have this office of God, and not of themselves.

Q. It is the Office of the Spirit alone to nourish our faith?

A. Yet Sacraments are added as effectual instruments of the Spirit.

Q. Where then does the efficacy of the Sacraments come from?

A. From God's Holy Spirit only.

Q. What moved God to employ this kind of teaching?

A. Because it is natural to us to understand heavenly things by sensible and earthly things.

Q. May we be saved without the Sacraments?

A. Yes, for our salvation does not absolutely depend upon them.

Q. May we refuse to use the Sacraments?

A. No, for then we would refuse the favour of God.

Q. Do all men receive the favour of God by means of them?

A. No. Only the faithful receive it.

Q. How then are they true seals to all men?

A. They offer Christ truly to all men.

Q. When are the Sacraments fruitful?

A. When we receive them with faith.

Q. Is there any virtue enclosed in them?

A. None at all, for they are but signs of heavenly mysteries.

Q. What is our faith to seek by means of them?

A. To be led directly to Jesus Christ.

Q. If they require faith first, how can they nourish faith?

A. They require some faith first, and then they nourish it.

Q. Are we not infidels when we need signs?

A. No. Rather are we weak in faith.

Q. What then is our state in this life?

A. We are always imperfect and weak in faith.

Q. What then should we do?

A. We should diligently use the Word and the Sacraments.

HOW THE SACRAMENTS AND THE WORD DIFFER AND AGREE

Q. How do the Sacraments differ from the Word?

A. They speak to the eye, and the Word to the ear.

Q. Do they say anything different from the Word?

A. No. They say the same thing in a different way.

Q. But the Word does teach us sufficiently.

A. Yet the Sacraments with the Word do it more effectually.

Q. What then are the Sacraments to the Word?

A. They are sure and authentic seals given by God.

Q. May the Sacraments be without the Word?

A. No, for the Word is their life.

Q. May the Word be fruitful without the Sacraments?

A. Yes, no doubt, but it works more plenteously with them.

Q. What is the reason for that?

A. Because more senses are moved to the comfort of our faith.

THE PARTS OF THE SACRAMENTS

Q. What are the principal parts of the Sacrament?

A. The external action, and the inward signification.

Q. How are they joined together?

A. As the word and the signification are joined together.

Q. What similitude have the Sacraments with the sign signified by them?

A. Great similitude in substance and in qualities.

Q. What does the substance of the elements signify?

A. The very substance of Christ's body.

Q. What if the substance of the elements were not there?

A. Then they would not be true Sacraments of Christ's body.

Q. What do the natural qualities of the elements mean?

A. The spiritual qualities given by Christ.

Q. What does our near conjunction with the Sacraments signify?

A. Our spiritual union with Jesus Christ, and among ourselves.

Q. What does the outward giving and taking mean?

A. The spiritual giving or taking of Christ.

Q. What does the natural operation of the elements mean?

A. The spiritual operation of Christ in us.

Q. Are these things only signified by the Sacraments?

A. No. They are also given and sealed up by the Spirit.

Q. Who may give the seal of these things?

A. God only may give the seal of His promise.

THE MINISTER, AND ORDER OF THE SACRAMENTS

Q. Who may administer the Sacraments?

A. Only the minister of the Word of God.

Q. How are they to be ministered?

A. According to the order given by Christ.

Q. How are they sanctified, consecrated, or blessed?

A. By the practice of the order commanded by Christ.

Q. What is it to consecrate or bless a Sacrament?

A. It is to apply a common thing to a holy use.

Q. Who may do this?

A. God only, and we at His commandment.

Q. Does the consecration or blessing change the substance of the elements?

A. No. It changes the use only.

Q. How long do they remain holy?

A. As long as they are used in that action.

Q. What are they after that use?

A. Common things as before.

Q. Do the Sacraments benefit all the receivers, when they are administered?

A. No. They are received by some without faith for a while.

Q. Then the words of consecration have no force?

A. They have no power to imprint any quality of virtue or holiness in the elements.

Q. To whom are they spoken?

A. To the receivers, and to the elements.

Q. What is the function of these words of blessing?

A. To testify the will of God to the people.

Q. In what language should they be spoken?

A. In the receivers' own language.

Q. Where are the Sacraments to be administered?

A. Publicly before the congregation.

THE RECEIVERS

Q. To whom should the Sacraments be given?

A. To all the members of the Church in due time.

Q. How should the Sacraments be received?

A. In a lively faith and true repentance.

Q. What if there is no faith and repentance?

A. Then double condemnation is sealed up.

Q. Can the sin of the Ministers or others hurt us?

A. No, for they are God's ordinances.

Q. How should we prepare ourselves?

A. We should test our knowledge, faith, and repentance.

Q. Should these gifts be perfect in us?

A. No, but they should be there and without hypocrisy.

THE CAUSES AND NUMBER OF THE SACRAMENTS

Q. Why are the Sacraments used?

A. For the nourishment of our faith, and for an open protestation of our religion before men.

Q. What other end do they serve?

A. They crave the increase of newness of life, with brotherly love and concord.

Q. Did the Sacraments of the Old Testament serve the same uses?

A. Yes no doubt, as the Prophets and Apostles testify.

Q. How many Sacraments has Christ given us?

A. Two only, Baptism and the Lord's Supper.

Q. Why do we have only these two Sacraments?

A. Because we need both to be received, and also to be fed in God's family.

Q. The fathers had very many Sacraments?

A. Yet they had but two principals, that is Circumcision and the Passover.

Q. What did these two testify to them?

A. Their reception, and continual feeding, in God's household.

THE SACRAMENT OF BAPTISM

Q. What is the signification of Baptism?

A. Remission of our sins, and regeneration.

Q. What similitude has Baptism with remission of sins?

A. As washing cleanses the body so Christ's blood cleanses our souls.

Q. In what does this cleansing consist?

A. In the putting away of sin and the imputation of justice.

Q. In what does our regeneration consist?

A. In mortification and newness of life.

Q. How are these things sealed up in Baptism?

A. By the laying on of water.

Q. What does the laying on of the water signify?

A. Our dying to sin and rising to righteousness.

Q. Does the external washing work these things?

A. No, it is the work of God's Holy Spirit alone.

Q. Then the Sacrament is a bare figure?

A. No. It has the reality joined with it.

Q. *Do all men receive these graces with the Sacraments?*
A. No. Only the faithful.

Q. *What is the ground of our regeneration?*
A. The death, burial, and resurrection of Christ.

Q. *When are we partakers of His death and resurrection?*
A. When we are made one with Him through His Spirit.

Q. *How are we to use Baptism aright?*
A. We should use it in faith and repentance.

Q. *How long does Baptism work?*
A. All the days of our life.

THE BAPTISM OF CHILDREN

Q. *How then may little children receive Baptism?*
A. Even as they received circumcision under the Law.

Q. *On what ground were they circumcised?*
A. On the promise made to the fathers, and their seed (Gen. 17; Acts 7:8).

Q. *Have we the same promise for us and our children?*
A. Without doubt, since Christ came to accomplish the same for the faithful.

Q. *What if our children die without Baptism?*
A. Then they are saved by the promise.

Q. *Why are they baptised, when they are young and do not understand?*
A. Because they are of the seed of the faithful.

Q. *What comfort do we have in their Baptism?*
A. This, that we rest persuaded that they are inheritors of the Kingdom of Heaven.

Q. *What should that work in us?*
A. Diligence in teaching them the way of salvation.

Q. *What admonition are they given through this Baptism?*
A. That they are to be thankful when they come to age.

Q. *What then is Baptism for our children?*

A. An entry into the Church of God, and to the Holy Supper.

Q. How does Baptism differ from the Supper?

A. In the element, action, rites, and signification

Q. Why is Baptism administered only once?

A. Because it is enough to be received once into God's family.

Q. Why is the Lord's Supper so often administered?

A. Because we need to be fed continually.

Q. Why is the Lord's Supper not ministered also to infants?

A. Because they cannot examine themselves.

THE SACRAMENT OF THE LORD'S SUPPER

Q. What does the Lord's Supper signify to us?

A. That our souls are fed with the body and blood of Christ.

Q. Why is this represented by bread and wine?

A. Because what the one does to the body, the other does to the soul spiritually.

Q. But our bodies are joined corporally with the elements, or outward signs?

A. Even so are our souls joined spiritually with Christ's body.

Q. What need is there of this union with Him?

A. Otherwise we cannot enjoy His benefits.

Q. Explain that in the Sacraments?

A. As we see the elements given to feed our bodies, even so we see by faith that Christ gave His body to us, to feed our souls.

Q. Did He not give it upon the Cross for us?

A. Yes, but here He gives the same body to be our spiritual food, which we receive and feed on by faith.

Q. When is His body and blood our food?

A. When we feel the efficacy and power of His death in our consciences.

Q. In what way is this done?

A. By His offering, and our receiving of it.

Q. How does He offer His body and blood?

A. By the Word and Sacraments.

Q. How do we receive His body and blood?

A. By our own lively faith alone.

Q. What follows upon this receiving by faith?

A. That Christ dwells in us, and we in Him.

Q. Is not this done by the Word and Baptism?

A. Yes, but our union with Christ is more evident and manifest here.

Q. Why is it more evident?

A. Because it is expressed by meat and drink joined with us inwardly in our bodies.

THE PARTS OF THE SACRAMENT AND THEIR SIGNIFICATION

Q. What does this bread and wine signify to us?

A. Christ's body and blood once offered upon the Cross for us and now given to us to be the food of our souls.

Q. What does the breaking of the bread signify?

A. The breaking and suffering of Christ's body upon the Cross.

Q. What does the pouring out of the wine mean?

A. The shedding of His blood, even to the death.

Q. Where does the Supper lead us?

A. Directly to the Cross and death of Christ.

Q. Should we offer Him again for our sins?

A. No, for Christ did that once for all upon the Cross.

Q. What are we commanded here?

A. To take it, eat it, and drink it in remembrance of Him.

Q. What does the giving of the bread and wine mean?

A. The giving of Christ's body and blood to our souls.

Q. Is it not first given to our bodies?

A. No, for it is the only food of our souls.

Q. What does the taking of that bread and wine signify?

A. The spiritual receiving of Christ's body in our souls.

Q. What does our corporal eating and drinking here mean?

A. Our spiritual feeding upon the body and blood of Christ.

Q. In what way is this done?

A. By the continual exercise of our faith in Christ.

Q. What does the close conjunction we have with meat and drink mean?

A. The spiritual union which we have with Jesus Christ.

Q. What does the strength which we receive from meat and drink signify?

A. The spiritual fruits which we receive from Christ.

Q. Why are both meat and drink given here?

A. To testify that Christ only is the whole food of our souls.

Q. Does the Cup pertain to the common people?

A. Yes, for so the wisdom of God taught and commanded us (Matt. 26:27).

Q. Are Christ's body and blood in the bread and wine?

A. No. His body and blood are only in Heaven.

Q. Why then are the elements called His body and blood?

A. Because they are sure seals of His body and blood given to us.

CHRIST'S NATURAL BODY IS RECEIVED

Q. Then we receive only the tokens, and not His body?

A. We receive His very substantial body and blood by faith.

Q. How can that be proved?

A. By the truth of His Word, and the nature of a Sacrament.

Q. But His natural body is in Heaven?

A. Without doubt, and yet we receive it on earth by faith.

Q. *How can that be?*

A. By the wonderful working of the Holy Spirit.

Q. *What are we to behold in this Sacrament?*

A. The visible food of our bodies, and the inward food of our souls.

Q. *Should we seek the food of our souls in the elements of bread and wine?*

A. No, for they were not given to that end.

Q. *To what end then were they given?*

A. To lead us directly to Christ, who only is the food of our souls.

Q. *What profit should our bodies have by this Sacrament?*

A. It is a pledge of our resurrection by Christ.

Q. *How is that?*

A. Because our bodies are partakers of the sign of life.

THE ORDER AND USE OF THIS SACRAMENT

Q. *How should this Sacrament be administered and used?*

A. As Christ with His Apostle did practise and command.

Q. *May the Minister alone use it in the name of the rest?*

A. No, for it is a common and public banquet.

Q. *What makes this action holy?*

A. Christ's ordinance practised by the lawful Minister.

Q. *How is it made fruitful?*

A. Through the true faith of the receivers.

Q. *To whom should this Sacrament be given?*

A. To all who believe and can examine themselves.

HOW WE SHOULD PREPARE OURSELVES

Q. *What should they examine?*

A. Whether they are lively members of Christ.

Q. *How are they to know this secret?*

A. By their own faith and repentance.

Q. How are faith and repentance to be known?

A. By their fruits, agreeable to the first and second Table.

Q. But all men's faith and repentance are imperfect?

A. Therefore we come to the Sacrament for healing.

Q. What kind of faith and repentance is required?

A. That which is true, upright, and not counterfeited.

Q. What do they receive who come with a guilty conscience?

A. They eat and drink their own damnation.

Q. How can Christ received bring damnation?

A. He is not received by the wicked, but refused through dissimulation and abuse of the Sacrament.

Q. Then it is best to abstain from the Sacrament?

A. We are not so commanded, but to examine and prepare ourselves.

Q. What if men cannot examine themselves?

A. Then they should read the Scriptures and consult with their Pastors.

Q. What if men will not use these means?

A. Then they deceive themselves, and abuse the Sacrament.

Q. What if the Minister admit such careless men?

A. Then he profanes this holy Sacrament.

THE MINISTRY OF MEN, AND THE DISCIPLINE

Q. How are men to be excluded from the Sacrament?

A. By the judgement of the elders of the Church.

Q. What kind of men should be excluded?

A. All infidels and public slanderers of the Church.

Q. What if their crime is secret?

A. Then they should be left to their own judge.

Q. Why are men excluded from the Sacraments?

A. Lest they should hurt themselves, slander the Church, and dishonour God.

Q. By whom and when should such persons be admitted?

A. By the eldership, after just trial of their repentance.

Q. Who established this order in the Church?

A. Jesus Christ by His Word and the Apostles.

Q. What is the office of this eldership?

A. They should watch over the manners of men and exercise the discipline.

Q. What authority do they have?

A. Authority to bind and loose on earth.

Q. May they do this at their own pleasure?

A. No, for their authority is bound to the Word.

Q. What is the service of the civil magistrate?

A. He should cause all things to be done according to God's Word, and defend the discipline.

Q. Does the care of the Religion pertain to him?

A. No doubt, seeing he is raised up chiefly for this cause.

Q. May the Magistrate use the office of the ministers?

A. No, but he charges them to use their own office.

Q. What may the eldership do to the magistrate?

A. Admit him to the Sacraments, or exclude, according to the Word of God.

Q. May the minister use the office of the magistrate?

A. No, for they should not be entangled with worldly affairs.

TWO JURISDICTIONS IN THE CHURCH

Q. How many jurisdictions are there in the Church?

A. Two, one spiritual and another civil.

Q. How do they agree in the Church?

A. As the mouth and hand of God.

Q. To what end were they established in the Church?

A. For the planting and preservation of the same.

Q. How far should we obey these jurisdictions?

A. So far as their commandment agrees with the Word.

Q. What should we do, when they are both against the Church?

A. We should remain with the Church of God.

Q. But they will say the Church ought to be with them?

A. We should test their sayings by the signs of the true Church.

Q. What are these signs or marks?

A. The Word, the Sacraments, and Discipline rightly used.

Q. What if no order of discipline exists among them?

A. Then we should remain with the Word and Sacraments.

Q. But what if both the Word and Sacraments are corrupted?

A. Then we should not join ourselves with that company.

Q. But what if they receive the name of the true Church?

A. So did Satan clothe himself with the Angel of Light, for the further blinding of the world.

Q. But what shall men do when they do not know any other Church?

A. Let them content themselves with true faith in Christ.

Q. But then they are divided from the Church?

A. Not from the true Church and Body of Christ.

Q. How can that be proved?

A. Thus: all that are united with Christ are joined with the Church.

Q. Which of these two unions is first and cause of the other?

A. Our mystical and spiritual union with Jesus Christ. For we are joined with all the saints of God, because we are joined first with God in Christ.

Q. What comfort to us, then, is our society with the Church?

A. A singular comfort, chiefly when we are persecuted by the bastard church, and tyrants of the world.

Q. What is the comfort to us?

A. This, that they cannot separate us from Christ and His members, even if they separate us from their wicked society.

9. THE FIRST CAUSE AND PROGRESS OF SALVATION AND THE END OF ALL FLESH

Q. *From what source does our stability derive?*

A. From God's eternal and constant election in Christ.

Q. *How does this election come to us?*

A. By His effectual calling in due time.

Q. *What does this effectual calling work in us?*

A. The obedience of faith.

Q. *What does faith work?*

A. Our perpetual and inseparable union with Christ.

Q. *What does this union with Christ work?*

A. A mutual communion with Him and His graces.

Q. *What does this communion work?*

A. Remission of sins and imputation of justice.

Q. *What do remission of sins and imputation of justice work?*

A. Peace of conscience and continual sanctification.

Q. *What does sanctification work?*

A. The hatred of sin and the love of godliness.

Q. *What does the hatred of sin work?*

A. A continual battle against sin.

Q. *What does this battle work?*

A. Continual desire to profit in godliness.

Q. *What does this desire work?*

A. An earnest study of the Word of God.

Q. *What does this earnest study work?*

A. Further knowledge of our own weakness and God's goodness.

Q. *What does this knowledge work in us?*

A. An earnest calling upon God for help.

Q. *What does this earnest calling work?*

A. Victory against Satan and sin.

Q. *What does this victory work?*

U

A. A lively experience of God's favour.

Q. *What does this lively experience work?*

A. Boldness to fight and sure hope of further victory.

Q. *What does this sure hope work?*

A. An unspeakable joy of heart in trouble.

Q. *What does this joy of heart work?*

A. Patience to the end of the battle.

Q. *What does patience work in us?*

A. Stoutness of heart to the final triumph.

Q. *What does this stoutness of heart work?*

A. A plain defiance against Satan and sin.

Q. *What is this defiance?*

A. The beginning of the eternal life in us.

Q. *What is this beginning to us?*

A. A sure seal of our election and glorification.

THE CERTAINTY OF ADOPTION

Q. *May not this seal be abolished through sin?*

A. No, for these gifts are without repentance.

Q. *But many fall shamefully from God.*

A. The Spirit of adoption raises up again all the chosen.

Q. *But many are never raised up again?*

A. These were never the chosen of God.

Q. *Yet both they and the Church believed otherwise?*

A. They deceived themselves, but the Church judges charitably.

Q. *Then faith is not certain?*

A. True faith is ever certain to the believers.

Q. *What certainty has every one of his faith?*

A. The testimony of the Spirit of adoption with the fruits.

Q. *But many glory in this testimony in vain?*

A. Yet this testimony is most sure and certain.

Q. *Why then are so many deceived in this way?*

A. Because they glory in a faith without fruits.

Q. How may we eschew this danger?

A. By the right trial of our adoption.

THE TRIAL OF OUR ADOPTION

Q. Where should we begin our trial?

A. With the fruits of faith and repentance. Because they are best known to ourselves and others.

Q. What if we begin at election?

A. Then we shall wander in darkness.

Q. But God's election is most clear and certain?

A. It is clear and certain in itself: but it is not always certain to us in particular.

Q. When is it certain to every one of us?

A. When it may be felt and known by its fruits.

Q. But this exact trial has brought some to desperation?

A. Yet God's elect are always sustained, and finally comforted.

Q. Yet this trial is troublesome to men's consciences?

A. But at length it brings great peace of conscience.

Q. When and how is that?

A. When after the feeling of God's judgements we taste of His mercy again more abundantly.

Q. Why are God's elect so often thus troubled in mind?

A. That they may the better feel and know the mercy of God.

Q. Why do worldly men esteem so little the mercy of God?

A. Because they do not have a thorough taste of His justice.

Q. What then is trouble with the comfort of the Spirit?

A. A seal of God's love, and a preparation for life eternal.

Q. What is prosperity without the taste of the Spirit?

A. A token of God's wrath, and a way to perdition.

Q. But some are troubled in mind without any relief?

A. Such men begin their hell with Cain.

THE FINAL AND ETERNAL STATE OF MANKIND

Q. What then will be the final end of all flesh?

A. Either life, or death eternal, without any change.

Q. With whom and where shall the faithful be?

A. With God in heaven, full of all joy and felicity.

Q. With whom and where shall the wicked be?

A. With Satan in hell, oppressed with infinite miseries.

Q. Are these two ends certain and sure?

A. Yes no doubt, since the means are certain and sure.

Q. Which are these sure means?

A. Faith and infidelity with their fruits.

Q. What makes these means sure?

A. God's most just and constant will revealed in His Word.

Q. When did He ordain these means and ends?

A. Before all beginnings in His secret counsel.

Q. Why did He do this?

A. That His mercy and justice might shine perfectly in mankind.

Q. How was this brought to pass?

A. Through the creation of man in uprightness and his fall from that state.

Q. What followed upon this fall of man?

A. All men once were concluded under sin and most just condemnation.

Q. How did this serve His mercy and justice?

A. Occasion was thus offered both of mercy and justice.

Q. To whom was mercy promised and given?

A. Only to His chosen children in Christ, who are called the vessels of mercy.

Q. How does He show mercy to them?

A. He gives them the means whereby they come assuredly to life eternal.

Q. On whom does He show justice?

A. On all the rest of Adam's posterity, who are called the children of wrath.

Q. When does He do this?

A. When He suffers them to walk patiently according to their own corrupt nature.

Q. What follows upon that walking?

A. Eternal perdition infallibly, according to God's eternal decree.

Q. Does God compel them to walk that way?

A. No. They willingly embrace it against His Word.

Q. How can men willingly embrace the way of perdition?

A. Because they are blinded and corrupted by Satan and their own lusts.

Q. May they embrace the way of life?

A. No, they refuse it necessarily, and yet freely without any compulsion.

Q. Where does this necessity come from?

A. From the bondage of sin, in which they were cast by the fall of Adam.

Q. Is all Adam's posterity equally in the same bondage?

A. Yes no doubt, but the chosen are redeemed through Christ, and the others justly left in their natural state.

Q. What is to be seen perpetually in vessels of wrath?

A. The glory of God's eternal and fearful justice.

Q. What is to be seen in the vessels of mercy?

A. The perpetual praise of His mercy and goodness, through Jesus Christ our Lord. To whom with the Father and the Holy Spirit, be all honour and glory eternally. Amen.

THE NEW CATECHISM, 1644

The New Catechism
according to the form of the Kirk of Scotland

The New Catechism of 1644 represents on the doctrinal side a stage of development in the Reformed Church of Scotland parallel to that which characterised the old *Book of Common Order*, the last edition of which was published in the same year. This Catechism was an enlargement of the *Catechism for Young Children* published three years earlier, but judging from the words on its title page, *Set forth for the general good of both Kingdoms*, its publication in London was evidently intended to influence the work of the Westminster Divines. It is much nearer in its teaching to the earlier Reformed Catechisms, and shows little, if any, of the rationalistic schematism of the Federal theology, although that had its beginning in Scotland as far back as Robert Rollock and its great champion in David Dickson. Of all the official Catechisms of the Church of Scotland, this had the shortest life, for it was hardly put into effective use when it was superseded by the productions of Westminster.

Question 1. Who made the Heavens and the Earth, and all things contained in them?
Answer. God.
Q.2. Of what was man created?
A. Of the earth.
Q.3. To what end was he made?
A. To serve God.
Q.4. How many principal parts are there in God's service?
A. Four: Faith, Obedience, Prayer, and Thanksgiving.
Q.5. What is the rule of our faith?

A. The Word of God, the sum of which is in the Articles of the Belief.

Q.6. What is the rule of our obedience?

A. The Ten Commandments.

Q.7. What is the rule of our Prayers?

A. The Lord's Prayer.

Q.8. What is the common rule of our thanksgiving?

A. The Confession at the end of the Lord's Prayer, For Thine is the kingdom, the power, and the glory, etc.

Q.9. In what estate was man created?

A. In the image of God, perfect and holy in soul and body.

Q.10. How did he fall from that happy estate?

A. By sin and disobedience.

Q.11. What was the occasion?

A. Satan speaking out of the serpent, tempted Eve in Paradise, and she persuaded Adam to eat of the forbidden tree.

Q.12. What punishment did they deserve therefore?

A. The curse of God and eternal condemnation.

Q.13. Do we deserve to be punished for that sin?

A. Yes: for we sinned in Adam, being in his loins, and so we were a part of him.

Q.14. Who then shall be saved?

A. Only those who believe that they will be saved by Christ.

I. The Twelve Articles of the Belief

Q.15. Repeat the 12 Articles of the Belief?

A. I believe in God the Father Almighty, etc.

Q.16. What is the content of the first article?

A. Our confidence in a loving and powerful God.

Q.17. How many Gods are they?

A. One.

Q.18. How many persons are there in the Godhead?

A. Three: God the Father, the Son, and the Holy Ghost.

Q.19. What is it to believe in God?

A. To put our whole confidence in Him, trusting that He will provide for us in all things needful for this life, and the life to come.

Q.20. How is God our Father?

A. First by creation, because He made us; next, by adoption, and regeneration, through the blood and Spirit of Christ.

Q.21. Why is He called Almighty?

A. Because He may do all things whatsoever He pleases, and He may do more than He will by His absolute power; for of stones He may raise up children unto Abraham.

Q.22. By what works is He known to be Almighty?

A. By the making of heaven and earth, and of all things that are in them.

Q.23. What is the content of the second article?

A. The names and titles of God the Son.

Q.24. Why is He called Jesus?

A. Because He is our Saviour.

Q.25. Why is He named Christ?

A. Because He is anointed as our King, Priest, and Prophet.

Q.26. What does He do to us as a King?

A. He governs us, and defends us from our enemies.

Q.27. What does He do to us as a Priest?

A. He has offered Himself once in a sacrifice for our sins, and He intercedes for us.

Q.28. What does He do to us as a Prophet?

A. He reveals the will of God to us by the preaching of His Word, and by His Spirit.

Q.29. Why is He called the only Son of God, seeing we are His sons by adoption and regeneration?

A. Because God has no other sons by nature.

Q.30. How is Christ more particularly our Lord than the Lord of other creatures?

A. In that He is our Head and has redeemed us by the price of His blood.

Q.31. What kind of person is He?

A. Very God and very Man in one person.

Q.32. Why did it behove Him to be Man?

A. That He might die for us.

Q.33. Why did it behove Him to be God in the same person?

A. That He might overcome death and merit our salvation.

Q.34. What is the content of the third article?

A. His coming into this world.

Q.35. By whom was He conceived?

A. By the Holy Ghost.

Q.36. Who was His mother who bore Him?

A. The Virgin Mary.

Q.37. What is the content of the fourth article?

A. The sufferings of Christ.

Q.38. Under what judge was He condemned?

A. Under Pontius Pilate.

Q.39. What punishment did He suffer?

A. He was crucified.

Q.40. What is meant by His crucifixion?

A. His hands and feet were nailed to the cross, a crown of thorns wounded His head, His back was beaten with scourges, a spear pierced His side, and all the sufferings that accompanied His cross.

Q.41. What was the result of His sufferings?

A. He died.

Q.42. What was done with His body?

A. It was buried.

Q.43. What is the meaning of the words, He descended into hell?

A. The extremity of His sufferings, wherein His soul was tormented with the sense of God's wrath, which is the most horrible bitterness of hell.

Q.44. What is the content of the fifth article?

A. His resurrection on the third day after His death.

Q.45. What benefit do we have through it?

A. In that He rose from the dead, we are the more assured that He can raise us.

Q.46. What does the sixth article contain?

A. His further exaltation unto glory, and its fruition.

Q.47. Which are the words that speak of His further exaltation?

A. He ascended into heaven.

Q.48. Which are the words that speak of the fruition of that glory?

A. He sitteth at the right hand of God.

Q.49. What does He do for us in heaven?

A. He prepares a place for us, and intercedes for us.

Q.50. What is expressed in the seventh article?

A. The coming of Christ unto judgement.

Q.51. To what end will He come to judgement?

A. To judge the quick and the dead.

Q.52. Who will summon them to appear before the great Judge?

A. The voice of the Archangel, with a terrible sound of a trumpet.

Q.53. Where shall every man be placed?

A. Christ's sheep shall be placed on His right hand, and the goats on His left hand.

Q.54. What shall be their reward?

A. The godly shall inherit the Kingdom of glory. The wicked shall be punished with everlasting fire in hell, prepared for the Devil and his angels.

Q.55. What is the content of the eighth article?

A. Our confidence in the Holy Ghost.

Q.56. Why is He only called holy, seeing the Father and the Son are also holy?

A. Because He makes us holy by His immediate power.

Q.57. What is the content of the ninth article?

A. That a chosen number of people are united to Christ, and also among themselves, in a spiritual fellowship.

Q.58. What do you call this number?

A. The Holy Universal Kirk.

Q.59. What is God's Kirk?

A. A society of religious professors called out from the profane people of the world.

Q.60. Why is the Kirk called holy, and also called saints?

A. Because they are sanctified by the Holy Ghost.

Q.61. Why is the Kirk called universal?

A. Because it is gathered out of all sorts of people in all ages.

Q.62. In what does the communion of saints consist?

A. In a common union with Christ their Head, and among themselves.

Q.63. By what bonds are we united to Christ?

A. By His Spirit, He binds us to Himself, and by faith we take hold on Him.

Q.64. By what bond are we united among ourselves?

A. By Christian love.

Q.65. What advantage do we have from this communion?

A. Christ and all His benefits are made ours.

Q.66. What is the content of the tenth article?

A. That all our sins are pardoned.

Q.67. How do we get this benefit?

A. By faith in Christ, who died for us.

Q.68. What is mentioned in the eleventh article?

A. The resurrection of our bodies at the last day.

Q.69. Is no more meant in it than arising from death?

A. We shall also rise from every sense of misery, such as shame, sorrow, pain, hunger, thirst, weakness, and mortality.

Q.70. Repeat the twelfth article?

A. Life everlasting.

Q.71. What is included in these words?

A. The enjoyment of endless life, joy, glory, and every happiness for ever.

Q.72. What shall become of the earth, and of the creatures in it, at the last day?

A. They shall be destroyed with fire, and the elements shall melt with heat.

Q.73. What shall succeed in their place?

A. We shall look for a new heaven and a new earth, wherein dwells righteousness.

II. The Ten Commandments

Q.74. What is the second principal part of God's service?

A. Obedience.

Q.75. What is obedience?

A. The keeping of God's commandments.

Q.76. How many commandments are there?

A. Ten.

Q.77. Repeat the Ten Commandments?

A. I am the Lord, etc.

Q.78. How many commands are in the first table?

A. Four.

Q.79. What duty is contained in the first table?

A. My duty towards God, which is to love Him with all my heart, with all my soul, and with my whole strength.

Q.80. How many commands are in the second table?

A. Six.

Q.81. What duty is contained in it?

A. My duty towards my neighbour.

Q.82. What duty is that?

A. To love him as myself.

Q.83. To whom did God give His Law?

A. To His people Israel.

Q.84. Where did He give it?

A. On Mount Sinai.

Q.85. How did He give it?

A. With a fearful and horrible voice, and with the sound of a trumpet.

Q.86. What should this print in our hearts?

A. That the trial of the transgressors of the law shall be more terrible at the last day.

Q.87. What is commanded in the first precept?

A. To love, fear, and reverence God, to believe in Him above all things that are most excellent, and to confess Him before men accordingly.

Q.88. What is forbidden in it?

A. We are forbidden to believe in any other, to love, fear, or reverence any other above the true God, or equally with Him.

Q.89. What is commanded in the second precept?

A. To worship God as His own Word has prescribed.

Q.90. What is forbidden in it?

A. To worship Him by bowing to any image, or by any other human device.

Q.91. What is commanded in the third precept?

A. To praise and glorify God, to honour His Name, and to speak reverently of His attributes, His Word, and His works.

Q.92. What is forbidden in it?

A. All perjury, blasphemy, cursing or swearing, vain and false oaths, all rash and irreverent use of God's Name.

Q.93. What is commanded in the fourth command?

A. To spend the Sabbath day solemnly in God's worship and service.

Q.94. In what service?

A. In hearing and reading God's Word, in praying unto God, and praising Him, in holy conference, in heavenly meditations, and in works of piety and charity.

Q.95. What is forbidden in it?

A. Beside the committing of that which is sin in itself, also all civil labours, judicatories, pastimes, and plays are forbidden.

Q.96. Why are they forbidden?

A. Because the doing of them is not a sanctifying of the Sabbath.

Q.97. What is commanded in the fifth command?

A. To honour and obey our natural Parents, Rulers, Masters, Pastors, Teachers, and all our Superiors.

Q.98. What is forbidden in it?

A. All ungodly disobedience and irreverent behaviour towards them.

Q.99. What is commanded in the sixth precept?

A. To take care of the safety of our neighbour's health and life, and to keep him from hurt by others; and therefore to banish away envy, hatred, malice, contempt of our neighbour, whereby his hurt is procured.

Q.100. What is commanded in the seventh precept?

A. To live chastely and soberly in thought, word, deed, and behaviour.

Q.101. What is forbidden in it?

A. All uncleanness in our thoughts, words, deeds, and therefore we are commanded to eschew all filthy talk, bawdy songs, drunkenness, gluttony, wantonness, and evil company, which breed unlawful lusts.

Q.102. What is commanded in the eighth precept?

A. To be content with the means of living which God gives us in a lawful way, and to help others as we are able in their necessity.

Q.103. What is forbidden in it?

A. All covetousness, whereby we unlawfully take our neighbour's goods and property, as by oppression or robbery, or under cover of the law, by theft, by false measures or false weights.

Q.104. What is commanded in the ninth precept?

A. To defend the fame and good name of others, and to repress defamatory talk.

Q.105. What is forbidden in it?

A. All lying, slandering, backbiting, all speaking to the discredit or infamy of others; all giving ready ear to calumnies, lies, and reproaches.

Q.106. What is commanded in the tenth command?

A. To rejoice at the prosperity of others, or when any good is done; and to be sorry at the hard condition of others, or when any evil is done.

Q.107. What is forbidden in it?

A. All concupiscence, whereby we covet things which do not lawfully belong to us, and whereby we approve in our hearts the doing of evil, or the hurt of others.

Q.108. How does the duty of this precept differ from the inward duty of other precepts?

A. We obey or disobey this precept in our desires, not intending actually to do the thing desired, but in other precepts the intention concurs with the desire, whether the purpose is put into effect or not.

Q.109. Are we able to obey these commandments?

A. No.

Q.110. What punishment do we deserve for breaking them?

A. The curse of God, and endless torments in hell.

Q.111. How then shall we be saved?

A. By Christ, who died for our sins and rose again for our righteousness.

Q.112. For whom did He die?

A. Only for the faithful.

Q.113. What is faith?

A. An assurance of God's endless favour and mercy towards us for Christ's sake.

Q.114. Who works lively faith in us?

A. The Holy Ghost, by hearing of the Word.

Q.115. By what means is our faith confirmed?

A. By the hearing of the same Word, and by the right using of the Sacraments.

Q.116. How is lively faith known to be in us?

A. By true repentance.

Q.117. What is repentance?

A. Sorrow for our past sins, and an active zeal for good works and amendment of life.

Q.118. What shall we do that we may obtain lively faith and true repentance?

A. We should pray continually that God would bless the Word and Sacraments to that end.

III. PRAYER

Q.119. What is the third principal part of God's service?

A. Prayer.

Q.120. What is prayer?

A. A seeking from God of things needful for setting forth His glory, and for the supplying of our wants.

Q.121. How should we pray?

A. As Christ taught us in the most perfect form of prayer.

Q.122. Repeat the Lord's Prayer?

A. Our Father which art in heaven, etc.

Q.123. Repeat the preface of the Prayer?

A. Our Father which art in heaven.

Q.124. Why do you call God our Father?

A. To stir up our confidence in His fatherly love, and to persuade ourselves that He will hear us.

w

Q.125. Why do you say "which art in heaven", seeing God is also in the earth, and in all other places?

A. Because as we speak boldly in calling Him Father, so we reverently honour Him in naming the most glorious place of His residence.

Q.126. How many petitions does this Prayer have?

A. Six.

Q.127. What is contained in the first three petitions?

A. Things that concern the setting forth of God's glory.

Q.128. What is contained in the last three?

A. Things that concern man's necessity.

Q.129. What do you seek in the first petition?

A. That we should glorify God in a holy remembrance of His Name.

Q.130. What do you seek in the second petition?

A. That His Kingdom may increase in the means of His providence, in the ministry and increase of grace, and in hastening the consummation thereof in glory.

Q.131. What do you seek in the third petition?

A. That in doing and suffering we should always obey His will sincerely and willingly, as the angels obey His will in heaven.

Q.132. What do you seek in the fourth petition?

A. All things needful for maintaining this present life.

Q.133. Why do you call them bread?

A. Because they sustain our life as bread does.

Q.134. Why do you say "our bread"?

A. Because it should be ours by faithful labouring in our calling, and by other lawful means.

Q.135. What do you seek in the fifth petition?

A. Remission of sins.

Q.136. Upon what condition do you seek this?

A. If we forgive them that sin against us.

Q.137. Why do you say "our sins", and not "my sins", and why do you include others with yourself so often in this Prayer?

A. Because we should pray for others as we do for ourselves.

Q.138. What do you seek in the sixth petition?

A. That God would keep us from the temptation of sin, and deliver us from its evil.

Q.139. What is the greatest evil of temptation?

A. The fearful state into which Satan would draw us by sin; despair, presumption, impenitence, and the wrath of God.

Q.140. Repeat the confession immediately following this Prayer.

A. For thine is the kingdom, the power, and the glory, for ever.

Q.141. How does this confession help us to pray?

A. It shows God's all-sufficiency and goodness, and so stirs up our confidence in Him.

Q.142. How is it a rule of our thanksgiving?

A. In that by using this confession we praise God for His bountifulness.

Q.143. What is the meaning of the words "for thine is the kingdom"?

A. That the whole world is God's Kingdom of providence, by an absolute right.

Q.144. What does the word "power" mean?

A. That He has absolute authority and power to do whatsoever He pleases.

Q.145. What does the word "glory" mean?

A. That all good things are affected by His almighty power in His Kingdom of providence, and so the praise and glory thereof is His.

Q.146. What is the meaning of the words "for ever"?

A. That His Kingdom, power, and glory are not limited by time, but are eternal.

Q.147. What does the word "Amen" signify?

A. So be it: that is, O Lord, let these my desires be granted.

IV. The Sacraments

Q.148. What is the fourth principal part of God's service?

A. Thanksgiving.

Q.149. What is thanksgiving?

A. An acknowledgement of the goodness of God, and of His bountifulness towards us, and a praising of God for it.

Q.150. Which is the common rule of thanksgiving?

A. The confession in the Lord's Prayer.

Q.151. What are the rules of solemn thanksgiving in remembrance that Christ by His death has purchased our salvation?

A. The institution of the Sacraments.

Q.152. What is a Sacrament?

A. A representing of Christ's sufferings, and of the benefits thereby purchased, by outward visible signs, as Christ has ordained in His Word.

Q.153. How many Sacraments are ordained by Christ in the New Testament?

A. Two, Baptism and the Lord's Supper.

Q.154. What is Baptism?

A. The seal of the remission of our sins, and of our regeneration and entry unto God's Kirk.

Q.155. What does the washing with water signify?

A. That Christ by the merit of His blood, and by His Spirit, washes away all our sins.

Q.156. Declare the meaning of our spiritual washing?

A. God has forgiven us all our sins, and renewed us by His Holy Spirit, because Christ has shed His precious blood for us.

Q.157. What duty did your parents in your name promise at Baptism?

A. That I should forsake the Devil, and all his works, and all the sinful lusts of the flesh, and believe all God's Word, which is summarily contained in the Articles of the Faith, and live in holiness all my lifetime.

Q.158. What is the Lord's Supper?

A. The seal of our daily and spiritual nourishment in God's Kirk.

Q.159. What are its outward elements?

A. Bread and Wine.

Q.160. What do they represent?

A. The body and blood of Christ.

Q.161. What does the breaking of the bread signify?

A. The breaking of His body, and all His sufferings.

Q.162. What does the pouring out of the wine signify?

A. The shedding of His blood.

Q.163. What does the eating of the bread and drinking of the wine signify?

A. The spiritual eating of His body, and drinking of His blood by faith.

Q.164. Declare its meaning.

A. It means that we should seriously meditate upon the love and the sufferings of Christ, and apply them to us, assuring ourselves that the Son of God, eternal life, happiness and glory, and all His benefits are made ours, through the breaking of His body and shedding of His blood; that the sweetness of this assurance may comfort and strengthen our souls, as men after long fasting are refreshed by meat and drink.

Q.165. What do they eat and drink, who come worthily to the Lord's Table?

A. They eat Christ's body, and drink His blood, spiritually and sacramentally, and thereby they eat and drink their own salvation.

Q.166. What do they eat and drink, who come unworthily?

A. They eat and drink their own damnation.

Q.167. How shall we prepare ourselves that we may come worthily?

A. We should try and examine ourselves as to where we have sinned, and humbly, with sorrowful hearts, confess our sins, crying earnestly to God for mercy, both in private and in the public assembly; and that we may be assured that God will hear us, and forgive us, we should forgive them that offend us; and seeking the graces of increase of faith and sanctification, we should resolve and promise by His grace to live a better life hereafter.

THE WESTMINSTER LARGER
CATECHISM, 1648

The Larger Catechism
agreed upon by the Assembly of Divines at Westminster, with the
assistance of Commissioners from the Church of Scotland, as part of
the convenanted uniformity in Religion between the Churches of
Christ in the Kingdoms of Scotland, England and Ireland, and
approved anno 1648 by the General Assembly of the Church of
Scotland to be a Directory for catechising such as have made some
proficiency in the knowledge and grounds of Religion.

ALONG with the *Confession of Faith* the Westminster Assembly prepared two Catechisms, a *Larger* and a *Shorter Catechism*. Great care was taken over their production to make them adequate statements of reformed teaching and valuable instruments for its inculcation. The *Larger Catechism* was designed chiefly as a directory for ministers in their teaching of the reformed faith Sunday by Sunday. The preparation of the Catechisms made use of the Reformation Catechisms and also of later productions (some of which were only in draft form), such as those of Rutherford, Palmer, Ussher, Goudge, Rogers, Ball, etc., but the person mainly responsible for them was Anthony Tuckney of Cambridge. They were presented to Parliament for examination late in 1647 and approved in their final form in September 1648. The *Larger Catechism* was adopted by the General Assembly of the Church of Scotland in July, 1648, finding it "to be agreeable to the Word of God and in nothing contrary to the received Doctrine, Worship, Discipline, and Government of this Kirk", and approving it "as a part of uniformity, agreeing, on their part, that it be a common Catechism for the Three Kingdoms, and a Directory for catechising such as have made some proficiency in the Knowledge of the grounds of Religion". Its adoption was ratified by act of the Scottish Parliament in February 1649.

Right from its adoption, the *Larger Catechism* assumed a place of supreme importance among the doctrinal standards of the Church, superseding the previous catechisms in pre-eminence, if not ousting them from the affection and use of the Church. According to an act of the Assembly in 1649, every minister was ordained "with the assistance of the elders of their several kirk-sessions, to take course, that in every house, there be at least one copy of the *Shorter* and *Larger Catechism*, *Confession of Faith*, and *Directory for Family Worship*".

Although the Act of Parliament ratifying the adoption of the Catechisms in Scotland was repealed under Charles II, in 1661, and although the Acts of Parliament which restored the Presbyterian Church of Scotland in 1690 made no express mention of either of the Catechisms, they still retained their authoritative use in the Kirk.

In this edition outstanding archaisms have been removed from the original.

THE LARGER CATECHISM

Question 1. What is the chief and highest end of man?

Answer. Man's chief and highest end is to glorify God, and fully to enjoy Him for ever.

Q.2. How does it appear that there is a God?

A. The very light of nature in man, and the works of God, declare plainly that there is a God; but His Word and Spirit only do sufficiently and effectually reveal Him unto men for their salvation.

Q.3. What is the Word of God?

A. The Holy Scriptures of the Old and New Testament are the Word of God, the only rule of faith and obedience.

Q.4. How does it appear that the Scriptures are the Word of God?

A. The Scriptures reveal themselves to be the Word of God by their majesty and purity; by the consent of all the parts, and the scope of the whole, which is to give all glory to God; by their light and power to convince and convert sinners, to comfort and build up believers unto salvation; but the Spirit of God bearing witness by and with the Scriptures in the heart of man, is alone able fully to persuade it that they are the very Word of God.

Q.5. What do the Scriptures principally teach?

A. The Scriptures principally teach, what man is to believe concerning God, and what duty God requires of man.

WHAT MAN OUGHT TO BELIEVE CONCERNING GOD

Q.6. What do the Scriptures make known of God?

A. The Scriptures make known what God is, the persons in the Godhead, His decrees, and the execution of His decrees.

Q.7. What is God?

A. God is a Spirit, in and of Himself infinite in being, glory, blessedness, and perfection; all-sufficient, eternal, unchangeable, incomprehensible, everywhere present, almighty, knowing all things, most wise, most holy, most just, most merciful and gracious, long-suffering, and abundant in goodness and truth.

Q.8. Are there more Gods than one?

A. There is but One only, the living and true God.

Q.9. How many persons are there in the Godhead?

A. There are three persons in the Godhead, the Father, the Son, and the Holy Spirit; and these three are one true, eternal God, the same in substance, equal in power and glory; although distinguished by their personal properties.

Q.10. What are personal properties of the three persons in the Godhead?

A. It is proper to the Father to beget the Son, and to the Son to be begotten of the Father, and to the Holy Spirit to proceed from the Father and the Son from all eternity.

Q.11. How does it appear that the Son and the Holy Spirit are God equal with the Father?

A. The Scriptures manifest that the Son and the Holy Spirit are God equal with the Father, ascribing unto Them such names, attributes, works, and worship, as are proper to God only.

Q.12. What are the decrees of God?

A. God's decrees are the wise, free, and holy acts of the counsel of His will, whereby, from all eternity, He has, for His own glory, unchangeably foreordained whatsoever comes to pass in time, especially concerning angels and men.

Q.13. What has God especially decreed concerning angels and men?

A. God, by an eternal and immutable decree, out of His mere love, for the praise of His glorious grace, to be manifested in due time, has elected some angels to glory; and in Christ, has chosen some men to eternal life, and the means thereof; and also, according to His sovereign power, and the unsearchable counsel of His own will (whereby He extends or withholds favour as He pleases), has passed by and fore-ordained the rest to dishonour and wrath, to be for their sin inflicted, to the praise of the glory of His justice.

Q.14. How does God execute His decrees?

A. God executes His decrees in the works of creation and providence, according to His infallible foreknowledge, and the free and immutable counsel of His own will.

Q.15. What is the work of creation?

A. The work of creation is that wherein God did in the beginning, by the Word of His power, make of nothing the world, and all things therein, for Himself, within the space of six days, and all very good.

Q.16. How did God create angels?

A. God created all the angels spirits, immortal, holy, excelling in knowledge, mighty in power, to execute His commandments, and to praise His name, yet subject to change.

Q.17. How did God create man?

A. After God had made all other creatures, He created man male and female; formed the body of the man of the dust of the ground, and the woman of the rib of the man; endued them with living, reasonable, and immortal souls; made them after His own image, in knowledge, righteousness, and holiness; having the law of God written in their hearts, and power to fulfil it, with dominion over the creatures; yet subject to fall.

Q.18. What are God's works of providence?

A. God's works of providence are His most holy, wise, and powerful preserving and governing of all His creatures; ordering of them, and all their actions, to His own glory.

Q.19. What is God's providence towards the angels?

A. God by His providence permitted some of the angels, wilfully and irrecoverably, to fall into sin and damnation, limiting and ordering that, and all their sins, to His own glory; and established the rest in holiness and happiness; employing them all, at His pleasure, in the administrations of His power, mercy, and justice.

Q.20. What was the providence of God toward man in the state in which he was created?

A. The providence of God toward man in the state in which he was created, was the placing of him in paradise, appointing him to dress it, giving him liberty to eat of the fruit of the earth; putting the creatures under his dominion, and ordaining marriage for his help; affording him communion with Himself; instituting the Sabbath; entering into a covenant of life with him, upon condition of personal, perfect, and perpetual obedience, of which the tree of life was a pledge; and forbidding to eat of the tree of the knowledge of good and evil, upon the pain of death.

Q.21. Did man continue in that state wherein God at first created him?

A. Our first parents being left to the freedom of their own will, through the temptation of Satan, transgressed the commandment of God in eating the forbidden fruit; and thereby fell from the state of innocency in which they were created.

Q.22. Did all mankind fall in that first transgression?

A. The covenant being made with Adam as a public person, not for himself only, but for his posterity, all mankind descending from him by ordinary generation, sinned in him, and fell with him in that first transgression.

Q.23. Into what state did the fall bring mankind?

A. The fall brought mankind into a state of sin and misery.

Q.24. What is sin?

A. Sin is any want of conformity unto, or transgression of, any law of God, given as a rule to the reasonable creature.

Q.25. Wherein consists the sinfulness of that state into which man fell?

A. The sinfulness of that state into which man fell, consists in the guilt of Adam's first sin, the want of that righteousness in which he was created, and the corruption of his nature, whereby he is utterly indisposed, disabled, and made opposite unto all that is spiritually good, and wholly inclined to all evil, which is commonly called Original Sin, and from which proceed all actual transgressions.

Q.26. How is original sin conveyed from our first parents to their posterity?

A. Original sin is conveyed from our first parents to their posterity by natural generation, so that all who proceed from them in that way are conceived and born in sin.

Q.27. What misery did the fall bring upon mankind?

A. The fall brought upon mankind the loss of communion with God, His displeasure, and curse; so that we are by nature children of wrath, bond-slaves to Satan, and justly liable to all punishments in this world, and that which is to come.

Q.28. What are the punishments of sin in this world?

A. The punishments of sin in this world are either inward, like blindness of mind, a reprobate sense, strong delusions, hardness of heart, horror of conscience, and vile affections; or outward, like the curse of God upon the creatures for our sakes, and all other evils that befall us in our bodies, names, estates, relations, and employments; together with death itself.

Q.29. What are the punishments of sin in the world to come?

A. The punishments of sin in the world to come, are everlasting separation from the comfortable presence of God, and most grievous torments in soul and body, without intermission, in hell-fire for ever.

Q.30. Does God leave all mankind to perish in the state of sin and misery?

A. God does not leave all men to perish in the state of sin and misery, into which they fell by the breach of the first covenant, commonly called the covenant of works; but of His mere love and mercy delivers His elect out of it, and brings them into a state of salvation by the second covenant, commonly called the covenant of grace.

Q.31. With whom was the covenant of grace made?

A. The covenant of grace was made with Christ as the second Adam, and in Him with all the elect as His seed.

Q.32. How is the grace of God manifested in the second covenant?

A. The grace of God is manifested in the second covenant, in that He freely provides and offers to sinners a Mediator, and life and salvation by Him; and requiring faith as the condition to interest them in Him, promises and gives His Holy Spirit to all His elect, to work in them that faith, with all other saving graces; and to enable them unto all holy obedience, as the evidence of the truth of their faith and thankfulness to God, and as the way of salvation which He has appointed for them.

Q.33. Was the covenant of grace always administered in one and the same way?

A. The covenant of grace was not always administered in the same way, but the administrations of it under the Old Testament were different from those under the New.

Q.34. How was the covenant of grace administered under the Old Testament?

A. The covenant of grace was administered under the Old Testament, by promises, prophecies, sacrifices, circumcision, the passover, and other types and ordinances, which did all fore-signify Christ then to come, and were for that time sufficient to build up the elect in faith in the promised Messiah, by whom they then had full remission of sin and eternal salvation.

Q.35. How is the covenant of grace administered under the New Testament?

A. Under the New Testament, when Christ the substance was exhibited, the same covenant of grace was and still is to be administered in the preaching of the Word, and the administration of the Sacraments of Baptism and the Lord's Supper; in which grace and salvation are held forth in more fulness, evidence, and efficacy, to all nations.

Q.36. Who is the Mediator of the covenant of grace?

A. The only Mediator of the covenant of grace is the Lord Jesus Christ, who, being the eternal Son of God, of one substance and equal with the Father, in the fulness of time became man, and so was and continues to be God and Man, in two entire distinct natures, and one person, for ever.

Q.37. How did Christ, being the Son of God, become man?

A. Christ the Son of God became man, by taking to Himself a true body, and a reasonable soul, being conceived by the power of the Holy Spirit in the womb of the Virgin Mary, of her substance, and born of her, yet without sin.

Q.38. Why was it requisite that the Mediator should be God?

A. It was requisite that the Mediator should be God, that He might sustain and keep the human nature from sinking under the infinite wrath of God, and the power of death; give worth and efficacy to His sufferings, obedience, and intercession; and to satisfy God's justice, procure His favour, purchase a peculiar people, give His Spirit to them, conquer all their enemies, and bring them to everlasting salvation.

Q.39. Why was it requisite that the Mediator should be man?

A. It was requisite that the Mediator should be man, that He might advance our nature, perform obedience to the law, suffer and make intercession for us in our nature, have a fellow-feeling of our infirmities; that we might receive the adoption of sons, and have comfort and access with boldness to the throne of grace.

Q.40. Why was it requisite that the Mediator should be God and Man in one person?

A. It was requisite that the Mediator, who was to reconcile God and man, should Himself be both God and Man, and this in one person, that the proper works of each nature might be accepted of God for us, and relied on by us, as the works of the whole person.

Q.41. Why was our Mediator called Jesus?

A. Our Mediator was called Jesus, because He saved His people from their sins.

Q.42. Why was our Mediator called Christ?

A. Our Mediator was called Christ, because He was anointed with the Holy Spirit above measure; and so set apart, and fully furnished with all authority and ability to execute the offices of Prophet, Priest, and King of His Church, in the state both of His humiliation and exaltation.

Q.43. How does Christ execute the office of a Prophet?

A. Christ executes the office of a Prophet, in His revealing to the church, in all ages, by His Spirit and Word, in different ways of administration, the whole will of God, in all things concerning their edification and salvation.

Q.44. How does Christ execute the office of a Priest?

A. Christ executes the office of a Priest, in the offering of Himself once as a sacrifice without spot to God, to be a reconciliation for the sins of His people; and in making continual intercession for them.

Q.45. How does Christ execute the office of a King?

A. Christ executes the office of a King, in calling out of the world a people to Himself, and giving them officers, laws, and censures, by which He visibly governs them; in bestowing saving grace upon His elect, rewarding their obedience, and correcting them for their sins, preserving and supporting them under all their temptations and sufferings, restraining and over-coming all their enemies, and powerfully ordering all things for His own glory, and their good; and also in taking vengeance on the rest, who know not God, and obey not the Gospel.

Q.46. What was the state of Christ's humiliation?

A. The state of Christ's humiliation was that lowly condition, in which He for our sakes, emptying Himself of His glory, took upon Him the form of a servant, in His conception and birth, life, death, and after His death, until His resurrection.

Q.47. How did Christ humble Himself in His conception and birth?

A. Christ humbled Himself in His conception and birth, in that, being from all eternity the Son of God, in the bosom of the Father, He was pleased in the fulness of time to become the Son of Man, made of a woman of low estate, and to be born of her; with various circumstances of more than ordinary abasement.

Q.48. How did Christ humble Himself in His life?

A. Christ humbled Himself in His life, by subjecting Himself to the law, which He perfectly fulfilled; and by conflicting with the indignities of the world, temptations of Satan, and infirmities in His flesh, whether common to the nature of man, or particularly accompanying His lowly condition.

Q.49. How did Christ humble Himself in His death?

A. Christ humbled Himself in His death, in that having been betrayed by Judas, forsaken by His disciples, scorned and rejected by the world, condemned by Pilate, and tormented by His persecutors; having also come into conflict with the terrors of death, and the powers of darkness, felt and bore the weight of God's wrath, He laid down His life an offering

x

for sin, enduring the painful, shameful, and cursed death of the Cross.

Q.50. In what did Christ's humiliation after His death consist?

A. Christ's humiliation after His death consisted in His being buried, and continuing in the state of the dead, and under the power of death till the third day; which has been expressed otherwise in these words, *He descended into hell.*

Q.51. What was the state of Christ's exaltation?

A. The state of Christ's exaltation includes His resurrection, ascension, sitting at the right hand of the Father, and His coming again to judge the world.

Q.52. How was Christ exalted in His resurrection?

A. Christ was exalted in His resurrection, in that, without being corrupted in death (for that was not possible), and having the very same body in which He suffered, with its essential properties (but without mortality, and other common infirmities belonging to this life), really united to His soul, He rose again from the dead the third day by His own power; whereby He declared Himself to be the Son of God, to have satisfied divine justice, to have vanquished death, and him who has the power of it, and to be Lord of the living and the dead. He did all this as a public person, the Head of His Church, for their justification, quickening in grace, support against enemies, and to assure them of their resurrection from the dead at the last day.

Q.53. How was Christ exalted in His ascension?

A. Christ was exalted in His ascension, in that having after His resurrection often appeared unto and conversed with His apostles, speaking to them of the things pertaining to the Kingdom of God, and giving them commission to preach the gospel to all nations, forty days after His resurrection, He, in our nature, and as our Head, triumphing over enemies, visibly went up into the highest heavens, there to receive gifts for men, to raise up our affections thither, and to prepare a place for us, where He Himself is, and shall continue till His second coming at the end of the world.

Q.54. How is Christ exalted in His sitting at the right hand of God?

A. Christ is exalted in His sitting at the right hand of God, in that as God-Man He is advanced to the highest favour with God the Father, with all fulness of joy, glory, and power over all things in heaven and earth; and gathers and defends His Church, and subdues their enemies; furnishes His ministers and people with gifts and graces, and makes intercession for them.

Q.55. How does Christ make intercession?

A. Christ makes intercession, by His appearing in our nature continually before the Father in heaven, in the merit of His obedience and sacrifice on earth, declaring His will to have it applied to all believers; answering all accusations against them, and procuring for them quiet of conscience, notwithstanding daily failings, access with boldness to the throne of grace, and acceptance of their persons and services.

Q.56. How is Christ to be exalted in His coming again to judge the world?

A. Christ is to be exalted in His coming again to judge the world, in that He, who was unjustly judged and condemned by wicked men, shall come again at the last day in great power, and in the full manifestation of His own glory, and of His Father's, with all His holy angels, with a shout, with the voice of the archangel, and with the trumpet of God, to judge the world in righteousness.

Q.57. What benefits has Christ procured by His mediation?

A. Christ, by His mediation, has procured redemption, with all other benefits of the covenant of grace.

Q.58. How do we come to be made partakers of the benefits which Christ has procured?

A. We are made partakers of the benefits which Christ has procured, by their application to us, which is the work especially of God the Holy Spirit.

Q.59. Who are made partakers of redemption through Christ?

A. Redemption is certainly applied, and effectually communicated, to all those for whom Christ has purchased it; who are in time by the Holy Spirit enabled to believe in Christ according to the Gospel.

Q.60. Can they who have never heard the gospel, and so do not know Jesus Christ, or believe in Him, be saved by their living according to the light of nature?

A. They who, having never heard the gospel, do not know Jesus Christ, and do not believe in Him, cannot be saved, no matter how diligently they order their lives according to the light of nature, or the laws of the religion which they profess; neither is there salvation in any other, but in Christ alone, who is the only Saviour of His Body the Church.

Q.61. Are they all saved who hear the gospel, and live in the Church?

A. All who hear the Gospel and live in the visible Church, are not saved; but only those who are true members of the Church invisible.

Q.62. What is the visible Church?

A. The visible Church is a society made up of all those in all ages and places of the world who profess the true religion, and their children.

Q.63. What are the special privileges of the visible Church?

A. The visible Church has the privilege of being under God's special care and government; of being protected and preserved in all ages, in spite of the opposition of all enemies; and of enjoying the Communion of Saints, the ordinary means of salvation, and offers of grace by Christ to all the members of it in the ministry of the Gospel, testifying, that whoever believes in Him shall be saved, and excluding none who will come to Him.

Q.64. What is the invisible Church?

A. The invisible Church is the whole number of the elect, who have been, are, or shall be gathered into one under Christ the Head.

Q.65. What special benefits do the members of the invisible Church enjoy through Christ?

A. The members of the invisible Church through Christ enjoy union and communion with Him in grace and glory.

Q.66. What is that union which the elect have with Christ?

A. The union which the elect have with Christ is the work of God's grace, by which they are spiritually and mystically, yet really and inseparably, joined to Christ as their Head and Husband, which is done in their effectual calling.

Q.67. What is effectual calling?

A. Effectual calling is the work of God's almighty power and grace, in which (out of His free and special love to His elect, and not from anything in them moving Him to it), He invites and draws them to Jesus Christ, by His Word and Spirit, in His accepted time, savingly enlightening their minds, renewing and powerfully determining their wills, so that (although in themselves dead in sin) they are thus made willing and able freely to answer His call, and to accept and embrace the grace offered and conveyed in it.

Q.68. Are the elect only effectually called?

A. All the elect, and they only, are effectually called; although others may be, and often are, outwardly called by the ministry of the Word, and have some common operations of the Spirit; who, for their wilful neglect and contempt of the grace offered to them, being justly left in their unbelief, never truly come to Jesus Christ.

Q.69. What is the communion in grace which the members of the invisible Church have with Christ?

A. The communion in grace which the members of the invisible Church have with Christ, is their partaking of the virtue of His mediation, in their justification, adoption, sanctification, and whatever else, in this life, manifests their union with Him.

Q.70. What is justification?

A. Justification is an act of God's free grace unto sinners, in which He pardons all their sins, accepts and accounts their persons righteous in His sight; not for any thing wrought in them, or done by them, but only for the perfect obedience and full satisfaction of Christ, by God imputed to them, and received by faith alone.

Q.71. How is justification an act of God's free grace?

A. Although Christ, by His obedience and death, did make a proper, real and full satisfaction to God's justice on the behalf of those who are justified; yet in as much as God accepts the satisfaction from a surety, which He might have demanded from them, and did provide this surety, His own only Son, imputing His righteousness to them, and requiring nothing of them for their justification but faith, which also is His gift, their justification is for them an act of free grace.

Q.72. What is justifying faith?

A. Justifying faith is a saving grace, wrought in the heart of a sinner by the Spirit and Word of God, by which he, being convinced of his sin and misery, and of the disability in himself and all other creatures to recover himself out of his lost condition, not only assents to the truth of the promise of the Gospel, but receives and rests upon Christ and His righteousness, held forth in it, for pardon of sin, and for the accepting and accounting of his person righteous in the sight of God for salvation.

Q.73. How does faith justify a sinner in the sight of God?

A. Faith justifies a sinner in the sight of God, not because of those other graces which always accompany it, or because of good works which are the fruits of it, nor as if the grace of faith, or any act of faith, were imputed to him for his justification. Faith is only an instrument by which he receives and applies Christ and His righteousness.

Q.74. What is adoption?

A. Adoption is an act of the free grace of God, in and for His only Son Jesus Christ, whereby all those who are justified are received into the number of His children, have His name put upon them, the Spirit of His Son given to them, are under His fatherly care and dispensations, admitted to all the liberties and privileges of the sons of God, made heirs of all the promises, and fellow-heirs with Christ in glory.

Q.75. What is sanctification?

A. Sanctification is a work of God's grace, in which those whom God, before the foundation of the world, has chosen to be holy, are in time, through the powerful operation of His Spirit applying the death and resurrection of Christ to them, renewed in their whole man after the image of God; having the seeds of repentance unto life, and all other saving graces, put into their hearts, and those graces so stirred up, increased, and strengthened, that more and more they die to sin, and rise to newness of life.

Q.76. What is repentance unto life?

A. Repentance unto life is a saving grace, wrought in the heart of a sinner by the Spirit and Word of God, in which at the recognition not only of the danger, but also of the filthiness and odiousness of his sins, and on learning of God's mercy in Christ to the penitent, he so grieves for and hates his sins, as that he turns from them all to God, purposing and endeavouring constantly to walk with Him in all the ways of new obedience,

Q.77. Wherein do justification and sanctification differ?

A. Although sanctification is inseparably joined to justification, yet they differ, in that God in justification imputes the righteousness of Christ; in sanctification His Spirit infuses grace, and enables to the exercise thereof; in the former, sin is pardoned; in the latter, it is subdued: the one frees all believers equally from the revenging wrath of God, and that perfectly in this life, so that they never fall into condemnation; the other is neither equal in all, nor in this life perfect in any, but grows up into perfection.

Q.78. Where does the imperfection of sanctification in believers come from?

A. The imperfection of sanctification in believers arises from the remnants of sin abiding in every part of them, and the perpetual lustings of the flesh against the Spirit; by which they are often foiled with temptations, and fall into many sins, are hindered in all their spiritual services, and their best works are imperfect and defiled in the sight of God.

Q.79. May not true believers, by reason of their imperfections, and the many temptations and sins they are overtaken with, fall away from the state of grace?

A. True believers, by reason of the unchangeable love of God, and His decree and covenant to give them perseverance, their inseparable union with Christ, His continual intercession for them, and the Spirit and seed of God abiding in them, can neither totally nor finally fall away from the state of grace, but are kept by the power of God through faith unto salvation.

Q.80. Can true believers be infallibly assured that they are in the state of grace, and that they shall persevere in it unto salvation?

A. Those who truly believe in Christ, and endeavour to walk in all good conscience before Him, may, without extraordinary revelation, by faith grounded upon the truth of God's promises, and by the Spirit enabling them to discern in themselves those graces to which the promises of life are made, and bearing witness with their spirits that they are the children of God, be infallibly assured that they are in the state of grace, and will persevere in it unto salvation.

Q.81. Are all true believers at all times assured of their being in the state of grace in the present, and that they will be saved?

A. Since assurance of grace and salvation are not of the essence of faith, true believers may wait long before they obtain it; and, after the enjoyment of it, may have it weakened and intercepted, through manifold disorders, sins, temptations, and desertions; yet they are never left without a presence and support of the Spirit of God, keeping them from sinking into utter despair.

Q.82. What is the communion in glory which the members of the invisible Church have with Christ?

A. The communion in glory, which the members of the invisible Church have with Christ, is in this life, immediately after death, and at last perfected at the resurrection and day of judgement.

Q.83. What is the communion in glory with Christ which the members of the invisible Church enjoy in this life?

A. The members of the invisible Church have communicated to them in this life the first-fruits of glory with Christ, since they are members of Him their Head, and so in Him are interested in that glory which He fully possesses; and, as an earnest of it, enjoy the sense of God's love, peace of conscience, joy in the Holy Spirit, and hope of glory. On the other hand, a sense of God's revenging wrath, horror of conscience, and a fearful expectation of judgement, are to the wicked the beginning of their torments which they will endure after death.

Q.84. Will all men die?

A. Death is threatened as the wages of sin. Therefore it is appointed unto all men once to die, for all have sinned.

Q.85. If death is the wages of sin, why are not the righteous delivered from death, since all their sins are forgiven in Christ?

A. The righteous will be delivered from death itself at the last day, and even in death are delivered from its sting and curse; so that, although they die, yet God in His love frees them perfectly from sin and misery, and makes them capable of further communion with Christ, in glory upon which they then enter.

Q.86. What is the communion in glory with Christ, which the members of the invisible Church enjoy immediately after death?

A. The communion in glory with Christ, which the members of the invisible Church enjoy immediately after death, is in that their souls are then made perfect in holiness, and received into the highest heavens, where they behold the face of God in light and glory, waiting for the full redemption of their bodies, which even in death continue united to Christ, and rest in their graves as in their beds, till at the last day they are again united to their souls. But the souls of the wicked are at their death cast into hell, where they remain in torments and utter darkness, and where their bodies are kept in their graves, as in their prisons, till the resurrection and judgement of the great day.

Q.87. What are we to believe concerning the resurrection?

A. We are to believe, that at the last day there will be a general resurrection of the dead, both of the just and unjust: when they that are then found alive shall in a moment be changed; and the self-same bodies of the dead which were laid in the grave, being then again united to their souls for ever, will be raised up by the power of Christ. The bodies of the just, by the Spirit of Christ, and by virtue of His resurrection as their Head, shall be raised in power, spiritual, incorruptible, and made like to His glorious body; and the bodies of the wicked shall be raised up in dishonour by Him, as an offended Judge.

Q.88. What shall immediately follow after the resurrection?

A. Immediately after the resurrection will follow the general and final judgement of angels and men. No man knows its day and hour, that all may watch and pray, and be ever ready for the coming of the Lord.

Q.89. What shall be done to the wicked at the day of judgement?

A. At the day of judgement, the wicked shall be set on Christ's left hand, and, upon clear evidence, and full conviction of their own consciences, shall have the fearful but just sentence of condemnation pronounced against them; and shall then be cast out from the favourable presence of God, and the glorious fellowship with Christ, His saints, and all His holy angels, into hell, to be punished with unspeakable torments, both of body and soul, with the devil and his angels for ever.

Q.90. What shall be done to the righteous at the day of judgement?

A. At the day of judgement, the righteous, being caught up to Christ in the clouds, will be set on His right hand, and there openly acknowledged and acquitted, will join with Him in the judging of reprobate angels and men, and will be received into heaven, where they will be fully and for ever freed from all sin and misery; filled with inconceivable joys, made perfectly holy and happy both in body and soul, in the company of innumerable saints and holy angels, but especially in the immediate vision and fruition of God the Father, of our Lord Jesus Christ, and of the Holy Spirit, to all eternity. And this is the perfect and full communion, which the members of the invisible Church shall enjoy with Christ in glory, at the resurrection and day of judgement.

HAVING SEEN WHAT THE SCRIPTURES PRINCIPALLY TEACH US TO
BELIEVE CONCERNING GOD, IT REMAINS TO CONSIDER WHAT
THEY REQUIRE AS THE DUTY OF MAN.

Q.91. What is the duty which God requires of man?

A. The duty which God requires of man, is obedience to
His revealed will.

*Q.92. What did God at first reveal to man as the rule of His
obedience?*

A. The rule of obedience revealed to Adam in the state of
innocence, and to all mankind in him, besides a special command not to eat of the fruit of the tree of the knowledge of
good and evil, was the moral law.

Q.93. What is the moral law?

A. The moral law is the declaration of the will of God to
mankind, directing and binding every one to personal,
perfect, and perpetual conformity and obedience to it, in the
frame and disposition of the whole man, soul and body, and in
performance of all those duties of holiness and righteousness
which he owes to God and man: promising life upon the
fulfilling, and threatening death upon the breach of it.

*Q.94. Is there any use of the moral law to man since the
fall?*

A. Although no man, since the fall, can attain to righteousness and life by the moral law, yet there is great use for it,
common to all men, as well as peculiar to the unregenerate, or
the regenerate.

Q.95. Of what use is the moral law to all men?

A. The moral law is of use to all men, to inform them of the
holy nature and will of God, and of their duty, binding them
to walk accordingly; to convince them of their inability to
keep it, and of the sinful pollution of their nature, hearts, and
lives; to humble them in the sense of their sin and misery, and

so to help them to a clearer sight of the need they have of Christ, and of the perfection of His obedience.

Q.96. What particular use is there of the moral law to un-regenerate men?

A. The moral law is of use to unregenerate men, to awaken their consciences to flee from wrath to come, and to drive them to Christ; or, if they continue in the state and way of sin, to leave them inexcusable, and under its curse.

Q.97. What special use is there of the moral law to the regenerate?

A. Although those who are regenerate, and believe in Christ, are delivered from the moral law as a covenant of works, so that they are neither justified nor condemned for it; yet, apart from its general uses common to them with all men, it is of special use, to show them how much they are bound to Christ for His fulfilment of it, and for enduring its curse in their stead, and for their good, and so to provoke them to more thankfulness, and to express this in greater care to conform themselves to it as the rule of their obedience.

Q.98. Where is the moral law summarily comprehended?

A. The moral law is summarily comprehended in the Ten Commandments, which were delivered by the voice of God on Mount Sinai, and written by Him in two tables of stone. These are recorded in the twentieth chapter of Exodus, the four first commandments containing our duty to God, and the other six our duty to man.

Q.99. What rules are to be observed for the right understanding of the Ten Commandments?

A. For the right understanding of the Ten Commandments these rules are to be observed:

1. The law is perfect, and binds every one to full conformity in the whole man to the righteousness it requires and to entire obedience for ever. Then it requires the utmost perfection in every duty, and forbids sin in any degree.

2. It is spiritual, and so reaches the understanding, will, affections, and all other powers of the soul, as well as words, works, and gestures.

3. One and the same thing, in different respects, is required or forbidden in several commandments.

4. Where a duty is commanded, its contrary is forbidden; and, where a sin is forbidden, its contrary is commanded, so, where a promise is given, the threat of judgement is included; and, where judgement is threatened, the promise is included.

5. What God forbids, is at no time to be done; what He commands, is always our duty; and yet every particular duty is not to be done at all times.

6. Under one sin or duty, all similar sins and duties are forbidden or commanded, with all their causes, means, occasions, and appearances, and all their provocations.

7. What we ourselves are forbidden or commanded to do in our own situations we must try to help others to avoid or perform as required in their circumstances.

8. According to our places and callings we are bound to help others in doing what they are commanded, and we must beware of participating with others in doing what they are forbidden.

Q.100. What special things are we to consider in the Ten Commandments?

A. We are to consider, in the Ten Commandments, the preface, the substance of the commandments themselves, and the reasons attached to some of them, to help to enforce their fulfilment.

Q.101. What is the preface to the Ten Commandments?

A. The preface to the Ten Commandments is contained in these words, *I am the Lord Thy God, which have brought thee out of the land of Egypt, out of the house of bondage.* Here God manifests His sovereignty, as JEHOVAH, the eternal, immutable, and almighty God, who has His being in and of Himself, and who gives being to all His words and works. He is a God in covenant, not only with Israel of old, but with all His people, who delivers us from our spiritual thraldom, as He brought Israel out of their bondage in Egypt. Therefore we are bound to take Him for our God alone, and to keep all His commandments.

Q.102. What is the essence of the four commandments about our duty to God?

A. The essence of the four commandments about our duty to God, is, to love the Lord our God with all our heart, and with all our soul, and with all our strength, and with all our mind.

Q.103. Which is the first commandment?

A. The first commandment is, *Thou shalt have no other gods before me.*

Q.104. What are the duties required in the first commandment?

A. The duties required in the first commandment, are to know and acknowledge God to be the only true God, and our God; and to worship and glorify Him accordingly, by thinking of Him, meditating, remembering, highly esteeming, honouring, adoring, choosing, loving, desiring, fearing Him; by believing Him, trusting, hoping, delighting, rejoicing in Him; by being zealous for Him; calling upon Him, giving all praise and thanks, and yielding all obedience and submission to Him with the whole man; being careful in all things to please Him, and grieved when we offend Him in anything; and walking humbly with Him.

Q.105. What are the sins forbidden in the first commandment?

A. The sins forbidden in the first commandment are: atheism, in denying, or not having a God; idolatry, in having or worshipping more gods than one, or any with or instead of the true God; the refusal to have or acknowledge Him as God, and our God; the omission or neglect of anything due to Him, required in this commandment; ignorance, forgetfulness, misapprehensions, false opinions, unworthy and wicked thoughts of Him; bold and curious searching into His secrets; all profaneness, hatred of God, self-love, self-seeking, and all other inordinate and immoderate setting of our mind, will, or affections upon other things, and taking them off from Him in whole or in part; vain credulity, unbelief, heresy, wrong belief, distrust, despair, incorrigibleness, and insensibleness under judgements, hardness of heart, pride, presumption, carnal security, tempting of God; using unlawful means, and trusting in lawful means; carnal delights and joys; corrupt, blind, and indiscreet zeal; lukewarmness, and deadness in the things of God; estranging ourselves, and apostatising from God; praying, or giving any religious worship, to saints, angels, or any other creatures; all compacts and consulting with the devil, and hearkening to his suggestions; making men the lords of our faith and conscience; slighting and despising God and His commands; resisting and grieving His Spirit, discontent and impatience at His dispensations, charging Him foolishly for the evils He inflicts on us; and ascribing the praise of any good we either are, have, or can do, to fortune, idols, ourselves, or any other creature.

Q.106. What are we specially taught by these words "before me" in the first commandment?

A. The words "before me" or before my face, in the first commandment, teach us, that God, who sees all things, takes special notice of, and is much displeased with, the sin of having any other God. They are intended to show that this sin is a grievous provocation of God and so to dissuade us from it, but also to persuade us to do all that we undertake in His service and in His sight.

Q.107. Which is the second commandment?

A. The second commandment is, *Thou shalt not make unto thee any graven image, or any likeness of any thing that is in heaven above, or that is in the earth beneath, or that is in the water under the earth: Thou shalt not bow down thyself to them, nor serve them: for I the Lord thy God am a jealous God, visiting the iniquity of the fathers upon the children unto the third and fourth generation of them that hate me; and showing mercy unto thousands of them that love me, and keep my commandments.*

Q.108. What are the duties required in the second commandment?

A. The duties required in the second commandment are: to receive, observe, and keep pure and entire, all the religious worship and ordinances which God has instituted in His Word, particularly prayer and thanksgiving in the name of Christ, the reading, preaching, and hearing of the Word, the administration and receiving of the Sacraments, Church government and discipline, the ministry and its maintenance, religious fasting, swearing by the name of God, and vowing unto Him. We are also required to disapprove of, to detest and oppose all false worship, and according to the place and calling of each, to remove it, and all monuments of idolatry.

Q.109. What are the sins forbidden in the second commandment?

A. The sins forbidden in the second commandment are: all devising, counselling, commanding, using, and any approval of any religious worship not instituted by God Himself; tolerating any false religion; making any representation of God, of all or of any of the three persons, either inwardly in our mind, or outwardly in any kind of image or likeness of any creature whatsoever; all worshipping of it, or God in it or by it; the making of any representation of feigned deities, and all worship of them, or service belonging to them; all superstitious devices, corrupting the worship of God, adding to it, or taking from it, whether invented and taken up by ourselves, or received by tradition from others, even if under the name of

Y

antiquity, custom, devotion, good intent, or any other pretence whatsoever; Simony; sacrilege; all neglect, contempt, hindering, and opposing of the worship and ordinances which God has appointed.

Q.110. What are the reasons for enforcing the second commandment?

A. The reasons for enforcing the second commandment are contained in these words: *For I the Lord thy God am a jealous God, visiting the iniquity of the fathers upon the children unto the third and fourth generation of them that hate me; and showing mercy unto thousands of them that love me, and keep my commandments.* In other words, apart from God's sovereignty over us, and His claims upon us, His fervent zeal for His own worship, and His righteous indignation against all false worship, as spiritual infidelity, reckoning those who break this commandment as His enemies, and threatening to punish them for several generations; and esteeming those who observe it as loving and faithful toward Him, and promising mercy to them unto many generations.

Q.111. Which is the third commandment?

A. The third commandment is, *Thou shalt not take the name of the Lord thy God in vain; for the Lord will not hold him guiltless that taketh his name in vain.*

Q.112. What is required in the third commandment?

A. The third commandment requires, that the name of God, His titles, attributes, ordinances, His Word, Sacraments, prayer, oaths, vows, lots, His works, and all through which He makes Himself known, be used in thought, meditations, word, and writing with holiness and reverence, that is, in a holy profession of faith and a corresponding life, all to the glory of God, the good of ourselves and others.

Q.113. What are the sins forbidden in the third commandment?

A. The sins forbidden in the third commandment are: the

refusal to give glory to God's name; and its abuse in ignorant, vain, irreverent, profane, superstitious, or wicked speech, or in other ways the misuse of His titles, attributes, ordinances, or works, in blasphemy or perjury; all sinful cursing, oaths, vows, and lots; the violating of lawful oaths and vows, and the fulfilling of unlawful ones; murmuring, complaining, and wilful disrespect with regard to God's decrees and providences; misinterpreting, misapplying, or in any way perverting the Word, or any part of it, in profane jests, curious or unprofitable questions, vain discussion, or in maintaining false doctrines; abusing God's name, along with creatures, or any thing contained under His name, for charms, or sinful lusts and practices; maligning, scorning, reviling, or any wise opposing God's truth, grace, and ways; making profession of religion in hypocrisy, or for sinister ends; being ashamed of it, or bringing shame upon it, by unconformable, unwise, unfruitful, and offensive living or backsliding from it.

Q.114. What reasons are annexed to the third commandment?

A. The reasons annexed to the third commandment, in these words, "The Lord thy God" and "For the Lord will not hold him guiltless that taketh his name in vain", are: Because He is the Lord and our God, His name is not to be profaned, or any way abused by us. So far from acquitting and sparing the transgressors of this commandment, He will not suffer them to escape His righteous judgement, although many such escape the censures and punishments of men.

Q.115. Which is the fourth commandment?

A. The fourth commandment is, *Remember the sabbath day, to keep it holy. Six days shalt thou labour, and do all thy work: but the seventh day is the sabbath of the Lord thy God: in it thou shalt not do any work, thou, nor thy son, nor thy daughter, thy man-servant, nor thy maid-servant, nor the stranger that is within thy gates: For in six days the Lord made heaven and earth, the sea, and all that in them is, and rested the seventh day: wherefore the Lord blessed the sabbath-day, and hallowed it.*

Q.116. *What is required in the fourth commandment?*

A. The fourth commandment requires of all men the sanctifying or keeping holy to God such set times as He has appointed in His Word, namely, one whole day in seven; from the beginning of the world to the resurrection of Christ this was the seventh day; but ever since, and so to the end of the world, the first day of the week. This is the Christian Sabbath, and in the New Testament is called The Lord's Day.

Q.117. *How is the Sabbath or the Lord's Day to be sanctified?*

A. The Sabbath or Lord's Day is to be sanctified by a holy resting all day, not only from works that are at any time sinful, but even from worldly employments and recreations that are lawful on other days, and making it our delight to spend the whole time (except so far as it is to be taken up in works of necessity and mercy) in the public and private worship of God. Therefore we are to prepare our hearts, and arrange and dispatch our worldly business with such foresight and care that we may be free and fitted for the duties of that day.

Q.118. *Why is the charge of keeping the Lord's Day more specially directed to governors of families, and other superiors?*

A. The charge of keeping the Lord's Day is more specially directed to governors of families, and other superiors, because they are bound not only to keep it themselves, but to see that it is observed by all those under their charge; and because they often tend to hinder them by employments of their own.

Q.119. *What are the sins forbidden in the fourth commandment?*

A. The sins forbidden in the fourth commandment are: all omission of the duties required, all careless, negligent, and unprofitable performance of them, or tiring of them; all profaning the day by idleness, and sinful acts, and by all needless works, words, and thoughts, about our worldly employments and recreations.

Q.120. What are the reasons for enforcing the fourth commandment?

A. The reasons for enforcing the fourth commandment are taken: from its equity in which God allows us six days out of seven for our own affairs, and reserves but one for Himself, in these words, *Six days shalt thou labour and do all thy work*; from God's special claim upon that day, *The seventh day is the sabbath of the Lord thy God;* from the example of God, who *in six days made heaven and earth, the sea, and all that in them is, and rested the seventh day*; and from that blessing which God put upon that day, not only in sanctifying it to be a day for His service, but in ordaining it to be a means of blessing to us in our sanctifying of it; *Wherefore the Lord blessed the sabbath-day, and hallowed it.*

Q.121. Why is the word "Remember" set in the beginning of the fourth commandment?

A. The word *Remember* is set in the beginning of the fourth commandment, partly, because by remembering it, we are helped in our preparation to keep it, and, in keeping it, to keep better all the rest of the commandments, and continue in thankful remembrance of the two great benefits of creation and redemption, which contain a short abridgment of religion; and, partly, because we are very ready to forget it, for the following reasons: that there is less light of nature in it, although it restrains our natural liberty in things at other times lawful; that it comes once in seven days, and much worldly business comes between, and too often keeps our minds from thinking of it, either to prepare for it, or to sanctify it; and that Satan seeks by all means to blot out the glory, and even the memory of it, and so to bring in irreligion and impiety.

Q.122. What is the essence of the six commandments which contain our duty to man?

A. The essence of the six commandments which contain our duty to man, is, to love our neighbour as ourselves, and to do to others what we would have them do to us.

Q.123. Which is the fifth commandment?

A. The fifth commandment is, *Honour thy father and thy mother; that thy days may be long upon the land which the Lord thy God giveth thee.*

Q.124. Who are meant by "father" and "mother" in the fifth commandment?

A. By *father* and *mother*, in the fifth commandment, are meant, not only natural parents, but all superiors in age, and gifts; and especially those who, by God's ordinance, are placed in authority over us, whether in family, Church, or commonwealth.

Q.125. Why are superiors called "father" and "mother"?

A. Superiors are called *father* and *mother*, both to teach them in all duties towards their inferiors, like natural parents, to express love and tenderness to them, according to their several relations; and to bring inferiors to a greater willingness and cheerfulness in performing their duties to their superiors, as to their parents.

Q.126. What is the general scope of the fifth commandment?

A. The general scope of the fifth commandment is, the performance of those duties which we mutually owe to one another, as inferiors, superiors, or equals.

Q.127. What is the labour that inferiors owe to their superiors?

A. The honour which inferiors owe to their superiors is: all due reverence in heart, word, and behaviour, prayer and thanksgiving for them, imitation of their virtues and graces, willing obedience to their lawful commands and counsels, due submission to their corrections, fidelity to, defence and maintenance of their persons and authority, according to their rank, and status in life, bearing with their infirmities, and covering them in love, so that they may be an honour to them and to their government.

Q.128. What are the sins of inferiors against their superiors?

A. The sins of inferiors against their superiors are: all neglect of the duties required towards them, envying, contempt, and rebellion directed against their person and status, in their lawful counsels, commands, and corrections; cursing, mocking, and any refractory and scandalous behaviour that brings shame and dishonour to them and their government.

Q.129. What is required of superiors towards their inferiors?

A. It is required of superiors, according to the power they receive from God, and that relationship in which they stand to others, to love, bless and pray for their inferiors, to instruct, counsel and admonish them; favouring, commending, and rewarding those who do well; and hindering, reproving, and chastising those who do wrong; protecting and providing for them all things necessary for soul and body: and by grave, wise, holy, and exemplary behaviour, to bring glory to God, honour to themselves, and so to preserve the authority which God has given them.

Q.130. What are the sins of superiors?

A. The sins of superiors are: (apart from neglect of their duties) an inordinate seeking of themselves, their own glory, ease, profit, or pleasure; commanding things unlawful, or not in the power of inferiors to perform; counselling, encouraging, or favouring them in that which is evil; dissuading, discouraging, or discountenancing them in that which is good; correcting them unduly; careless exposing, or leaving them to wrong, temptation, and danger; provoking them to wrath; or any way dishonouring themselves, or lessening their authority, by unjust, indiscreet, rigorous, or remiss behaviour.

Q.131. What are the duties of equals?

A. The duties of equals are, to regard the dignity and worth of each other, in giving honour to go one before another; and to rejoice in each other's gifts and advancement, as their own.

Q.132. What are the sins of equals?

A. The sins of equals are: (apart from neglect of their duties) the undervaluing of the worth, envying the gifts, grieving at the advancement or prosperity one of another; and usurping preeminence one over another.

Q.133. What is the reason for enforcing the fifth commandment?

A. The reason for enforcing the fifth commandment, in these words, *That thy days may be long upon the land which the Lord thy God giveth thee*, is an express promise of long life and prosperity, as far as it serves God's glory and their own good, to all who keep this commandment.

Q.134. Which is the sixth commandment?

A. The sixth commandment is, *Thou shalt not kill.*

Q.135. What are the duties required in the sixth commandment?

A. The duties required in the sixth commandment are, all due care and endeavour to preserve the life of ourselves and others by resisting all thoughts and purposes, subduing all passions, and avoiding all occasions, temptations, and practices, which tend to the unjust taking of life; by just defence of life against violence, patient bearing of the hand of God, quietness of mind, cheerfulness of spirit; a sober use of meat, drink, medicine, sleep, labour, and recreations; by charitable thoughts, love, compassion, meekness, gentleness, kindness; peaceable, mild and courteous speech and behaviour; forbearance, readiness to be reconciled, patient bearing and forgiving of injuries, and requiting good for evil; comforting and succouring the distressed, and protecting and defending the innocent.

Q.136. What are the sins forbidden in the sixth commandment?

A. The sins forbidden in the sixth commandmant are, all taking of life, of ourselves or of others, except in public justice, lawful war, or necessary defence; the neglecting or with-drawing of the lawful and necessary means of preservation of life; sinful anger, hatred, envy, desire of revenge; all excessive passions, distracting cares; immoderate use of meat, drink, labour, and recreations; provoking words, oppression, quarrel-ling, striking, wounding, and whatever else tends to the destruction of life.

Q.137. *Which is the seventh commandment?*

A. The seventh commandment is, *Thou shalt not commit adultery.*

Q.138. *What are the duties required in the seventh command-ment?*

A. The duties required in the seventh commandment are, chastity in body, mind, affections, words, and behaviour; and the preservation of it in ourselves and others; watchfulness over the eyes and all the senses; temperance, keeping of chaste company, modesty in apparel; marriage by those that have not the gift of continency; conjugal love, and cohabitation; diligent labour in our callings; shunning all occasions of un-cleanness, and resisting temptations to it.

Q.139. *What are the sins forbidden in the seventh command-ment?*

A. The sins forbidden in the seventh commandment (apart from the neglect of the duties required) are: adultery, fornica-tion, rape, incest, sodomy, and all unnatural lusts; all unclean imaginations, thoughts, purposes, and affections; all corrupt or filthy communications, or listening to them; wanton looks, impudent or frivolous behaviour, immodest apparel; pro-hibiting of lawful, and dispensing with unlawful marriages; allowing, tolerating, keeping of brothels and resorting to them; entangling vows of single life, undue delay of marriage; having more wives or husbands than one at the same time; unjust divorce, or desertion; idleness, gluttony, drunkenness, unchaste company; lascivious songs, books, pictures, dancing, stage plays; and all other provocations to, or acts of uncleanness, either in ourselves or others.

Q.140. Which is the eighth commandment?

A. The eighth commandment is, *Thou shalt not steal.*

Q.141. What are the duties required in the eighth commandment?

A. The duties required in the eighth commandment are: truth, faithfulness, and justice in contracts and commerce between man and man; rendering to every one his due; restitution of goods unlawfully detained from the right owners; giving and lending freely, according to our ability, and the necessity of others; moderation in our judgements, wills, and affections concerning worldly goods; a provident care and effort to get, keep, use and dispose the things necessary and convenient for the sustaining of our nature, and suitable to our condition; a lawful calling, and diligence in it; frugality, avoiding unnecessary lawsuits, and pledges, or other like engagements, and an endeavour, by all just and lawful means, to procure, preserve, and further the wealth and outward estate of others, as well as our own.

Q.142. What are the sins forbidden in the eighth commandment?

A. The sins forbidden in the eighth commandment, apart from the neglect of the duties required, are: theft, robbery, man-stealing, and receiving anything that is stolen; fraudulent dealing, false weights and measures, removing land-marks, injustice and unfaithfulness in contracts between man and man, or in matters of trust; oppression, extortion, usury, bribery, vexatious lawsuits, unjust appropriations and evictions; increasing the weight of goods to enhance the price; unlawful callings, and all other unjust or sinful ways of taking or withholding from our neighbour what belongs to him, or of enriching ourselves; covetousness; inordinate love of worldly goods; unscrupulous ways of getting, keeping, and using them; envying the prosperity of others; likewise, idleness, prodigality, wasteful gambling; and all other ways in which we harm our own outward estate, and defraud ourselves of the proper use and comfort of what God has given us.

Q.143. Which is the ninth commandment?

A. The ninth commandment is, *Thou shalt not bear false witness against thy neighbour.*

Q.144. What are the duties required in the ninth commandment?

A. The duties required in the ninth commandment are, the preserving and promoting of truth between man and man, and the good name of our neighbour, as well as our own; appearing and standing for the truth; and from the heart, sincerely, freely, clearly, and fully, speaking the truth, and only the truth, in matters of judgement and justice, and in all other things whatsoever; a charitable esteem of our neighbours; loving, desiring, and rejoicing in their good name; sorrowing for, and overlooking their infirmities; free acknowledgment of their gifts and graces, defence of their innocence; a readiness to receive a good report, and an unwillingness to accept an evil report, concerning them; the discouraging of tale-bearers, flatterers, and slanderers; the love and care of our own good name, defending it when need requires; the keeping of lawful promises; the pursuit and practice of whatever things are true, honest, lovely, and of good report.

Q.145. What are the sins forbidden in the ninth commandment?

A. The sins forbidden in the ninth commandment are: all acts prejudicial to the truth, and the good name of our neighbours, as well as our own, especially in public judicature; giving false evidence, suborning false witnesses, wittingly appearing and pleading for an evil cause, misconstruing and overbearing the truth; passing unjust sentence, calling evil good, and good evil; rewarding the wicked according to the work of the righteous, and the righteous according to the work of the wicked; forgery, concealing the truth, undue silence in a just cause, and holding our peace when iniquity calls for either a reproof from ourselves, or complaint to others; speaking the truth unseasonably, or maliciously for a wrong end, or perverting it to a wrong meaning, or in doubtful and equivocal expressions, to the prejudice of truth or justice; speaking untruth, lying, slandering, backbiting, detracting, tale-bearing, whispering, scoffing, reviling, rash, harsh, and partial censuring; misconstruing intentions, words, and actions; flattering, vain-glorious boasting, thinking or speaking too highly or too meanly of ourselves or others; denying the gifts and graces of God; aggravating smaller faults; hiding, excusing, or extenuating sins, when called to a free confession; unnecessary discovering of infirmities; raising false rumours, receiving and countenancing evil reports, and stopping our ears against just defence; evil suspicion; envying or grieving at the deserved credit of any, endeavouring or desiring to impair it, rejoicing in their disgrace and infamy; scornful contempt, mad infatuation; breach of lawful promises; neglecting things of good report, and practising, or refusing to avoid ourselves, or not hindering what we can in others, such things as procure an ill name.

Q.146. Which is the tenth commandment?

A. The tenth commandment is, *Thou shalt not covet thy neighbour's house, thou shalt not covet thy neighbour's wife, nor his man-servant, nor his maid-servant, nor his ox, nor his ass, nor any thing that is thy neighbour's.*

Q.147. What are the duties required in the tenth commandment?

A. The duties required in the tenth commandment are, such a full contentment with our own condition, and such a charitable attitude of the whole soul toward our neighbour, that all our inward feelings concerning him, are directed to his good.

Q.148. What are the sins forbidden in the tenth commandment?

A. The sins forbidden in the tenth commandment are, discontent with our own state; envying and grieving at the good of our neighbour, together with all inordinate desires and feelings about what is his.

Q.149. Is any man able perfectly to keep the commandments of God?

A. No man is able, either by himself, or by any grace received in this life, perfectly to keep the commandments of God, but doth break them in thought, word, and deed.

Q.150. Are all transgressions of the law of God equally heinous in themselves, and in the sight of God?

A. Not all transgressions of the law of God are equally heinous; but some are more heinous in the sight of God than others, because of what they are in themselves and for other reasons.

Q.151. What is it that aggravates some sins, making them more heinous than others?

A. 1. Sins are aggravated when the persons committing them are older, of greater experience or grace, eminent in regard to profession, gifts, place, office, position of leadership, and when their example is likely to be followed by others.

2. Sins are aggravated when they are committed immediately against God, His attributes and worship; against Christ and His grace; the Holy Spirit, His witness and operations; against superiors, men of eminence, and those to whom we are related by kindred and duty; against any of the saints, particularly weak brethren, their souls, or the souls of any others; and the common good of all or many.

3. Sins are aggravated by the nature and quality of the offence; when they are against the express letter of the law, break many commandments, involve sinful acts; being not only conceived in the heart, but breaking forth in words and

actions, scandalising others, and admit of no reparation; when they are against means of grace, mercies, judgements, the light of nature, conviction of conscience, public or private admonition, censures of the Church, civil punishments; and against our prayers, purposes, promises, vows, covenants, and engagements to God or men; when they are done deliberately, wilfully, presumptuously, impudently, boastingly, maliciously, frequently, obstinately, with delight, continuance, or relapsing after repentance.

4. Sins are also aggravated through circumstances of time and place; if they are committed on the Lord's day, or other times of divine worship; or immediately before or after these, or other helps to prevent or remedy such misdeeds; if in public, or in the presence of others likely to be provoked or defiled by them.

Q.152. What does every sin deserve at the hands of God?

A. Every sin, even the least, being against the sovereignty, goodness and holiness of God, and against His righteous law, deserves His wrath and curse, both in this life, and that which is to come; and cannot be expiated but by the blood of Christ.

Q.153. What does God require of us, that we may escape His wrath and curse due to us for the transgression of the law?

A. That we may escape the wrath and curse of God due to us for the transgression of the law, He requires of us repentance toward God, and faith toward our Lord Jesus Christ, and the diligent use of the outward means by which Christ communicates to us the benefits of His mediation.

Q.154. What are the outward means by which Christ communicates to us the benefits of His mediation?

A. The outward and ordinary means by which Christ communicates to His Church the benefits of His mediation are all His ordinances; especially the Word, Sacraments, and prayer —all of which are made effectual to the elect for their salvation.

Q.155. How is the Word made effectual to salvation?

A. The Spirit of God makes the reading, but especially the preaching of the Word, an effectual means of enlightening, convincing, and humbling sinners; of driving them out of themselves, and drawing them to Christ; of conforming them to His image, and subduing them to His will; of strengthening them against temptations and corruptions; of building them up in grace, and establishing their hearts in holiness and comfort through faith unto salvation.

Q.156. Is the Word of God to be read by all?

A. Although all are not to be permitted to read the Word publicly to the congregation, yet all sorts of people are bound to read it apart by themselves, and with their families. For this purpose the Holy Scriptures are to be translated out of the original into the language of the people.

Q.157. How is the Word of God to be read?

A. The Holy Scriptures are to be read in high and reverent esteem; with a firm persuasion that they are the very Word of God, and that He only can enable us to understand them; with desire to know, believe, and obey the will of God revealed in them; with diligence, and attention to their matter and scope; with meditation, application, self-denial, and prayer.

Q.158. By whom is the Word to be preached?

A. The Word of God is to be preached only by those who are sufficiently gifted, and also duly approved and called to that office.

Q.159. How is the Word of God to be preached by those who are called?

A. Those who are called to labour in the ministry of the Word, are to preach sound doctrine, diligently, in season and out of season; plainly, not in the enticing words of man's wisdom, but in demonstration of the Spirit, and of power; faithfully, making known the whole counsel of God; wisely applying themselves to the necessities and capacities of the hearers; zealously, with fervent love to God and the souls of His people; sincerely, aiming at His glory, and their conversion, edification, and salvation.

Q.160. What is required of those who hear the Word preached?

A. It is required of those who hear the Word preached to attend upon it with diligence, preparation, and prayer; examine what they hear by the Scriptures; receive the truth with faith, love, meekness, and readiness of mind, as the Word of God; meditate and speak of it; hide it in their hearts, and bring forth the fruit of it in their lives.

Q.161. How do the Sacraments become effectual means of salvation?

A. The Sacraments become effectual means of salvation, not by any power in themselves, or any virtue derived from the piety or intention of him by whom they are administered, but only by the working of the Holy Spirit, and the blessing of Christ, by whom they are instituted.

Q.162. What is a Sacrament?

A. A Sacrament is a holy ordinance instituted by Christ in His Church, to signify, seal, and exhibit to those who are within the covenant of grace, the benefits of His mediation; to strengthen and increase their faith, and all other graces; to oblige them to obedience; to testify and cherish their love and communion one with another; and to distinguish them from those that are without.

Q.163. What are the parts of a Sacrament?

A. The parts of a Sacrament are two: the one, an outward and sensible sign, used according to Christ's own appointment; the other, an inward and spiritual grace thereby signified.

Q.164. How many Sacraments has Christ instituted in His Church under the New Testament?

A. Under the New Testament Christ has instituted in His

Church only two Sacraments, Baptism and the Lord's Supper.

Q.165. What is Baptism?

A. Baptism is a Sacrament of the New Testament, in which Christ has ordained the washing with water in the name of the Father, and of the Son, and of the Holy Spirit, to be a sign and seal of ingrafting into Himself, of remission of sins by His blood, and regeneration by His Spirit; of adoption, and resurrection unto everlasting life. By it the baptised are solemnly admitted into the visible Church, and enter into an open and professed engagement to be wholly and only the Lord's.

Q.166. Unto whom is Baptism to be administered?

A. Baptism is not to be administered to any who are outside of the visible Church, and so strangers from the covenant of promise, until they profess their faith in Christ and obedience to Him; but infants descended from parents (both or but one of them) professing faith in Christ and obedience to Him, are for that reason within the covenant, and to be baptised.

Q.167. How is our Baptism to be improved by us?

A. The needful but much neglected duty of improving our Baptism, is to be performed by us all our life long, especially in the time of temptation, and when we are present at the administration of it to others; by serious and thankful consideration of its nature, and of the ends for which Christ instituted it, the privileges and benefits conferred and sealed by it, and our solemn vow made in it; by being humbled for our sinful defilement, our falling short of, and walking contrary to, the grace of Baptism, and our engagements; by growing up to assurance of pardon of sin, and of all other blessings sealed to us in that Sacrament; by drawing strength from the death and resurrection of Christ, into whom we are baptised, for the mortifying of sin, and quickening of grace; and by endeavouring to live by faith, to have our conversation in holiness and righteousness, as those who have in it given up their

z

names to Christ; and to walk in brotherly love, as being baptised by the same Spirit into one Body.

Q.168. What is the Lord's Supper?

A. The Lord's Supper is a Sacrament of the New Testament, in which by giving and receiving bread and wine according to the appointment of Jesus Christ, His death is showed forth; and those who worthily communicate feed upon His body and blood, to their spiritual nourishment and growth in grace; have their union and communion with Him confirmed; testify and renew their thankfulness, and engagement to God, and their mutual love and fellowship with each other, as members of the same mystical Body.

Q.169. How has Christ appointed bread and wine to be given and received in the Sacrament of the Lord's Supper?

A. Christ has appointed the ministers of His Word, in the administration of this Sacrament of the Lord's Supper, to set apart the bread and wine from common use, by the word of institution, thanksgiving, and prayer; to take and break the bread, and to give both the bread and the wine to the communicants, who are, by the same appointment, to take and eat the bread, and to drink the wine, in thankful remembrance that the body of Christ was broken and given, and His blood shed, for them.

Q.170. How do they who worthily communicate in the Lord's Supper feed upon the body and blood of Christ in it?

A. As the body and blood of Christ are not corporally or carnally present in, with, or under the bread and wine in the Lord's Supper, and yet are spiritually present to the faith of the receiver, no less truly and really than the elements themselves are to their outward senses; so they who worthily communicate in the Sacrament of the Lord's Supper, do feed upon the body and blood of Christ, not after a corporal and carnal, but in a spiritual manner; yet truly and really, while by faith they receive and apply to themselves Christ crucified and all the benefits of His death.

Q.171. How are those who receive the Sacrament of the Lord's Supper to prepare themselves before they come unto it?

A. They that receive the Sacrament of the Lord's Supper are, before they come, to prepare themselves for it by examining themselves in regard to their being in Christ, their sins and wants; the truth and measure of their knowledge, faith, repentance, their love to God and the brethren, charity to all men, forgiving those who have done them wrong; their desires after Christ, and their new obedience; and by renewing the exercise of these graces, by serious meditation, and fervent prayer.

Q.172. May one who doubts of his being in Christ, or of his due preparation, come to the Lord's Supper?

A. One who doubts of his being in Christ, or of his due preparation for the Sacrament of the Lord's Supper, may have true interest in Christ, although he is not yet assured of it, and in God's account has it, if he duly realises his need of it, and sincerely desires to be found in Christ, and to depart from iniquity: in which case (because promises are made, and this Sacrament is appointed for the relief even of weak and doubting Christians) he is to bewail his unbelief, and labour to have his doubts resolved; and, so doing, he may and ought to come to the Lord's Supper, that he may be further strengthened.

Q.173. May any who profess the faith, and desire to come to the Lord's Supper, be kept from it?

A. Those who are found to be ignorant or scandalous, notwithstanding their profession of the faith, and desire to come to the Lord's Supper, may and ought to be kept from that Sacrament, by the power which Christ has left in His Church, until they receive instruction, and manifest their reformation.

Q.174. What is required of those who receive the Sacrament of the Lord's Supper in the time of its administration?

A. It is required of those who receive the Sacrament of the Lord's Supper, that, during the time of its administration, with all holy reverence and attention they wait upon God in that ordinance, diligently observe the sacramental elements and actions, heedfully discern the Lord's body, and affectionately meditate on His death and sufferings, and thereby stir themselves up to a vigorous exercise of their graces; in judging themselves, and sorrowing for sin; in earnest hungering and thirsting after Christ, feeding on Him by faith, receiving of His fullness, trusting in His merits, rejoicing in His love, giving thanks for His grace; in renewing their covenant with God, and love to all the saints.

Q.175. What is the duty of Christians after they have received the Sacrament of the Lord's Supper?

A. The duty of Christians after they have received the Sacrament of the Lord's Supper, is seriously to consider how they have behaved themselves in it, and with what success; if they find quickening and comfort, to bless God for it, ask for its continuance, watch against relapses, fulfil their vows, and encourage themselves to a frequent attendance at that ordinance: but if they find no present benefit, more exactly to review their preparation for, and behaviour at, the Sacrament; in both which, if they can approve themselves to God and their own consciences, they are to wait for the fruit of it in due time: but, if they see they have failed in either, they are to be humbled, and afterward to receive it with more care and diligence.

Q.176. Wherein do the Sacraments of Baptism and the Lord's Supper agree?

A. The Sacraments of Baptism and the Lord's Supper agree, in that the author of both is God; the spiritual part of both is

Christ and His benefits; both are seals of the same covenant, are to be dispensed by ministers of the Gospel, and by none other; and to be continued in the Church of Christ until His second coming.

Q.177. Wherein do the Sacraments of Baptism and the Lord's Supper differ?

A. The Sacraments of Baptism and the Lord's Supper differ, in that Baptism is to be administered but once, with water, to be as a sign and seal of our regeneration and ingrafting into Christ, and even to infants; whereas the Lord's Supper is to be administered often, in the elements of bread and wine, to represent and exhibit Christ as spiritual nourishment to the soul, and to confirm our continuance and growth in Him, and that only to those who are of years and ability to examine themselves.

Q.178. What is prayer?

A. Prayer is an offering up of our desires unto God, in the name of Christ, by the help of His Spirit, with confession of our sins; and thankful acknowledgement of His mercies.

Q.179. Are we to pray unto God only?

A. Since God only is able to search the hearts, hear the requests, pardon the sins, and fulfil the desire of all, and since He only is to be believed, and worshipped with religious worship, prayer, which is a special part of it is to be made by all to Him alone, and to no other.

Q.180. What is it to pray in the name of Christ?

A. To pray in the name of Christ is, in obedience to His command, and in confidence in His promises to ask mercy for His sake, not by bare mention of His name, but by drawing our encouragement to pray, and our boldness, strength, and hope of acceptance in prayer, from Christ and His mediation.

Q.181. Why are we to pray in the name of Christ?

A. Since the sinfulness of man, and because of it his distance from God are so great, that we can have no access into His presence without a Mediator; and since no one in heaven or earth is appointed or is fit for that glorious work except Christ, we are to pray in no other name than His alone.

Q.182. How does the Spirit help us to pray?

A. We do not know what to pray for as we ought, but the Spirit helps our infirmities, by enabling us to understand both for whom, and what, and how prayer is to be made; and by working and quickening in our hearts (although not in all persons, nor at all times, in the same measure) those apprehensions, affections, and graces which are requisite for the right performance of that duty.

Q.183. For whom are we to pray?

A. We are to pray for the whole Church of Christ on earth, for magistrates, and ministers; for ourselves, our brethren, even our enemies; and for all sorts of men living, or who will live hereafter; but not for the dead, nor for those who are known to have sinned the sin unto death.

Q.184. For what are we to pray?

A. We are to pray for all things tending to the glory of God, the welfare of the Church, our own or others' good, but not for anything that is unlawful.

Q.185. How are we to pray?

A. We are to pray with an awful apprehension of the majesty of God, and a deep sense of our own unworthiness, necessities, and sins; with penitent, thankful, and enlarged hearts; with understanding, faith, sincerity, fervour, love, and perseverance, waiting upon God with humble submission to His will.

Q.186. What rule has God given for our direction in the duty of prayer?

A. The whole Word of God is of use to direct us in the duty of prayer; but the special rule of direction is that form of prayer which our Saviour taught His disciples, commonly called *The Lord's Prayer.*

Q.187. How is the Lord's Prayer to be used?

A. The Lord's Prayer is not only for direction, as a pattern, according to which we are to make other prayers, but may also be used as a prayer to be used with understanding, faith, reverence, and other graces necessary to the right performance of the duty of prayer.

Q.188. Of how many parts does the Lord's Prayer consist?

A. The Lord's Prayer consists of three parts: a preface, petitions, and a conclusion.

Q.189. What does the preface of the Lord's Prayer teach us?

A. The preface of the Lord's Prayer (contained in these words, *Our Father, which art in heaven*), teaches us, when we pray, to draw near to God with confidence in His fatherly goodness, and our interest in it; with reverence, and all other childlike dispositions, heavenly affections, and due apprehensions of His sovereign power, majesty, and gracious condescension: as also, to pray with and for others.

Q.190. What do we pray for in the first petition?

A. In the first petition (which is, *Hallowed be thy name*), acknowledging the utter inability and indisposition that is in ourselves and all men to honour God aright, we pray that by His grace God may enable and incline us and others to know, to acknowledge, and highly to esteem Him, His title, attributes, ordinances, Word, works, and all through which He is pleased to make Himself known; and to glorify Him in thought, word, and deed; that He may prevent and remove atheism, ignorance, idolatry, profaneness, and whatever is dishonourable to Him; and, by His over-ruling providence, direct and dispose of all things to His own glory.

Q.191. What do we pray for in the second petition?

A. In the second petition (which is, *Thy kingdom come*),

acknowledging ourselves and all mankind to be by nature under the dominion of sin and Satan, we pray that the kingdom of sin and Satan may be destroyed, the Gospel propagated throughout the world, the Jews called, the fulness of the Gentiles brought in; the Church furnished with all gospel-officers and ordinances, purged from corruption, allowed and maintained by the civil magistrate; that the ordinances of Christ may be purely dispensed, and made effectual for the converting of those yet in their sins, and the confirming, comforting, and building up of those already converted: that Christ may rule in our hearts here, and hasten the time of His second coming, and our reigning with Him for ever: and that He may be pleased so to exercise the Kingdom of His power in all the world, as may best serve to these ends.

Q.192. *What do we pray for in the third petition?*

A. In the third petition (which is, *Thy will be done in earth, as it is in heaven*), acknowledging, that by nature we and all men are not only utterly unable and unwilling to know and do the will of God, but prone to rebel against His Word, to resent and murmur against His providence, and wholly inclined to do the will of the flesh, and of the devil: we pray, that God by His Spirit may take away from ourselves and others all blindness, weakness, unwillingness, and perverseness of heart; and by His grace make us able and willing to know, do, and submit to His will in all things, with a humility, cheerfulness, faithfulness, diligence, zeal, sincerity, and constancy, like that of the angels in heaven.

Q.193. *What do we pray for in the fourth petition?*

A. In the fourth petition (which is, *Give us this day our daily bread*), we acknowledge that in Adam, and by our own sin, we have forfeited our right to all the outward blessings of this life, and deserve to be wholly deprived of them by God, and to have them cursed to us in the use of them; that they by themselves cannot sustain us, and that we cannot merit or procure them by our own industry, but are prone to desire, get, and use them unlawfully. Therefore we pray for ourselves and others, that both they and we, waiting upon the providence of God from day to day in the use of lawful means, may by His free gift, and as it seems best to His fatherly wisdom, enjoy a sufficient share of them; and have them continued and blessed to us in our holy and comfortable use of them, and contentment in them; and be kept from all things that are contrary to our temporal support and comfort.

Q.194. What do we pray for in the fifth petition?

A. In the fifth petition (which is, *Forgive us our debts, as we forgive our debtors*), acknowledging that we and all others are guilty both of original and actual sin, and thus have become debtors to the justice of God; and that neither we, nor any other creature, can make the least satisfaction for this debt, we pray for ourselves and others, that God by His free grace may through the obedience and satisfaction of Christ, apprehended and applied by faith, acquit us both from the guilt and punishment of sin, accept us in His Beloved, continue His favour and grace to us, pardon our daily failings, and fill us with peace and joy, in giving us daily more and more assurance of forgiveness. We are more emboldened to ask for this and encouraged to expect it, when we have this testimony in ourselves, that we from the heart forgive others their offences.

Q.195. What do we pray for in the sixth petition?

A. In the sixth petition (which is, *And lead us not into temptation, but deliver us from evil*), we acknowledge that the most wise, righteous, and gracious God, for diverse holy and just ends, may so order things, that we may be assaulted, foiled, and for a time led captive by temptations; that Satan, the world, and the flesh, are ready powerfully to draw us aside, and ensnare us; and that we, even after the pardon of our sins, because of our corruption, weakness, and want of watchfulness, are not only subject to be tempted, and ready to expose ourselves to temptations, but we are unable of ourselves and unwilling to resist them, to withdraw from them, and to learn from them, and are worthy to be left under their power. Therefore we pray that God may so over-rule the world and all in it, subdue the flesh, and restrain Satan, order all things, bestow and bless all means of grace, and quicken us to watchfulness in their use, that we and all His people may by His providence be kept from being tempted to sin; or, if tempted, that by His Spirit we may be powerfully supported and enabled to stand in the hour of temptation, or when fallen, may be raised again and restored, learning from this experience and making a sanctified use of it. We further pray that our sanctification and salvation may be perfected, Satan trodden under our feet, and we fully freed from sin, temptation, and all evil, for ever.

Q.196. What does the conclusion of the Lord's Prayer teach us?

A. The conclusion of the Lord's Prayer (which is, *For thine is the kingdom, and the power, and the glory, for ever. Amen*), teaches us to enforce our petitions with arguments, taken not from any worthiness in ourselves, or in any other creature, but from God; and with our prayers to join praises, ascribing to God alone eternal sovereignty, omnipotence, and glorious excellency. Wherefore, since He is able and willing to help us, we by faith are emboldened to plead with Him that He may, and dare quietly to rely upon Him in fulfilling our requests. And to testify this desire and assurance in our heart, we say *Amen*.

FINIS

Part II

THE SHORTER CATECHISMS

THE LITTLE CATECHISM, 1556

The Manner of examining children before they are admitted to the Lord's Supper

EARLY in the Reformation there had grown up a custom of using two Catechisms, a larger one for purposes of full and careful instruction, and a smaller one for purposes of teaching and examining young children before admission to Holy Communion. A little Catechism of this kind was used in Geneva in 1553 when it was added on to the *Geneva Catechism*. This was subsequently enlarged, and reproduced in later Manuals, while a third and longer redaction was printed at the end of the Genevan *Psaltery* of 1562. *The Little Catechism* used in Scotland represents an adaptation of this little Catechism in Geneva. It is first found in *The Forme of prayers and ministration of the Sacraments, etc. used in the Englishe Congregation at Geneva: and approved by the famous and godly learned man, John Calvyn, 1556.* It was carried over into the editions of the *Book of Common Order* from 1564 to 1611 where it continued to be appended to *Calvin's Catechism*, and into the edition of 1615 when it was appended to the *Palatine Catechism*.

THE LITTLE CATECHISM

The Manner to examine Children, before they are admitted to the Lord's Supper

1. *Minister. In whom do you believe?*
Child. I believe in God the Father, and in Jesus Christ His Son, and in the Holy Spirit, and look for salvation by no other means.

2. *M. Are the Father, the Son, and the Holy Spirit any more than one God?*
C. No, although they are distinct in persons.

3. *M. What is the effect of your faith?*
C. That God the Father of our Lord Jesus Christ (and through Him of us all), is the beginning and principal cause of all things, which He governs in such a way that nothing can be done without His ordinance and providence. Next, that Jesus Christ His Son came down into this world, and accomplished all things, which were necessary for our Salvation; and ascended into heaven, where He sits at the right hand of the Father, that is, that He has all power in heaven and in earth; and shall come again from thence to judge the whole world. Furthermore that the Holy Spirit is very God, because He is the virtue and power of God, and prints in our hearts the promises made unto us in Jesus Christ. And finally, that the Church is sanctified, and its members are delivered from their sins through the mercies of God, and shall after this life rise again to life everlasting.

4. *M. Must we serve God according as He has commanded, or else as the traditions of men teach us?*
C. We must serve Him as He has taught us by His word and

commandments, and not according to the commandments of men.

5. *M. Can you keep God's commandments by yourself?*

C. No indeed.

6. *M. Who then keeps and fulfils them in you?*

C. The Holy Spirit.

7. *M. When God then gives you His Holy Spirit, can you perfectly observe them?*

C. No.

8. *M. Why? God curses and rejects all who do not in every point fulfil His commandments.*

C. It is true.

9. *M. How then will you be saved, and delivered from the curse of God?*

C. By the death and passion of our Lord Jesus Christ.

10. *M. How so?*

C. Because by His death He has restored us to life, and reconciled us to God our Father.

11. *M. To whom do you make your prayers?*

C. I pray to God in the name of our Lord Jesus Christ our Advocate and Mediator, referring all my prayers to that pattern, in which Christ our Saviour has left us a most sufficient and absolute rule.

12. *M. How many Sacraments are there in Christ's Church?*

C. Two: Baptism and the Lord's Supper.

13. *M. What is meant by Baptism?*

C. First it signifies that we have forgiveness of our sins by the blood of Christ. Secondly it sets before our eyes our regeneration or new spiritual birth.

14. *M. What does the Supper of the Lord signify?*

C. That by the spiritual eating and drinking of the body and blood of our Lord Jesus Christ, our souls are nourished unto life everlasting.

15. *M. What do the bread and wine represent in the Lord's Supper?*

C. That as our bodies are nourished by them, so our souls are sustained, and nourished with the virtue of Christ's body and blood: not that they are inclosed in the bread and wine, but we must seek Christ in heaven and in the glory of God His Father.

16. *M. By what means may we attain unto Him there?*

C. By faith, which God's Spirit works in our hearts, assuring us of God's promises made to us in His holy Gospel.

CRAIG'S SHORT CATECHISM, 1592

Craig's Short Catechism
A Form of Examination before the Communion,
Approved by the General Assembly of the Kirk of Scotland:
And appointed to be used in Families and Schools.

THE General Assembly in 1590 called for a uniform order to be used in examination of young people admitted to Holy Communion, and remitted the task of drawing one up to John Craig, Robert Pont, Thomas Buchanan, and Andrew Melville. By July the following year a *Form of Examination before the Communion*, penned by John Craig, and representing an abridgement of his longer Catechism, was presented to the Assembly and sent to be printed. In May 1592 at the Assembly presided over by Robert Bruce Craig's *Short Catechism* was given the full authority of the Kirk, while ministers were asked to have it purchased by congregations and to see that it was read in families. The Assembly also enjoined it to be read and learned in Lectors' Schools in place of *The Little Catechism*. As such it continued in constant use until it was finally displaced by the *Westminster Shorter Catechism*.

CRAIG'S SHORT CATECHISM
A FORM OF EXAMINATION BEFORE COMMUNION

I. OUR MISERABLE BONDAGE THROUGH ADAM

Q.1. What are we by nature?

A. The children of God's wrath (Eph. 2:3).

Q.2. Were we thus created by God?

A. No. He made us according to His own image (Gen. 1:26).

Q.3. How came we to this misery?

A. Through the Fall of Adam from God (Gen. 3).

Q.4. What has happened to us as a result of the Fall?

A. Original sin and natural corruption (Rom. 5:12, 18, 19).

Q.5. What power have we to turn to God?

A. None at all, for we are dead in sin (Eph. 2:1).

Q.6. What is the punishment of our sin?

A. Death eternal, both in body and soul (Rom. 6:23).

II. OUR REDEMPTION BY CHRIST

Q.7. Who may deliver us from this bondage?

A. God only who brings life out of death.

Q.8. How do we know that He will do it?

A. By His promise, and the sending His Son Christ Jesus in our flesh (John 3:16, 17).

Q.9. What kind of Person is Christ?

A. Perfect God and perfect Man, without sin (Matt. 1:23; Luke 1:31).

Q.10. What was the need for this wonderful union?

A. That He might be a suitable Mediator for us.

Q.11. How did He redeem us?

A. Through His obedience to the Law, and death on the Cross (Phil. 2:8).

Q.12. Did He suffer only natural death?

A. No, He suffered also the curse of God, in body and soul (Gal. 3:13).

Q.13. How do we know that His death brought life to us?

A. By His glorious resurrection and ascension.

Q.14. How is that?

A. For if He has not satisfied for all our sins perfectly, He has not risen, nor we by Him (1 Cor. 15:14, 17).

Q.15. Do we need to believe these Mysteries?

A. Without doubt, but that is not enough (James 2:17, 20).

Q.16. What more is required?

A. That we be made partakers of Christ and His merits (John 15:4-7).

III. OUR PARTICIPATION WITH CHRIST

Q.17. How is that wrought?

A. Through His continual intercession for us in Heaven (Heb. 7:25).

Q.18. Explain how that is done.

A. Hereby the Holy Spirit is sent (John 14:16, 26).

Q.19. What does the Spirit do in this work?

A. He offers Christ and His graces to us, and moves us to receive Him.

Q.20. How does He offer Christ to us?

A. By the preaching of the Evangel (Rom. 10:13, 14, 15).

Q.21. How does He move us to receive Him?

A. Through printing in our hearts true faith in Christ (Acts. 16:14).

Q.22. What is faith in Christ?

A. A sure persuasion that He is the only Saviour of the world, but ours in particular, who believe in Him (John 6).

Q.23. What does this fruit work?

A. Our inseparable union with Christ and His graces (Eph. 3:16-19).

Q.24. What is the first fruit of this union?

A. A remission of our sins, and imputation of justice (Rom. 6:19).

Q.25. What is the next fruit of our union with Him?

A. Our sanctification and regeneration to the image of God (John 3:3, 5).

Q.26. Who does this, and how?

A. The Holy Spirit through our union with Christ, in His death, burial and resurrection (Rom. 6).

Q.27. What are the chief parts of our regeneration?

A. Mortification of sin, and rising to righteousness (Rom. 6).

Q.28. How do we know sin and righteousness?

A. By the just and perfect Law of God (Rom. 7).

IV. THE WORD

Q.29. Where shall we find the Word of God?

A. Only in the holy Scriptures (Rom. 15:4).

Q.30. Are the Scriptures sufficient for our instruction?

A. Without doubt, as the Apostles do testify (John 20:31; Gal. 1:8; 2 Tim. 3:16).

Q.31. How should we receive and use the Word?

A. We should read it privately and publicly with all reverence (Deut. 31:21).

Q.32. Is this sufficient for our instruction?

A. Not if public teaching may be had (Eph. 4:11, 12).

Q.33. Why?

A. Because God not only raises up public teachers and pastors, but He has commanded us to hear them (Mal. 2:7).

Q.34. How long should we continue in this School?

A. All the days of our lives, since we are ignorant, forgetful, and easily deceived (Col. 3:16).

Q.35. What is the purpose of the Sacraments?

A. They are added for our further comfort and admonition as a visible Word (Gen. 17:9, 10, 11; Exod. 12).

V. OUR FREEDOM TO SERVE GOD

Q.36. What good things may we do once we are regenerated?

A. We may serve our God freely and uprightly (Rom. 12).

Q.37. May we do it perfectly according to the Law?

A. No truly, for our regeneration is not perfect (Gal. 5:17; Eccles. 7:22).

Q.38. What followed from that?

A. A certain rebellion of the flesh against the Spirit (Rom. 7:15-25).

Q.39. Is not this rebellion cursed by the Law?

A. Yes indeed, but it is not imputed to us (2 Cor. 5:19).

Q.40. Why is that, seeing it is sin, and the root of all our sins?

A. Because Christ offered satisfaction for us in all the points of the Law (Rom. 3:21, etc.).

Q.41. What are we, then, who believe in Christ?

A. Just in Him, but sinners in ourselves (Rom. 8).

Q.42. What does this confession require of us?

A. A constant faith in Christ, and continual repentance.

Q.43. What then is our only joy in life and death?

A. That all our sins past, present, and future, are buried; and Christ only is made our Wisdom, Justification, Sanctification, and Redemption (1 Cor. 1:30).

Q.44. What fruit springs from this faith?

A. Peace of conscience, and joy in the Spirit, in all our troubles within and without (Rom. 5:2; 2 Cor. 6:4).

Q.45. What do we learn from all this?

A. How miserable we are through Adam, and how blessed through Christ (Phil. 3:8).

Q.46. When are we to remember this teaching?

A. At all times, but especially when we are touched with a proud opinion of our worthiness, or are troubled in conscience for sin (Luke 18:19).

Q.47. Then this meditation serves as a preparation for the holy Sacraments?

A. Yes indeed, provided we think of them rightly.

VI. THE SACRAMENTS

Q.48. Explain that in Baptism.

A. We see there the seal of our spiritual uncleanness through our communion with Adam, and of our cleansing by our communion with Christ.

Q.49. Expound that also in the Supper.

A. We see, feel, and taste there also the seal of our spiritual needs, and death through Adam; and likewise of our spiritual treasures and life through Christ only.

Q.50. How do we contract our spiritual uncleanness from Adam?

A. Through our natural communion with him (Rom. 5:12, etc.).

Q.51. How do we get our spiritual cleansing and life by Christ?

A. Through our spiritual communion with our Second Adam, Head, and Spouse (Eph. 5:30).

Q.52. Do the Word and the Sacraments work this Communion?

A. No. It is the work of the Spirit only (Eph. 3:16).

Q.53. Where do the Word and Sacraments lead us?

A. Directly to the Cross and death of Christ (1 Cor. 1:17, 18, 23, 24).

Q.54. Why is that?

A. Because through His Cross and death, the wrath of God was quenched, and all His blessings made ours (Gal. 3:13, 14).

Q.55. Why was this high mystery represented by these weak and common elements?

A. Because they express most vividly our spiritual cleansing and feeding, which we have by Christ (John 6:32, etc.).

Q.56. When does He actually do these things to us?

A. When He is so joined with us, and we with Him, that He abides in us, and we in Him spiritually (John 15:4, 5).

Q.57. How is this union and abiding expressed here?

A. By natural washing, eating, drinking, digesting, feeding, and abiding in us.

Q.58. How may we feel and know this spiritual abiding in us?

A. By the testimony of the Spirit in us, and external actions in conformity with Christ in us (Matth. 7:6; Rom. 8:16).

Q.59. Then Christ is not an idle Guest in us?

A. No indeed, for He came not only with water and blood, but also with the Spirit, to assure us, in some measure, of His Presence in us (1 John 5:6).

VII. BAPTISM

Q.60. What does Baptism signify to us?

A. That we are unclean by nature, and are cleansed by the blood of Christ (Tit. 3:5).

Q.61. What is the meaning of our union with the water?

A. Our spiritual union with Jesus Christ (Rom. 6:3, 8; Gal. 3:27).

Q.62. What follows from our union with Him?

A. Remission of sins and regeneration (Rom. 6:4, 18, 22).

Q.63. Where does our regeneration come from?

A. From communion with the death, burial, and resurrection of Christ (Rom. 6:4, 5, 8).

Q.64. How long, and in what way does Baptism work in us?

A. All the days of our life, through faith and repentance (1 Cor. 6:19, 20).

Q.65. How then are infants baptised?

A. Upon the promise made to the faithful and their seed (Gen. 17:7, 10).

Q.66. How does Baptism differ from the Supper?

A. In regard to the elements, action, rites, signification, and use.

Q.67. Why is Baptism ministered only once?

A. It is enough to be received once in the House of God (Rom. 8:16).

Q.68. Explain the reason for that.

A. Those who are once truly received in His Society are never cast out (John 6:37).

Q.69. Why is the Supper ministered so often?

A. We need to be fed continually (John 6:55).

Q.70. Why is the Supper not ministered to infants?

A. Because they cannot examine themselves (1 Cor. 11:18).

VIII. THE SUPPER

Q.71. What does the action of the Supper signify?

A. That our souls are fed spiritually, by the body and blood of Jesus Christ (John 6:54).

Q.72. When is this done?

A. When we feel the efficacy of His death in our conscience by the Spirit of faith (John 6:63).

Q.73. Why is this Sacrament given in meat and drink?

A. To seal up our intimate conjunction with Christ.

Q.74. Why are both meat and drink given?

A. To testify that Christ is the whole food of our souls (John 6).

Q.75. Is Christ's body in the elements?

A. No. It is in Heaven (Acts 1:11).

Q.76. Why then is the element called His body?

A. Because it is a sure seal of His body given to our souls.

Q.77. To whom should this Sacrament be given?

A. To the faithful only, who can examine themselves.

Q.78. Wherein should they examine themselves?

A. In faith and repentance, with their fruits.

Q.79. What should the pastors do when men are negligent and abuse the Sacraments?

A. They should use the Order of Discipline established in the Word.

IX. DISCIPLINE

Q.80. Who should use this Discipline?

A. The pastors and elders by their mutual consent and judgement.

Q.81. What is the office of the eldership?

A. To watch over their flock and exercise the discipline.

Q.82. How is this done?

A. By private and public admonition, and other censures of the Kirk, as need requires.

Q.83. Who ought to be excluded from the Sacraments?

A. All infidels and public slanderers.

Q.84. Why are these excluded?

A. Lest they should hurt themselves, slander the Kirk, and dishonour God.

X. THE MAGISTRATE

Q.85. What is the office of the Christian Magistrate in the Kirk?

A. He should defend the true religion and discipline, and punish all who disturb and despise them.

XI. THE TABLE

Q.86. Why do we use a Table here, and not an Altar as the Fathers did at God's commandment?

A. Because we convene, not to offer a sacrifice for sin, but to eat and drink of that sacrifice, which Christ once offered on the Cross for us (Heb. 7:23, 24, 27 and 10:11, 12, 14, 18).

Q.87. What do we profess when we come to the Table?

A. That we are dead in ourselves, and seek our life only in Christ.

Q.88. Will this confession of our unworthiness hinder us from coming to Communion?

A. No indeed. It is rather a preparation for it, if accompanied by faith and repentance (Mark 2:17).

Q.89. Why is mention made here of Christ's body and blood particularly?

A. To testify to His death, by which alone He was made our spiritual meat and drink (John 6:51, 55).

Q.90. For what reason is this action called the Communion?

A. Because it is the real cause of our mutual fellowship with Christ in all things, good and evil.

Q.91. Explain how it takes place.

A. Here He removes all the evil things from us which we have by nature, and we receive of Him all good things, which we lack by nature.

Q.92. Declare these things more plainly?

A. The wrath of God and sin are removed, which we have by nature and the favour of God, and adoption, with the joy of Heaven, are restored to us, things which we do not have by nature (Rom. 8).

Q.93. What then may the faithful soul say?

A. Now I live, yet not I, but Christ lives in me. It is God who justifies. Who shall condemn?

Q.94. Let us therefore give thanks, and turn to this holy action, every one of us, saying and singing in his heart: The Lord is the Portion of mine inheritance and of my cup: Thou maintainest my lot. The lines are fallen unto me in pleasant places; yea, I have a goodly heritage (Psalm 16:5, 6).

A. So let it be done, with heart and mouth, to the confusion of all idolators, and to the Glory of our God.

XII. THE END OF OUR REDEMPTION

Q.95. To what end are we thus redeemed, and brought in hope of that endless joy to come?

A. To teach us effectually to deny all ungodliness, worldly lusts, and unrighteousness, and so to live godly, soberly, and righteously in this present world, looking for the Coming of Christ, for our full redemption (Titus 2:11, 12, 13).

Q.96. What will be the final end of all these graces?

A. God will be glorified for ever in mercy, and we shall enjoy that endless life with Christ our Head, to whom with the Father, and the Holy Spirit be all Honour and Glory for ever. Amen.

THE A, B, C

A CATECHISM FOR YOUNG CHILDREN, 1641

THIS little Catechism is built, in traditional style, round the Apostles' Creed, the Ten Commandments, and the Lord's Prayer, and represents a new attempt to provide the Church with something really suitable for children, longer than *The Little Catechism* first used in Scotland, and shorter than the *Short Catechism* of John Craig. It was "appointed", as the title page indicates, "by the act of the Church and Council of Scotland to be learned in all families and Lector Schools in the said Kingdom", and published in 1641, along with some prayers and graces suitable for the young. It went through several editions before the *Shorter Catechism* took the field and swept everything before it, but because the Westminster Assembly provided nothing which could actually take its place with young children, the succeeding centuries saw the production of many privately produced catechisms designed for this end.

THE A, B, C,

A CATECHISM FOR YOUNG CHILDREN

Q.1. Who made man?

A. God.

Q.2. In what estate did He make him?

A. Perfectly holy in body and soul.

Q.3. How did he fall from the good estate?

A. By breaking the commandment of God.

Q.4. What punishment followed?

A. Death and condemnation to him and his posterity.

Q.5. How are we delivered therefrom?

A . By God's free mercy in Jesus Christ.

Q.6. What kind of person is Jesus Christ?

A. He is very God and very Man in one person.

Q.7. Why do you call Him very God?

A. Because He is the eternal Son of God, of one and the selfsame Godhead with the Father and Holy Ghost.

Q.8. Why do you call Him very Man?

A. Because He is like us in all things, apart from sin.

Q.9. Why was He without sin?

A. That He might be an unspotted sacrifice for sin.

Q.10. What has He done for us?

A. He died for our sins and rose for our righteousness.

Q.11. Are all men who perish in Adam saved by Christ?

A. No, only those who have true faith in Him.

Q.12. What do you call true faith?

A. It is the true knowledge of Jesus Christ with assurance of salvation in Him.

Q.13. Repeat the Articles of your Faith.

B1

*A.*1. I believe in God the Father Almighty, Maker of heaven and earth.

2. And in Jesus Christ, His only Son our Lord.

3. Who was conceived of the Holy Ghost; born of the Virgin Mary,

4. Suffered under Pontius Pilate, was crucified, dead, and buried.

He descended into Hell.

5. The third day He rose again from the dead.

6. He ascended into heaven, and sitteth at the right hand of God the Father Almighty.

7. From thence He shall come to judge the quick and the dead.

8. I believe in the Holy Ghost.

9. The Holy Church Universal.

10. The Communion of Saints.

11. The forgiveness of sins.

12. The resurrection of the body and the life everlasting.

Q.14. By what means does God's Spirit work this faith in you?

A. By the Word of God.

Q.15. What do you call the Word of God?

A. The Holy Scripture of the Old and New Testament.

Q.16. By what means does God's Spirit confirm this faith in you?

A. By the same Word and by the Sacraments.

Q.17. What do you call the Sacraments?

A. They are visible signs and seals ordained of God for the confirmation of my faith.

Q.18. How do they confirm your faith?

A. By receiving them as pledges that Christ crucified (represented and offered in them) is given to me in particular to be my Saviour.

Q.19. How many Sacraments are there?

A. Two: Baptism and the Lord's Supper.

Q.20. Why were you baptised as an infant?

A. That thereby I might be ingrafted into Christ, and entered in His Church, which is His mystical Body.

Q.21. What profit do you have by Baptism now?

A. It seals up the remission of my sins in Christ's blood; and advances the renovation of my heart in His Spirit: which are my spiritual washing.

Q.22. What do you call the Lord's Supper?

A. It is the Sacrament of my spiritual nourishment in the body and blood of Christ.

Q.23. How do you eat His body and drink His blood?

A. By believing assuredly that His body was broken and His blood was shed for me.

Q.24. What thankfulness do you owe to God for giving His Son to shed His blood for you?

A. I ought to deny myself and walk in His Commandments all the days of my life.

Q.25. Repeat the Commandments.

A. Hearken and take heed O Israel, for I am the Lord thy God, who has brought thee out of the land of Egypt and out of the house of bondage;

1. Thou shalt have none other Gods but me, etc.

Lord, have mercy upon us, and write all these laws in our hearts, we beseech Thee.

Q.26. What is the sum and effect of all these Commandments?

A. Thou shalt love the Lord thy God with all thy heart, mind, and strength, and thy neighbour as thyself.

Q.27. Is any man able to do these things perfectly in this life?

A. None at all.

Q.28. Why so?

A. Because no man is perfectly sanctified in this life.

Q.29. Yet must not we press toward perfection in fulfilling God's commandments?

A. Doubtless, for otherwise there is neither faith nor fear of God in us.

Q.30. What must we do then, when we break any of these Commandments?

A. We must run to God by repentance and prayer.

Q.31. What do you call repentance?

A. It is the turning of my heart to God with unfeigned sorrow for offending His majesty, and a constant resolution to amend my life.

Q.32. What do you call prayer?

A. It is calling upon God in the name of Christ for things belonging to God's glory and our necessity.

Q.33. Why is it not lawful to pray to creatures as to Angels and Saints glorified?

A. Because God has commanded us to worship Himself alone.

Q.34. Why must we pray only in Christ's name?

A. Because He is our only Mediator and Intercessor.

Q.35. How then should we pray?

A. According to that pattern of prayer that our Master has set before us, saying, When ye pray, say: Our Father, which art in heaven, etc.

Q.36. How are you assured that God will hear your prayers?

A. By Christ's own Word promising that whatever we ask the Father in His name, it shall be given us.

Q.37. What is the fruit of all this, your religion and your serving of God?

A. Hereby God is glorified and I am saved, through Jesus Christ my Lord, to whom be everlasting praise and glory. Amen.

THE WESTMINSTER SHORTER
CATECHISM, 1648

*Agreed upon by the Assembly of Divines at Westminster, with the
assistance of Commissioners from the Church of Scotland, as part of
the covenanted uniformity in religion between the Churches of Christ
in the Kingdoms of Scotland, England, and Ireland.*

WORK on the Westminster *Shorter Catechism* was not taken
in hand until the *Larger Catechism* was more or less completed,
but as A. F. Mitchell has shown (*Catechisms of the Second Reformation*) it retains more of the earlier draft for the *Larger
Catechism* considered by the Assembly, and is less directly
dependent on the *Confession of Faith*. In its final form, however,
it owed less to the Scottish Commissioners than the other
Westminster Documents, and like the *Larger Catechism*, its
chief author seems to have been Anthony Tuckney. It was
approved by the General Assembly of the Church of Scotland
eight days after its approval of the *Larger Catechism* in July,
1648, and ratified like it by the Scottish Parliament in February
of the following year. It became at once the most popular and
widely used Catechism in Scotland as in England, and has been
more influential than any other document in shaping religious
thought and temperament in Scotland ever since.

The *Shorter Catechism* stands out in marked contrast to the
other short catechisms in use in the Church, in two main
respects.

(1) Its catechetical method is determined not so much by
the capacities of the child, but by what the child ought to
know in due course.

(2) It is directed not like Craig's Catechisms so much to the

inner life and growth of the faithful within the Church, as to the inquirer who may enter into it through learning and discipline. On the other hand the *Shorter Catechism* is less influenced by the schematism of the Federal Theology than the *Larger Catechism*, and is certainly less moralistic, even if it omits almost entirely anything about the Church. It is typical of the Westminster theology that it should replace the order of the Apostles' Creed for a more scholastic scheme of exposition. Taken all in all, it is one of the greatest and most remarkable documents in the whole history of Christian theology. It is reproduced here without the Scripture proofs which were added to it by the Westminster Assembly, while the spelling and sometimes the expressions have been altered to suit modern readers.

THE SHORTER CATECHISM

Q.1. What is the chief end of man?

A. Man's chief end is to glorify God, and to enjoy Him for ever.

Q.2. What rule has God given to direct us how to glorify and enjoy Him?

A. The Word of God, which is contained in the Scriptures of the Old and New Testaments is the only rule to direct us how to glorify and enjoy Him.

Q.3. What do the Scriptures principally teach?

A. The Scriptures principally teach what man is to believe concerning God, and what duty God requires of man.

Q.4. What is God?

A. God is a Spirit, infinite, eternal, and unchangeable, in His being, wisdom, power, holiness, justice, goodness, and truth.

Q.5. Are there more Gods than one?

A. There is but One only, the living and true God.

Q.6. How many persons are there in the Godhead?

A. There are three persons in the Godhead; the Father, the Son, and the Holy Spirit, and these three are one God the same in substance, equal in power and glory.

Q.7. What are the decrees of God?

A. The decrees of God are, His eternal purpose, according to the counsel of His will, whereby, for His own glory, He has foreordained whatever comes to pass.

Q.8. How does God execute His decrees?

A. God executes His decrees in the works of creation and providence.

Q.9. What is the work of creation?

A. The work of creation is, God's making all things of

nothing, by the Word of His power, in the space of six days, and all very good.

Q.10. How did God create man?

A. God created man male and female, after His own image, in knowledge, righteousness, and holiness, with dominion over the creatures.

Q.11. What are God's works of providence?

A. God's works of providence are, His most holy, wise, and powerful preserving, and governing of all His creatures, and all their actions.

Q.12. What special act of providence did God exercise towards man in the state in which he was created?

A. When God had created man, He entered into a covenant of life with him, upon condition of perfect obedience; forbidding him to eat of the tree of the knowledge of good and evil, upon the pain of death.

Q.13. Did our first parents continue in the state in which they were created?

A. Our first parents, being left to the freedom of their own will, fell from the state in which they were created, by sinning against God.

Q.14. What is sin?

A. Sin is any want of conformity to, or transgression of, the Law of God.

Q.15. What was the sin whereby our first parents fell from the state in which they were created?

A. The sin whereby our first parents fell from the state in which they were created, was their eating the forbidden fruit.

Q.16. Did all mankind fall in Adam's first transgression?

A. Since the covenant was made with Adam, not only for himself, but for his posterity, all mankind, descending from him by ordinary generation, sinned in him, and fell with him, in his first transgression.

Q.17. Into what state did the fall bring mankind?

A. The fall brought mankind into a state of sin and misery.

Q.18. Wherein consists the sinfulness of that state into which man fell?

A. The sinfulness of that state into which man fell, consists in the guilt of Adam's first sin, the want of original righteousness, and the corruption of his whole nature, which is commonly called original sin, together with all actual transgressions which proceed from it.

Q.19. What is the misery of that state into which man fell?

A. All mankind by their fall lost communion with God, are under His wrath and curse, and so made liable to all miseries in this life, to death itself, and to the pains of hell for ever.

Q.20. Did God leave all mankind to perish in the state of sin and misery?

A. God having, out of His mere good pleasure, from all eternity, elected some to everlasting life, did enter into a covenant of grace to deliver them out of the state of sin and misery and to bring them into a state of salvation by a Redeemer.

Q.21. Who is the Redeemer of God's elect?

A. The only Redeemer of God's elect is the Lord Jesus Christ, who, being the eternal Son of God, became Man, and so was, and continues to be, God and Man in two distinct natures, and one person, for ever.

Q.22. How did Christ, being the Son of God, become Man?

A. Christ, the Son of God, became man, by taking to Himself a true body, and a reasonable soul, being conceived by the power of the Holy Spirit in the womb of the Virgin Mary, and born of her, yet without sin.

Q.23. What offices does Christ execute as our Redeemer?

A. Christ, as our Redeemer, executes the offices of a Prophet, of a Priest, and of a King, both in His state of humiliation and exaltation.

Q.24. How does Christ execute the office of a Prophet?

A. Christ executes the office of a Prophet, in revealing to us, by His Word and Spirit, the will of God for our Salvation.

Q.25. How does Christ execute the office of a Priest?

A. Christ executes the office of a Priest, in His once offering up of Himself a sacrifice to satisfy divine justice, and reconcile us to God, and in making continual intercession for us.

Q.26. How does Christ execute the office of a King?

A. Christ executes the office of a King, in subduing us to Himself, in ruling and defending us, and in restraining and conquering all His and our enemies.

Q.27. In what did Christ's humiliation consist?

A. Christ's humiliation consisted in His being born, and that in a low condition, made under the law, undergoing the miseries of this life, the wrath of God, and the cursed death of the Cross; in being buried, and continuing under the power of death for a time.

Q.28. In what does Christ's exaltation consist?

A. Christ's exaltation consists in His rising again from the dead on the third day, in ascending up into heaven, in sitting at the right hand of God the Father, and in coming to judge the world at the last day.

Q.29. How are we made partakers of the redemption purchased by Christ?

A. We are made partakers of the redemption purchased by Christ, by the effectual application of it to us by His Holy Spirit.

Q.30. How does the Spirit apply to us the redemption purchased by Christ?

A. The Spirit applies to us the redemption purchased by Christ, by working faith in us, and thereby uniting us to Christ in our effectual calling.

Q.31. What is effectual calling?

A. Effectual calling is the work of God's Spirit, whereby, convincing us of our sin and misery, enlightening our minds in the knowledge of Christ, and renewing our wills, He persuades and enables us to embrace Jesus Christ, freely offered to us in the Gospel.

Q.32. What benefits do those who are effectually called partake of in this life?

A. Those who are effectually called partake of justification, adoption, and sanctification in this life, and the several benefits which in this life either accompany or flow from them.

Q.33. What is justification?

A. Justification is an act of God's free grace, in which He pardons all our sins, and accepts us as righteous in His sight, for the sake of the righteousness of Christ alone, which is imputed to us, and received by faith alone.

Q.34. What is adoption?

A. Adoption is an act of God's free grace, through which we are received into the number, and have a right to all the privileges of the sons of God.

Q.35. What is sanctification?

A. Sanctification is the work of God's free grace, by which we are renewed in the whole man after the image of God, and are enabled more and more to die unto sin, and live unto righteousness.

Q.36. What are the benefits which in this life accompany or flow from justification, adoption, and sanctification?

A. The benefits which in this life accompany or flow from justification, adoption, and sanctification, are, assurance of God's love, peace of conscience, joy in the Holy Spirit, increase of grace, and perseverance therein to the end.

Q.37. What benefits do believers receive from Christ at death?

A. The souls of believers are at their death made perfect in holiness, and immediately pass into glory; and their bodies, being still united to Christ, rest in their graves, till the resurrection.

Q.38. What benefits do believers receive from Christ at the resurrection?

A. At the resurrection, believers being raised up in glory, shall be openly acknowledged and acquitted in the day of judgement, and made perfectly blessed in the full enjoying of God to all eternity.

Q.39. What is the duty which God requires of man?

A. The duty which God requires of man, is obedience to His revealed will.

Q.40. What did God at first reveal to man for the rule of his obedience?

A. The rule which God at first revealed to man for His obedience, was the moral law.

Q.41. Where is the moral law summarily comprehended?

A. The moral law is summarily comprehended in the ten commandments.

Q.42. What is the sum of the Ten Commandments?

A. The sum of the Ten Commandments is, to love the Lord our God with all our heart, with all our soul, with all our strength, and with all our mind; and our neighbour as ourselves.

Q.43. What is the preface to the Ten Commandments?

A. The preface to the Ten Commandments is in these words, "I am the Lord thy God, who hath brought thee out of the land of Egypt, out of the house of bondage."

Q.44. What does the preface to the Ten Commandments teach us?

A. The preface to the Ten Commandments teaches us, that because God is the Lord, and our God, and Redeemer, therefore we are bound to keep all His Commandments.

Q.45. Which is the first commandment?

A. The first commandment is, "Thou shalt have no other gods before me."

Q.46. What is required in the first commandment?

A. The first commandment requires us to know and acknowledge God to be the only true God, and our God; and to worship and glorify Him accordingly.

Q.47. What is forbidden in the first commandment?

A. The first commandment forbids the denying, or failure to worship and glorify the true God as God, and our God; and the giving of that worship and glory to any other, which is due to Him alone.

Q.48. What are we specially taught by these words in the first commandment?

A. These words in the first commandment teach us, that God, who sees all things, takes notice of, and is much displeased with, the sin of having any other God.

Q.49. Which is the second commandment?

A. The second commandment is, "Thou shalt not make unto thee any graven image, or any likeness of any thing that is in heaven above, or that is in the earth beneath, or that is in the water under the earth: Thou shalt not bow down thyself to them, nor serve them: for I the Lord thy God am a jealous God, visiting the iniquity of the fathers upon the children unto the third and fourth generation of them that hate me; and showing mercy unto thousands of them that love me, and keep my commandments."

Q.50. What is required in the second commandment?

A. The second commandment requires the receiving, observing, and keeping pure and entire, all such religious worship and ordinances as God has appointed in His Word.

Q.51. What is forbidden in the second commandment?

A. The second commandment forbids the worshipping of God by images, or any other way not appointed in His Word.

Q.52. What are the reasons annexed to the second commandment?

A. The reasons annexed to the second commandment are, God's sovereignty over us, His claim upon us, and the zeal He has for His own worship.

Q.53. Which is the third commandment?

A. The third commandment is, "Thou shalt not take the name of the Lord thy God in vain: for the Lord will not hold him guiltless that taketh his name in vain."

Q.54. What is required in the third commandment?

A. The third commandment requires the holy and reverent use of God's names, titles, attributes, ordinances, Word, and works.

Q.55. What is forbidden in the third commandment?

A. The third commandment forbids all profaning or abusing of any thing whereby God makes Himself known.

Q.56. What is the reason annexed to the third commandment?

A. The reason annexed to the third commandment is, that though the breakers of this commandment may escape punishment from men, yet the Lord our God will not suffer them to escape His righteous judgement.

Q.57. Which is the fourth commandment?

A. The fourth commandment is, "Remember the sabbathday to keep it holy. Six days shalt thou labour, and do all thy work: but the seventh day is the sabbath of the Lord thy God: in it thou shalt not do any work, thou, nor thy son, nor thy daughter, thy man-servant, nor thy maid-servant, nor thy cattle, nor thy stranger that is within thy gates: For in six days the Lord made heaven and earth, the sea, and all that in them is, and rested the seventh day: wherefore the Lord blessed the sabbath-day, and hallowed it."

Q.58. What is required in the fourth commandment?

A. The fourth commandment requires the keeping holy to God of such set times as He has appointed in His Word;

expressly one whole day in seven, to be a holy sabbath to Himself.

Q.59. *Which day of the seven has God appointed to be the weekly sabbath?*

A. From the beginning of the world to the resurrection of Christ, God appointed the seventh day of the week to be the weekly sabbath; and the first day of the week ever since, to continue to the end of the world, which is the Christian Sabbath.

Q.60. *How is the sabbath to be sanctified?*

A. The sabbath is to be sanctified by a holy resting all that day, even from such worldly employments and recreations as are lawful on other days; and spending the whole time in the public and private exercises of God's worship, except so much as is to be taken up in the works of necessity and mercy.

Q.61. *What is forbidden in the fourth commandment?*

A. The fourth commandment forbids the omission or careless performance of the duties required, and the profaning of the day by idleness, or doing what is in itself sinful, or by unnecessary thoughts, words, or works, about our worldly employments or recreations.

Q.62. *What are the reasons annexed to the fourth commandment?*

A. The reasons annexed to the fourth commandment are, God's allowing us six days of the week for our own employments, His special claim on the seventh day, His own example, and His blessing of the sabbath-day.

Q.63. *What is the fifth commandment?*

A. The fifth commandment is, "Honour thy father and thy mother; that thy days may be long upon the land which the Lord thy God giveth thee.

Q.64. *What is required in the fifth commandment?*

A. The fifth commandment requires our preserving the honour, and performing the duties, belonging to every one in their several places and relations, as superiors, inferiors, or equals.

Q.65. What is forbidden in the fifth commandment?

A. The fifth commandment forbids our neglecting or doing anything against, the honour and duty which belong to everyone in their several places and relations.

Q.66. What is the reason annexed to the fifth commandment?

A. The reason annexed to the fifth commandment, is a promise of long life and prosperity (as far as it shall serve God's glory and their own good) to all such as keep this commandment.

Q.67. Which is the sixth commandment?

A. The sixth commandment is, "Thou shalt not kill."

Q.68. What is required in the sixth commandment?

A. The sixth commandment requires all lawful endeavours to preserve our own life, and the life of others.

Q.69. What is forbidden in the sixth commandment?

A. The sixth commandment forbids the taking away of our own life, or the life of our neighbour unjustly, or anything tending to it.

Q.70. Which is the seventh commandment?

A. The seventh commandment is, "Thou shalt not commit adultery."

Q.71. What is required in the seventh commandment?

A. The seventh commandment requires the preservation of our own and our neighbour's chastity, in heart, speech, and behaviour.

Q.72. What is forbidden in the seventh commandment?

A. The seventh commandment forbids all unchaste thoughts, words, and actions.

Q.73. Which is the eighth commandment?

A. The eighth commandment is, "Thou shalt not steal."

Q.74. What is required in the eighth commandment?

A. The eighth commandment requires the lawful procuring and furthering of the wealth and outward estate of ourselves and others.

Q.75. What is forbidden in the eighth commandment?

A. The eighth commandment forbids whatever does or may unjustly hinder our own or our neighbour's wealth or outward estate.

Q.76. Which is the ninth commandment?

A. The ninth commandment is, "Thou shalt not bear false witness against thy neighbour."

Q.77. What is required in the ninth commandment?

A. The ninth commandment requires the maintaining and promoting of truth between man and man, and of our own and our neighbour's good name, especially in witness-bearing.

Q.78. What is forbidden in the ninth commandment?

A. The ninth commandment forbids whatever is prejudicial to truth, or injurious to our own or our neighbour's good name.

Q.79. Which is the tenth commandment?

A. The tenth commandment is, "Thou shalt not covet thy neighbour's house, thou shalt not covet thy neighbour's wife, nor his man-servant, nor his maid-servant, nor his ox, nor his ass, nor any thing that is thy neighbour's."

Q.80. What is required in the tenth commandment?

A. The tenth commandment requires full contentment with our own condition, with a right and charitable attitude towards our neighour, and all that is his.

Q.81. What is forbidden in the tenth commandment?

A. The tenth commandment forbids all discontent with our own state, envying or grieving at the good of our neighbour, and all inordinate desires and feelings about what is his.

Q.82. Is any man able perfectly to keep the commandments of God?

CI

A. No mere man since the fall is able in this life perfectly to keep the commandments of God, but daily breaks them in thought, word, and deed.

Q.83. Are all transgressions of the law equally heinous?

A. Some sins are more heinous in the sight of God than others, because of what they are in themselves, and because of certain aggravations.

Q.84. What does every sin deserve?

A. Every sin deserves God's wrath and curse, both in this life, and that which is to come.

Q.85. What does God require of us, that we may escape His wrath and curse due to us for sin?

A. To escape the wrath and curse of God due to us for sin, God requires of us faith in Jesus Christ, repentance unto life, with the diligent use of all the outward means whereby Christ communicates to us the benefits of redemption.

Q.86. What is faith in Jesus Christ?

A. Faith in Jesus Christ is a saving grace, whereby we receive and rest on Him alone for salvation, as He is offered to us in the gospel.

Q.87. What is repentance unto life?

A. Repentance unto life is a saving grace, whereby a sinner, out of a true sense of his sin, and apprehension of the mercy of God in Christ, with grief and hatred of his sin, turns from it unto God, and with full purpose of, and endeavour after, new obedience.

Q.88. What are the outward means whereby Christ communicates to us the benefits of redemption?

A. The outward and ordinary means whereby Christ communicates to us the benefits of redemption, are His ordinances, especially the Word, Sacraments, and prayer, all of which are made effectual to the elect for salvation.

Q.89. How is the Word made effectual for salvation?

A. The Spirit of God makes the reading, but especially the preaching of the Word, an effectual means of convincing and converting sinners, and of building them up in holiness and comfort, through faith, unto salvation.

Q.90. How is the Word to be read and heard, that it may become effectual for salvation?

A. That the Word may become effectual for salvation, we must attend to it with diligence, preparation, and prayer; receive it with faith and love, lay it up in our hearts, and practise it in our lives.

Q.91. How do the Sacraments become effectual means of salvation?

A. The Sacraments become effectual means of salvation, not because of any virtue in them, or in him who administers them, but only by the blessing of Christ, and the working of His Spirit in those who receive them by faith.

Q.92. What is a Sacrament?

A. A Sacrament is a holy ordinance instituted by Christ, in which, by sensible signs, Christ, and the benefits of the new covenant, are represented, sealed, and applied to believers.

Q.93. Which are the Sacraments of the New Testament?

A. The Sacraments of the New Testament are Baptism and the Lord's Supper.

Q.94. What is Baptism?

A. Baptism is a Sacrament, in which the washing with water in the name of the Father, and of the Son, and of the Holy Ghost, signifies and seals our ingrafting into Christ, and partaking of the benefits of the covenant of grace, and our engagement to be the Lord's.

Q.95. To whom is Baptism to be administered?

A. Baptism is not to be administered to any outside the visible Church, until they profess their faith in Christ, and obedience to Him; but the infants of members of the visible Church are to be baptised.

Q.96. What is the Lord's Supper?

A. The Lord's Supper is a Sacrament, in which, by giving and receiving bread and wine, according to Christ's appointment, His death is showed forth, and the worthy receivers are, not after a corporal and carnal manner, but by faith, made partakers of His body and blood, with all His benefits, to their spiritual nourishment, and growth in grace.

Q.97. What is required for worthy receiving of the Lord's Supper?

A. It is required of those who would worthily partake of the Lord's Supper, that they examine themselves as to their knowledge to discern the Lord's body, their faith to feed upon Him, their repentance, love, and new obedience; lest, coming unworthily, they eat and drink judgement to themselves.

Q.98. What is prayer?

A. Prayer is an offering up of our desires unto God, for things agreeable to His will, in the name of Christ, with confession of our sins, and thankful acknowledgment of His mercies.

Q.99. What rule has God given for our direction in prayer?

A. The whole Word of God is of use to direct us in prayer; but the special rule of direction is that form of prayer which Christ taught His disciples, commonly called *The Lord's Prayer.*

Q.100. What does the preface of the Lord's Prayer teach us?

A. The preface of the Lord's Prayer (which is, "Our Father which art in heaven") teaches us to draw near to God with all holy reverence and confidence, as children to a father, able and ready to help us; and that we should pray with and for others.

Q.101. What do we pray for in the first petition?

A. In the first petition (which is, "Hallowed be thy name"), we pray that God may enable us and others to glorify Him in all the ways in which He makes Himself known; and that He may dispose all things to His own glory.

Q.102. What do we pray for in the second petition?

A. In the second petition (which is, "Thy kingdom come") we pray that Satan's kingdom may be destroyed; and that the Kingdom of grace may be advanced, ourselves and others brought into it, and kept in it; and that the Kingdom of Glory may be hastened.

Q.103. What do we pray for in the third petition?

A. In the third petition (which is, "Thy will be done in earth, as it is in heaven") we pray that God, by His grace, may make us able and willing to know, obey, and submit to His will in all things, as the angels do in heaven.

Q.104. What do we pray for in the fourth petition?

A. In the fourth petition (which is, "Give us this day our daily bread") we pray that by God's free gift we may receive a sufficient share of the good things of this life, and enjoy His blessing with them.

Q.105. What do we pray for in the fifth petition?

A. In the fifth petition (which is, "And forgive us our debts, as we forgive our debtors") we pray that God, for Christ's sake, would freely pardon all our sins. We are more encouraged to ask for this because by His grace we are enabled from the heart to forgive others.

Q.106. What do we pray for in the sixth petition?

A. In the sixth petition (which is, "And lead us not into temptation, but deliver us from evil") we pray that God may either keep us from being tempted to sin, or support and deliver us when we are tempted.

Q.107. What does the conclusion of the Lord's Prayer teach us?

A. The conclusion of the Lord's Prayer (which is, "For thine is the kingdom, and the power, and the glory, for ever, Amen") teaches us to take our encouragement in prayer from God only, and in our prayers to praise Him, ascribing Kingdom, Power, and Glory to Him. And, in testimony of our desire, and assurance to be heard, we say, *Amen.*

THE SHORT LATIN CATECHISM

RUDIMENTA PIETATIS

SEVERAL Latin Catechisms were used in the Schools of Scotland, notably those of Geneva and Heidelberg. The former was done into Latin verse by Patrick Adamson in 1573 but was little used. In the same year Robert Pont published a brief catechism of his own composition, also in Latin verse, which came to see several editions. It was entitled *Parvus Catechismus quo examinari possunt iuniores qui ad Sacram Coenam admittuntur*. The *Rudimenta Pietatis*, however, was the Catechism most widely and continuously used in Latin instruction. It was first published in 1595 by Andrew Duncan, with a dedication to the Earl of Rothes. Duncan had been Rector of the Grammar School in Dundee since 1571, was Regent of St. Leonard's College when Andrew Melville was busy reconstructing the curriculum at St. Andrews, and in 1597 was ordained Minister of the Word of God at Crail. Thereafter he led an eventful and stormy life. In 1605 he was imprisoned in Blackness Castle for attending the Aberdeen Assembly earlier that year, and in 1606 he was banished to France. In November 1607 he became Professor of Theology at the College of La Rochelle, but returned to Scotland in 1613 to his parish at Crail. Once again, however, he came under the King's displeasure in 1619, and in the following year was deposed from the ministry and banished from his parish. He died in 1626.

In his earlier days Andrew Duncan was the author of several text-books on Latin: *Latinae Grammaticae Pars Prior, sive etymologia latina in usu rudiorum* was published in Edinburgh in 1595, while two years later he published *Appendix Etymologiae*, and *Studiorum Puerilium Clavis* embracing, as the subtitle indicates, *Latinae linguae ac Poeticae Rudimenta*. From his dedication to the Earl of Rothes it is clear that Duncan intended the *Rudimenta Pietatis* to be used along with *Pars Prior* in the grammatical instruction of scholars so that piety might be a companion, nay a guide, to learning. For this purpose he had translated into Latin for school use the teaching that had been handed on to him by "John Knox, the light of our Church". In a brief preface to the reader Duncan pointed out that the *Scholia* were added not so much to remove difficulties or obscurities (for what could be clearer or plainer?), as to excite the inquiry of readers and to kindle and inflame their desire toward God. They were not given to be thrust upon learners of tender years but to open up the way for those more advanced to direct their eyes and minds to the innermost mysteries of the Christian Religion.

The *Rudimenta Pietatis* went into many editions, but after Duncan's death came to be published together with the *Rudimenta Grammatices in Gratiam Juventutis Scoticae conscripta* of Andrew Simpson (who had been a schoolmaster at Perth and Dunbar, and then Minister at Dunbar and Dalkeith, where he died in 1590), and the *Vocabula cum aliis nonnullis Latinae Linguae subsidiis* of David Wedderburn. By 1653 Duncan's Catechism was published under the title *Rudimenta Pietatis quibus accessit Summula Catechismi ad piam iuniorem educationem apprime utilis*, and came to be bound together in one volume with the works of Simpson and Wedderburn mentioned above. Under this general title the *Rudimenta Pietatis* contained the Latin Alphabet, the Lord's Prayer, Apostles' Creed, the Ten Commandments, the Sum of the Law (Matt. 23:34 f.), Brief Questions and Answers on the institution and meaning of Baptism, with reference to Matt. 28:19, Matt. 21:12, Titus 3:5, and Acts 22:16, and of the

Lord's Supper, with reference to 1 Cor. 11:23 f. Then came the original *Rudimenta Pietatis* with the *Scholia*, and to this were added prayers of confession and thanksgiving and supplication, also in Latin, for the daily use of scholars. In these editions Andrew Duncan's dedication and preface to the reader were omitted, and in due course its authorship came to be ascribed to Andrew Simpson, so that by the beginning of the eighteenth century Dunlop (*Collection*, II, XI) could say: "This is the little Catechism which has always been taught in the Grammar Schools of Scotland. It is said to be composed by Mr. Andrew Simpson, the Author of the Latin Rudiments which begins, *Quum literarum consideratio*, who was Master of the Grammar School at Perth, before and in the time of the Reformation, and afterward the first Protestant Minister of Dunbar." That is reflected in the editions published after the Restoration, in 1692, 1709, 1711, and 1713, etc.

In this edition of the *Rudimenta Pietatis* there are reproduced only (what came to be called) the *Summula Catechismi*, and the *Scholia*. They are given not only because they played such a notable part in shaping the theological tradition of the Reformed Kirk in Scotland, but because they give some indication of the Latin terms regularly employed in theological instruction. The text has been taken from the original edition of 1595, from the copy in the National Library, Edinburgh, but several minor emendations from the later editions have been incorporated.

RUDIMENTA PIETATIS

Triplex hominis status
1. In sanctitate et sanitate
2. Sub peccato et morte
3. Sub Christi gratia

Questio. Quis hominem creavit?
Responsio 1. Deus

Q. Qualem creavit eum?
R.2. Sanctum et sanum, mundique dominum.

1. Homo liber, cum creatus

Q. In quem usum creatus est?
R.3. Ut Deo inserviret.

Q. Quod servitii genus ab eo exigebat Deus?
R.4. Legis suae praestationem.

Q. Num in legis Dei praestatione perstitit?
R.5. Nequaquam: sed eam foede transgressus est.

Q. Quae huius transgressionis poena?
R.6. Mors aeterna, tum animae, tum corporis, et ipsi et posteris.

2. Captivus, cum peccavit

Q. Quomodo inde liberamur?
R.7. Mera Dei gratia in Christo Jesu, absque nostris meritis.

3. Liberatus cum credit in Christum

Q. Cuiusmodi persona est Christus?
R.8. Vere Deus vereque homo, in persona una.

Q. Quomodo nos liberavit?
R.9. Morte sua: mortem enim nobis debitam pro nobis subiit, nosque eripuit.

Modus liberationis, per mortem Christi

Q. Num omnes liberantur per Christum?
R.10. Minime, sed ii tantum qui fide eum amplectuntur.

Qui liberati, fideles

Q. Quid est fides?

Fides quid

R.11. Cum mihi persuadeo, Deum me omnesque Sanctos amare, nobisque Christum cum omnibus suis bonis gratis donare.

Q. Recense summam tuae fidei.

Fidei summa

R.12. Credo in Deum Patrem, etc.

Q. Quis operatur hanc fidem in nobis?

Fidei Author
Spiritus
Sanctus
Instrumenta,
Verbum et
Sacramenta

R.13. Spiritus Sanctus per Verbum et Sacramenta.

Q. Quomodo eam operatur per Verbum et Sacramenta?

R.14. Aperit cor, ut Deo loquenti in Verbo et Sacramentis credamus.

Q. Quid est Dei Verbum?

Verbum Dei
quid, scz.
Scriptura

R.15. Quicquid veteris ac novi Testamenti libris continetur.

Q. Verbi Dei quot partes?

Verbi Dei
partes: Lex,
Evangelium

R.16. Duae, Lex et Evangelium.

Q. Quid Lex?

Lex quid

R.17. Doctrina Dei, debitum a nobis exigens, et quia non sumus solvendo, damnans.

Q. Quid Evangelium?

Evangelium
quid

R.18. Doctrina Christum cum omnibus suis bonis offerens, debitumque nostrum ab eo solutum, nosque liberos esse proclamans.

Q. Quid Sacramenta?

Sacramenta
quid

R.19. Sigilla Dei, significantia et donantia nobis Christum cum omnibus suis bonis.

Q. Quae haec Christi bona?

Beneficia
Sacramentis
obsignata

R.20. Amor Dei, Spiritus Sanctus, unio nostri cum Christo: unde remissio peccatorum, sanatio naturae, spiritualis nutritio et vita aeterna.

Q. Quot sunt novi Testamenti Sacramenta?

Sacramentor-
um numerus

R.21. Duo, Baptismus et Sacra Coena.

Q. Quid Baptismus?

R.22. Sacramentum insitionis nostri in Christum, et ablutionis a peccatis.

Q. Quid insitio nostri in Christum?

R.23. Unio nostri cum Christo, unde manat remissio peccatorum, et perpetua resipiscentia.

Q. Baptismus quid juvat fidem?

R.24. Testatur, ut aqua corpus abluitur, sic, operante Spiritu Sancto, a peccatorum reatu et radice per fidem in sanguine Christi nos repurgari.

Q. Quid est Sacra Coena?

R.25. Sacramentum spiritualis nutritionis nostri in Christo.

Q. Coena Domini, quid juvat fidem?

R.26. Testatur, ut pane et vino corpora nostra aluntur et augescunt; sic animas nostras corpore et sanguine Christi crucifixi ali et corroborari ad vitam aeternam.

Q. Corpore et sanguine Christi quomodo alimur?

R.27. Dum fide percipimus, et vi Spiritus Sancti, qui una adest ea nobis applicamus.

Q. Quando fide percipimus, et nobis applicamus corpus Christi crucifixi?

R.28. Dum nobis persuademus Christi mortem et crucifixionem non minus ad nos pertinere, quam si ipsi nos pro peccatis nostris crucifixi essemus: persuasio autem haec est verae fidei.

Q. Vera fides quomodo dignoscitur?

R.29. Per bona opera.

Q. Quomodo cognoscuntur bona opera?

R.30. Si Dei legi respondeant.

Q. Recita Dei Legem.

R.31. Audi Israel, Ego sum Dominus, etc.

Q. Haec Lex de quibus te admonet?

Baptismus quid

Insitio nostri in Christum quid, et eius effecta.

Baptismi usus ad fidem.

Coena Domini quid.

Coenae usus ad fidem.

Modus spiritualis nostri nutritionis.

Verae fidei examen per bona opera

Bonorum operum examen per Dei legem.

Summa legis et usus.

R.32. De officio meo erga Deum, et erga proximum.

Q. Quid officii debes Deo?

1. Tabula

R.33. Supra res omnes eum ut amem.

Q. Quid debes proximo?

2. Tabula.

R.34. Eum ut amem tanquam meipsum.

Q. Potis es haec praestare?

Praestatio legis homini impossibilis propter inhabitans peccatum.

R.35. Minime gentium: nam tantisper dum hic vivimus, habitat in nobis peccatum.

Intestina in homine dissensio inter carnem et spiritum.

Q. In Dei filiis, quid hinc existit?

R.36. Perennis pugna inter carnem et spiritum.

Remedium precatio.

Q. In hac pugna, quomodo nobis versandum?

R.37. Assidue orandum, ut Deus peccata nobis remittat, imbecillitatemque sustentet.

Q. Quomodo orandum?

Precatio Christi

R.38. Ut nos docuit Christus; Pater noster, etc.

Q. Quî tibi persuades, Deum donaturum quae petis?

Fiducia inter precandum unde, scz. ex Dei mandato et promissione.

R.39. Quia orare jussit, pollicitusque est, quicquid peterem in Christi nomine, se mihi largiturum.

Quae Deo debemus ob tot beneficia, scz. gratiarum actio et servitium.

Q. Quid debes Deo ob tot beneficia?

R.40. Ut ei gratias agam, perpetuoque serviam.

Norma servitii Dei, Scriptura.

Q. Quomodo Deo serviendum?

R.41. Ex Verbi ipsius praescripto, ut jam dictum est.

FINIS

SCHOLIA

1. Primaeva Dei in hominem beneficia. (1) Quod esset.
(2) Quod homo esset. (3) Quod Dei similis, nempe sanctus,
et sanus mundique dominus.

2. Ex lapsu enim cum in peccatum, tum in morbum
mortemque incidimus. Peccato enim non modo foedati,
rerumque dominio exuti, sed graviter vulnerati, atque adeo
trucidati sumus. Porro vide unde miser homo excidit, fuit
beatus primum in internis aeternisque, deinde in externis:
interna fuerunt sanctitas sanitasque omnium partium animae,
corporis, etc. Externa, rerum dominium, opes, et copiae, etc.
Sed fraude Diaboli his omnibus fuit eversus, factusque miser.

3. Nam (1) quid aequius, quam ut opifici opus suum serviat,
(2) quid nobis conducibilius, quam finem ob quem conditi
sumus assequi: ea enim est nostra felicitas. (3) Non es factus
in alium finem, quam ut servias Deo; unde ni ei servias, nulli es
usui, nisi ut in aeternum pereas, justitiae ejus declarandae causa.

6. Mors duplex: animae et corporis, in hac vita moritur
anima, simulac peccat: Deum enim qui animae vita est,
deserit. Moritur corpus, dum ab anima deseritur. In futura
utrumque morietur, dum saevissimis, sempiternisque suppliciis
totus homo mactabitur.

Haec poena inflicta est posteris, quia omnes in Adamo
peccavimus, qui autem peccat, jure punitur. Peccati enim
comes est poena, vindice justitia.

8. Homo fuit ut mori posset hominisque debitum ex-
solvere: Deus, ut moriendo mortem vinceret, ne mors, Dei
hominisque hostis, amplius in hominem dominaretur.

9. Ex peccato debitum contraximus, unde obligati sumus ut
aeternum moreremur, sed pertulit hanc mortem Christus pro
nobis, nosque exsolvit.

10. Nam justus ex fide vivit: et qui fide caret, ei sub morte et ira Dei aeternum habitandum est.

11. Nam in fide est duplex persuasio. (1) De amore Dei erga nos. (2) De Dei beneficiis, quae ex amore fluunt, Christo nimirum, cum omnibus suis bonis. Hinc duae Symboli partes. (1) De Dei Patris, Filii, et Spiritus Sancti amore erga nos, qui elucet ex iis quae nostri causa praestiterunt. (2) De Dei beneficiis in nos collatis. Ex gemina autem ea persuasione nascitur fiducia, cum in solidum a Deo pendemus. Expende symbolum.

14. Undique obstructum est cor hominis, tenebrisque, et omni perversitate refertum, ut nullus sit aditus Dei Verbo, aut ulli rei bonae. Sed Spiritus Sanctus accedens id aperit, facem coelestis veritatis infert, et hoc Augiae stabulum expurgat.

16. Deus Lege exigit debitum suum: debitum autem est, ut aut legem exequamur, aut aeternum pereamus: elucet hic Dei justitia. Evangelio declarat, et Sacramentis obsignat, hoc debitum esse solutum a Christo, nosque liberos, si Christus fiat noster: fit autem noster si credimus. Atque hic relucet Dei misericordia: utrobique vero hominis miseria absque Christo.

19. Nam Sacramenta non modo significant Christum, sed eum etiam donant cum omnibus quae habet: Imo esse nobis in Verbo donatum confirmant et obsignant: sunt enim sigilla. Ergo quid si sic definiam? Sacramenta sunt Dei Sigilla certum me facientia Christum esse mihi donatum cum omnibus suis bonis. Nam Deus Christum cum omnibus quae habet, Verbo nobis offert. Nos fide recipimus, et possidemus. Spiritus autem Sanctus hanc possessionem Sacramentis obsignat.

22. Baptismus obsignat coelestem nativitatem: Coena educationem nostri in Ecclesia.

23. Unum cum Christo facti, quicquid ille habet, nos accipimus; et quicquid ab eo praestitum est, Deus nos existimat id omne praestitisse, nos ergo in Christo satisfecimus pro peccatis: nos cum Christo peccatum crucifiximus, ne in nos

INDEX TO THE CATECHISMS

Acceptance before God, 24, 49, 198, 229, 233

Access to God, 11, 43f., 192, 195, 230, 288

Adam, 70, 72, 103f., 113, 165, 168, 188, 204, 232, 245, 248, 257, 264, 287
   Old Adam, 58, 119
   Second Adam, 190, 249

Adoption, sonship, 12, 46, 75, 108, 140f., 162ff., 169, 192, 199, 225, 253, 267

Advent, Christ's Second, 4, 7, 18, 77, 117, 123, 171, 194, 203, 229, 232, 239, 254, 266

Amen, meaning of, 96, 180, 234, 278

Angels, 41, 48, 137, 144, 171f., 178, 186ff., 195, 203, 208, 232, 260, 277

Anxiety, 208, 217, 218

Apostles, 3, 40, 49, 64, 85, 111, 152, 157, 159, 194, 247

Apostles' Creed, 7, 72, 106, 168, 181, 239, 258, 280, 284, 288

Ascension of Christ, 7, 17, 72, 77f., 106, 116, 168, 171, 181, 194, 239, 246, 258, 284

Assumption of flesh, manhood, etc., 12, 75, 77, 124, 191, 265
   of our curse, 14

Assurance, certainty, etc., 20, 22, 45f., 54, 58, 61, 69, 84, 86, 124, 137, 162f., 170, 177, 181, 200f., 225, 227, 233f., 241, 257, 267

Atheism, 98, 207f., 231

Authorities ordained of God, 34

Baptism, 56f., 61, 63f., 67, 81f., 84, 152ff., 180f., 191, 225f., 229, 240, 249ff., 258ff., 275, 280, 284f., 288
   Difference between Baptism and the Lord's Supper, 56, 63f., 154, 228f., 250f., 288
   Entry into Christ's Church, 56, 63f., 152, 154, 180, 225, 251, 259
   Ingrafting into Christ, union with Christ, etc., 58, 81, 152f., 155, 225, 229, 250, 259, 275, 285

Cleansing in Christ and remission of sins, 57, 81f., 84, 152f., 180, 225, 240, 249f., 259, 275, 285
   Regeneration or renewal in Christ, 57f., 81f., 152, 180, 225, 229, 240, 250, 259, 288
   Infant Baptism, 58f., 82, 153f., 225, 229, 250f., 259, 276
   Improvement of Baptism, 225f.
   Administered only once, 63, 154, 229, 251

Bondage in sin, 102, 120, 165, 189, 207, 232f., 245

Censures of the Church, 192, 222, 252

Charity, 46, 63, 162, 174, 216, 218ff., 227, 273

Christian, the, partaker of Christ's anointing, 74

Church, 3, 5, 7, 19ff., 49, 56f., 64f., 72, 78ff., 82, 85f., 100, 105ff., 119ff., 151f., 154, 158ff., 162, 172, 180, 192, 194f., 196ff., 201ff., 222, 224f., 227, 229f., 232, 240, 251f., 258f., 275ff., 288f.
   Belief in the Church, 20f., 119f.
   The Work of the Trinity, 107, 119
   Grounded in the Word, 3, 100, 105
   Fruit of the Death of Christ, 19f., 196
   Formed through union with Christ, 60f., 113, 120f., 124, 160, 172, 197, 202, 226, 246f.
   Chosen community existing in all ages, 78, 172, 192, 196
   Christ the Head of the Church, 18, 20, 60, 77f., 79, 120f., 124, 170, 192, 194f., 197, 249, 289
   Body of Christ, 120, 160, 172, 196f., 226, 259
   Outwith the Church no ground of salvation, 21, 121
   Forgiveness of sins in the Church, 21, 122, 196, 198
   Unity of the Church, 20, 78, 120f., 160, 226
   Holiness of the Church, 7, 20, 72, 106, 120, 172, 239, 258

DI*

Church—*cont.*
  Catholicity, 19f., 78, 120, 172, 196f.
  Church visible, 21, 121, 196, 225, 275
  Church invisible, 196f., 201f.
  Family or Household of God, 56, 152, 154, 251
  Power of the Keys in the Church, 85, 159, 227
  Government of the Church, 33, 64f., 158f., 192, 209, 228ff., 232, 252
  Two Jurisdictions in the Church, 159f.
  The Signs or Marks of the Church, 21, 121f., 160
  The Company of the Elect, 19, 21, 78, 119f., 172, 197
  The Communion of Saints, 20, 78f., 120f., 172, 196f., 258
  The Communion of the Faithful, 19, 21, 56, 78, 172
  Mutual participation in Christ and mutual fellowship in love, 20f., 160, 172, 196f., 224, 226
  Communion in Grace, 197f., 201
  Communion in Glory, 197f., 201f.
Circumcision, 58, 82, 152f., 190
Cleansing in Christ, 16, 19, 57, 81, 84, 115f., 152f., 180, 225, 249f., 259, 275, 285
Comfort, only, in life and death, 69, 248
Companions of Christ's Priesthood, 11
Confession of sin, 182, 229, 248, 253, 276
Confession of faith, 7, 107, 151, 210
Conformity to God, 23, 32, 48
  to Christ, 79, 223, 250
  to the Word, 53
  to Law, 80, 204f.
Conscience, 11, 24, 45, 50, 52, 54, 57, 74, 79, 102, 121, 124, 155, 158, 161, 163, 189, 200f., 203, 209, 222, 248f., 251
Conversion, 86f., 92, 103, 134, 185, 224, 232, 275
Covenant of God, 85
  Old Covenant, 82, 105
  New Covenant, 82, 275
  Covenant of Life, of Works, 188, 190, 204f., 264
  Covenant of Grace, of Promise, 82, 190, 195, 200, 224, 225, 265, 275
  Covenant of Christ, 105

Creation, 5, 8f., 31f., 70, 73, 99f., 108f., 164, 167, 169, 187, 213, 239, 245, 257, 263f., 283, 287

Death, 10, 15, 22, 25, 39, 57, 60, 69, 101, 123, 164, 188f., 193, 201f., 204, 245, 257, 264f., 267, 283, 287
Decree of God, 8, 113, 117, 164f., 185ff., 200, 211, 263
Devil, Satan, 11, 26, 47, 50f., 69f., 74f., 92, 94, 101, 109f., 119, 131, 136, 140, 143, 160f., 165, 168, 171, 180f., 188f., 193, 203, 208, 213, 232f., 277, 287, 289
Discipline, 44, 54, 77, 85, 111, 183, 209, 252
Dominion of man in creation, 187, 264, 283, 287
Doubt, 201, 227
Duty of man, 128f., 173f., 185, 204ff., 214ff., 263, 268, 286

Earnest of glory, 201
Effectual calling, 161, 197, 266f.
Elders, 158f., 184, 252
Election, 21, 29, 99, 119f., 145, 161f., 172, 186ff., 190, 193, 197, 199, 265, 274
Eschatology, 21f., 78f., 80, 95f., 116f., 164f., 171ff., 189, 194f., 201ff., 254, 267f.
Exaltation of Christ, 171, 194f., 265f.
Examination of self, 63, 182, 227, 229, 251, 276
Exchange, saving, 115, 253
Experience of God's favour, 162
Expiation, 222

Faith, 22f., 24f., 32, 37, 43, 55f., 58, 63, 72, 74, 78ff., 82, 86, 99, 101, 103f., 106ff., 119, 123ff., 125, 129, 147, 150f., 153, 155, 158, 162, 167, 169, 172, 176f., 181f., 190, 198, 200f., 207, 222, 224f., 227f., 233, 239, 246, 248, 251, 253, 257, 260, 266, 274, 276, 284f., 288f.
  Affiance, 24, 27, 60
  Reliance, 6, 41, 43, 46, 134, 234
  Justifying faith, 125, 198, 274
  Condition of interest in Christ, 190
Fall of man, 70, 99, 101f., 164, 168, 188f., 204, 245, 257, 264f., 274, 287
Fear of God, 25, 89, 126, 129, 174, 260
Feeling, religious, 19, 58, 79, 96, 103, 108, 137, 163, 250

Fencing of the Table, 64, 85, 158f., 227, 252

Filioque, 107, 117, 186

Foreknowledge, 187

Foreordination, 186f., 263

Forgiveness of sins, pardon, remission, etc., 14, 21, 44, 49, 52, 57, 72, 78f., 80f., 83f., 85, 95, 104, 122, 125, 142, 152, 161, 172, 178f., 180, 182, 191, 198, 202, 225, 233, 240, 247, 250, 259, 267, 277, 284, 288ff.

Form of a Servant, 193

Free-will, 100, 102, 187f., 264

Glorification of believers, 162, 173, 201ff.

God, Father, Son, and Holy Spirit, 8, 73, 78, 81, 107, 165, 168, 186, 203, 225, 239, 263, 275, 288

   Father, 6f., 22, 25, 33, 37, 43, 45, 50, 52, 56, 61f., 69, 72ff., 77, 94, 106ff., 139, 168, 177f., 186, 195, 203, 231, 239, 240f., 254

   Almighty, 7, 46, 72f., 94, 106, 109f., 139f., 168f., 186, 258

   Creator, 5, 8, 26, 70, 72f., 106f., 169, 187f., 239, 246, 257, 263f., 283

   Spirit, 27, 41, 137, 186, 263

   All-sufficiency, 179, 186

   Unchangeableness, immutability, 73, 134, 140, 186, 206f., 263

   Majesty, 27, 43, 46f., 70, 94, 128, 130, 139, 230, 260

   Holiness, 100, 140, 186, 204, 222, 263

   Glory, 5, 27f., 30, 42, 45f., 52, 62, 86f., 90, 119, 138, 178f., 185ff., 207, 210f., 215, 241, 254, 260, 263

   Goodness, Love, and Mercy, 6, 10, 29, 43, 48f., 50ff., 70, 86, 94, 100, 102, 106, 108ff., 124, 139f., 161, 163, 168, 177, 179f., 186, 201f., 222, 231, 239f., 257, 263, 284, 288

   God in Covenant, 207

   Wrath of God, 11, 35, 70f., 75, 85, 92, 101, 111, 114, 116, 163, 170, 179, 187, 191ff., 200, 222, 245, 249, 253, 265, 274

   Attributes or Perfections of God, 186, 206f., 210, 221, 231, 270

Good works, 24f., 80, 87ff., 110, 125f., 142, 174, 200, 248, 285, 290

Gospel, 22, 60f., 72, 80f., 85f., 90, 99, 104f., 126, 135ff., 193, 196, 229, 231, 240f., 246, 267, 274, 284

Grace, 11, 20, 22, 29, 39, 42f., 49f., 54f., 59f., 74ff., 77, 79, 80, 86, 95, 124, 178, 182, 186, 190, 192, 195, 198, 210, 211, 221, 223f., 225f., 228, 232f., 274, 276f., 283

Guilt, 39, 50, 71, 106, 114, 124, 158, 189, 233, 285, 289

Healing of nature, 284, 289f.

Hearing of the Word, 53, 146f., 174, 177, 209, 224f.

Heavenly Session of Christ, 18, 77, 84, 116, 171, 189, 194f., 239, 266

Heir of eternal life, of Kingdom of Heaven, etc., 59, 79, 116, 153, 171, 199

Hell, 7, 15, 22, 76, 111, 163, 170f., 176, 194, 202f., 265

   Why not in the Creed, 22

History of redemption, 7

Holy Spirit, the, 7, 8, 9f., 12f., 19f., 25, 31, 47, 53, 57f., 62, 69, 72f., 74f., 77f., 80ff., 84, 86, 90f., 93, 95, 103f., 107, 111f., 117f., 124, 135, 146ff., 152, 162f., 165, 170f., 180, 185f., 190, 192, 196, 198, 200f., 208, 221, 223f., 230, 232, 239ff., 246f., 248ff., 254, 258f., 265ff., 275, 284f., 288f.

   Co-eternal with God the Father, 8, 78, 117, 186, 239, 254

   Power and operation of God, 8, 13, 53, 58, 72, 75, 77, 78, 80, 82, 84, 90, 95, 103, 107, 112, 117ff., 139, 143, 146, 148, 152, 157, 170f., 190, 196f., 199, 202, 221, 223f., 230, 232, 239, 241, 249, 265, 275, 284f., 288

   Applies Christ and His salvation to us, 19, 57, 72, 78, 80ff., 84, 104, 111, 118f., 146, 152, 172, 180, 196, 239, 246, 259, 266, 275, 284f.

   Regenerates us, 19, 25, 39, 70, 81, 86, 93, 118, 191, 202, 246, 259, 288

   Enlightens, reveals, 19, 23, 54, 81, 103, 118, 192, 197, 201f., 223, 230, 239, 267, 288

   Seals, imprints truth within us, etc., 19, 23, 54, 124, 246

   Sanctifies, 25, 58, 118f., 120, 171f., 200, 275, 288

   Governs, 9, 31, 47, 50f., 74, 78, 118

   Confers gifts and graces, 7, 19, 77, 118, 190, 199f.

Holy Spirit—*cont.*
  Grace of the Spirit, 10, 93, 132, 199f.,
    232
  Indwelling Spirit, 19, 48, 78, 91, 112,
    137, 200f.
  Helper in our prayers, 42, 137f., 230
  Testimony, Witness of the Spirit, 146,
    162, 185, 201, 221, 250
  Anointing of the Spirit, 74, 111, 113,
    192
  The Spirit joined to the Gospel, not
    to the Law, 135
  The Spirit operates in the order of
    nature but is above nature, 118
Honour of God, 6, 27, 37, 99, 105f.,
    127ff., 136, 144, 207, 231
Humiliation of Christ, 193f., 265f.

Idolatry, 28, 41, 85, 89, 128f., 137, 144,
    207, 208f., 231
Image of God
  Man created according to the image
    of God, 70, 100, 104, 133, 168,
    187, 264, 287
  Image lost in the Fall, 101
  Man renewed in the image of God, 86,
    93, 142, 199, 247, 267
  Perfection of the image in the vision
    of God, 93, 202f.
  Two contrary images in mankind, 104
  Renewal in the image of Christ, 86
  The glory of God reflected in the
    Church, 20
  Images, representations of God, pro-
    hibited, 27f., 89, 129, 174, 209,
    268
Imputation, non-imputation, 24, 38, 60,
    75, 79, 95, 116, 124f., 152, 161,
    198, 200, 247f., 267
Incarnation, 75, 113, 191, 193, 239, 265
  saving significance of, 75, 112f., 193
Incorporation, ingrafting into Christ, 21,
    60f., 72, 80, 84, 124, 225, 259, 275,
    285
  Into the people of God, 21, 60, 82, 124
Infusion of grace, 200
Ingratitude, 27, 100, 143
Instruments of salvation, 54, 99, 104,
    136, 146, 199, 284
Intercession, Advocacy of Christ, 17,
    19, 44, 46, 74, 77, 116, 169, 171,
    191f., 195, 200, 240, 246, 260, 266
Irreligion, 213

Jesus Christ, 10ff., 74ff., 110ff., 169ff.,
    191ff., 240, 245ff., 257f., 265ff.,
    283f., 287f.
  True God, 8, 10, 12, 16, 71, 73, 75,
    77, 103, 107, 110, 165, 170, 191ff.,
    245, 257, 265f., 283
  True Man, 12f., 16, 71, 75f., 77, 103,
    110f., 170, 191ff., 245, 257, 265,
    283
  Son of God, 8, 12, 73ff., 81, 107, 112,
    168f., 181, 186, 191, 193f., 198,
    240, 245, 251f., 265f., 288f.
  Hypostatic Union, 77, 113, 170, 191ff.,
    245, 263, 283
  Virgin Birth, 12f., 75, 112f., 170, 191,
    193, 265f.
  Anointing as the Christ, 10, 12, 74,
    111, 169, 192
  Offices of Christ, 10, 12, 74, 111f., 169,
    192, 265
  Historical life of Jesus, 12f., 24, 75,
    112f., 170, 191f., 193f., 265f.
  Obedience, active and passive, 13f.,
    60, 75, 79, 84, 111, 125, 135, 170,
    191f., 193, 195, 198, 205, 233, 245
  Suffering of Christ, 14f., 75f., 85, 113f.,
    170, 180, 191, 228, 240, 245f.
  Death of Christ, 13f., 15, 16, 50, 57f.,
    60, 75f., 83, 110, 113f., 155f., 170,
    172, 176, 180f., 193f., 226f., 228,
    240, 245f., 249f., 259, 283, 285,
    287
  Merits of Christ, 72, 85, 122, 124, 170,
    180, 195, 228, 246, 289
  Mediator, the, 11, 13, 43, 71, 110, 112,
    116f., 137, 190ff., 230, 245, 260
  Proper works of divine and human
    natures, 13, 16, 71f., 77, 191f.
  Resurrection of Christ, 17, 57, 60, 76,
    116, 126, 171f., 176, 194, 212,
    246, 250, 258, 266, 271
  Christus Victor, 14, 16f., 75, 78, 111f.,
    116, 170, 191f., 194, 266, 288f.
  Atoning prayer of Jesus, 111, 114
  Head of men, 12, 112
    of angels, 112
    of the Church, 18, 20, 60, 77f., 79,
      120f., 124, 170, 192, 194f., 197,
      249, 289
  Atonement, see Mediation, Sacrifice,
    Satisfaction, Reconciliation, Re-
    demption, Expiation, Inter-
    cession, Justification.

Joy, 60, 78, 87, 117, 123, 162, 164, 173, 201, 203, 233, 248, 253f., 267

Judgement, condemnation, etc., 13f., 16, 18, 21ff., 39, 50, 70f., 75, 77f., 81, 85, 113f., 130, 134, 151, 158, 164, 168, 170, 173f., 181, 194, 200ff., 206, 211, 239, 266, 270, 284, 289
  Last Judgement, 18f., 22, 34, 47, 78, 117, 171, 173f., 194f., 201f., 239, 266, 268

Justification, 23f., 49f., 79, 120, 124f., 135, 176, 194, 198ff., 233, 248, 253, 267, 288f.

Justus et peccator, 136, 248

King, 10, 12, 95, 111, 169, 192, 265f.

Kingdom of God, 22, 45, 47, 52, 86f., 94, 178f., 194, 278
  of Christ, 10f., 12, 86, 111, 118, 232
  of Heaven, 85, 153
  of Glory, 171, 178, 277
  of Grace, 178, 277
  of Providence, 179
  of sin, 232, 277

Knowledge of God, 5ff., 8, 12, 46, 52, 89, 93, 97, 100, 104f., 124, 145, 169, 185ff., 207
  of good and evil, 188, 204, 264

Law, 25ff., 69, 80, 87ff., 104f., 125ff., 134, 173ff., 189, 191, 204ff., 221, 245, 247, 259, 264, 283f., 285, 288

Life Eternal, 52, 59, 69, 75f., 78f., 80, 83, 97, 111, 122f., 145, 162f., 164, 172f., 181, 188, 216f., 223, 239, 284

Light of nature, 185, 196, 213, 222

Lord's Supper, 56ff., 60ff., 67, 82ff., 154ff., 180ff., 226ff., 240f., 249, 251ff., 259, 275f., 281, 285
  Difference between the Lord's Supper and Baptism, 56, 63f., 154, 228f., 250f., 288
  Preparation for the Supper, 63, 157f., 182, 227ff., 249, 251f., 276
  Feeding upon Christ in God's Household, 56, 59f., 63, 83, 154f., 156, 181, 226f., 228f., 240f., 251f., 259, 276, 284f.
  Communion in the Body and Blood of Christ, 59f., 62, 83f., 154f., 156f., 226, 240f., 276
  Communion in the one sacrifice of Christ, 82, 252
  Partaking of Christ's obedience, 60, 84
  Sursum corda, 62, 241
  Thankful remembrance of Christ, 82, 84, 86f., 155, 180, 226, 228, 253, 259
  Union with Christ renewed, 61f., 83, 154f., 226, 251, 284f.
  Pledge of resurrection, eternal life, 62, 83f., 157
  Renewal of covenant with God, 228
  Administration of the Supper, 64, 85, 157f., 227f., 252

Magistrate, 91f., 131, 159, 230, 252

Man
  Creation in body and soul, 5, 9, 70, 73f., 100, 108, 167ff., 187, 245, 257, 264, 284, 287
  Chief end to glorify and serve God, 5, 70, 100, 167f., 184, 263, 283, 287
  Fall of man, 13, 70, 99, 101f., 164, 168, 188f., 204, 245, 257, 264f., 274, 287
  Misery, 6, 33, 69f., 73, 99f., 188, 204, 248, 265, 288
  Nature, 23, 28f., 38, 42, 55, 58, 69f., 75, 79, 93, 100f., 102, 108, 134, 165, 167, 187, 189, 191, 193, 198, 204, 229f., 232f., 250, 253, 265, 287f.

Means of grace, 54, 99, 104, 136, 146, 164, 190f., 199, 222, 224, 234, 274f., 284

Mediation, 20, 22, 190ff., 195, 198, 222, 224, 229f., 245

Ministry, 41, 54, 64f., 90, 99, 136f., 146f., 150f., 158ff., 178, 196f., 209, 223f., 226, 229f., 231

Members of Christ, 12, 16, 33, 45, 60, 63, 69, 86, 72, 74, 77f., 81, 86, 111, 117, 120, 157, 200f.

Moral Law, 204f., 268

Mortification, 16, 25, 31, 58, 76, 87, 126, 152, 225, 247

Mysteries of Christ, 148, 246, 249 280

Mystical Body, 226, 259

Neighbours, duty to, 26, 35, 38, 46, 49f., 58, 63, 86, 89, 92, 95, 128, 132f., 173f., 206f., 214, 219, 272f.

New heaven and new earth, 173

New man, 17ff., 48, 57f., 87, 116, 152, 199

Obedience, 6, 25f., 29, 33, 37, 40f., 47, 53, 58, 99f., 105, 126ff., 129, 140, 167, 173, 176, 178, 188, 190, 204, 214, 224f., 227, 233, 268, 274, 276

Order of God, 38, 41
  in the Church, 33, 53, 64f., 105, 150, 252
  of nature, 9, 13, 118

Ordinance of God, 34, 48, 137, 151, 209ff., 214, 228, 231, 239, 269f.,
  of Christ, 54, 85, 150, 157, 159, 222, 224, 274f.
  of the Apostles, 85, 157, 159
  of the Church, 67, 147, 159, 209f., 222

Original sin, corruption, etc., 13, 16, 18, 23, 57f., 70, 75, 101, 113, 118, 133, 168, 188f., 200, 204, 232f., 245, 248, 264f., 285, 286f., 289f.

Paradise, 25, 70, 72, 104, 168, 188

Participation in Christ and His salvation, 19, 50, 59f., 62, 78, 84, 120, 195f., 246f., 266

Passover, 152, 190

Pastors, 131, 147, 158, 175, 247, 252

Peace of conscience, 201, 233, 248, 267

Pentecost, 128, 130, 198

Perseverance, 53f., 200f., 230, 267

Pilgrim people, 2f., 62

Praise of God, 51f., 136f., 144ff., 165, 174, 179, 186f., 207f., 234, 278

Prayer, 32f., 39ff., 93ff., 99, 105, 129, 136ff., 145, 167, 174, 177ff., 209, 214, 222f., 226, 229f., 240, 260, 274, 276, 286
  The Lord's Prayer, 44f., 93f., 138f., 177f., 231f., 240, 260, 276f., 286
  Pattern of Prayer, 44f., 49, 51, 138, 144, 168, 177, 230f., 240, 260, 276, 290

Preaching, proclamation, 53, 64, 80, 85, 89, 104, 122, 125, 147, 191, 194, 209, 223, 246, 275

Pride, 102, 208, 220

Priest, 10f., 61, 74, 111, 169, 192, 265f.

Promise of God, 10, 29, 33, 54ff., 57f., 103, 105ff., 124, 131f., 137, 147, 153, 190, 204f., 210, 222, 240, 245, 250, 290
  of Christ, 17, 25, 60, 62, 81f., 93, 227, 229, 239, 260
  of the Gospel, 24, 72, 80, 85, 103f.

Prophet, 3, 11, 40, 72, 74, 105, 111, 152, 169, 192, 265f.

Providence, 8f., 50f., 69, 73, 109, 140, 143f., 178f., 187f., 231ff., 264
  Divine overruling, 109f., 211, 231, 234, 239

Punishment, 21, 28, 34, 52, 70f., 90, 101f., 110, 115f., 122, 128, 168, 170, 176, 189, 211, 233, 245, 257, 270, 283

Rebellion, 34, 48, 102, 124, 215, 248

Reconciliation, 11, 13, 60, 192, 240, 266

Redemption, 10, 13, 19, 62, 69, 71ff., 74f., 76, 82, 86, 110ff., 113ff., 165, 170, 180, 195, 202, 213, 245f., 248, 254, 265, 274, 283, 289

Regeneration, renovation, etc., 19, 25, 39, 48, 57, 70, 81, 86, 93, 118, 126, 152f., 169, 180, 199, 202f., 240, 247, 250, 259, 267, 289

Religion, 32, 105, 123, 131, 151, 159, 183f., 196, 209, 211, 213, 252, 261, 280

Repentance, 25, 58, 63, 86, 99, 103, 126ff., 151, 153, 158, 163, 199, 222, 227, 230, 248, 250f., 253, 260, 274, 276, 285, 289

Reprobate, 23, 47, 51, 203

Revelation, 11, 22, 72f., 89, 93, 105, 164, 169, 185, 192, 200, 204, 223

Reward, 25, 123, 126, 128, 171, 193

Rule of Faith, 167, 184

Sacraments, 33, 52f., 54ff., 80ff., 84, 90, 99, 104, 121f., 130, 139, 146, 147ff., 150f., 154, 177, 180ff., 191, 210, 222, 224f., 240, 247f., 249f., 258f., 274f., 284, 288
  What Sacraments are, 54, 80, 147f., 180, 224, 258, 285, 288
  Conjoined to the Word, 54, 64, 80, 104, 149, 248
  Visible Word, 149, 248
  Number of Sacraments, 56, 81, 151f., 180, 224f., 258, 284

Sacraments—*cont.*

  Signification, representation, 54f., 80,
    149f., 180, 258, 284, 288
  Matter, substance, 80, 149, 191, 224,
    228f.
  Operation, 56, 147f., 177, 224, 228f.,
    275, 284, 288
  Efficacy, 54f., 148, 150, 224, 249f.,
    274f., 284
  They lead us to Christ and His
    Sacrifice, 55f., 80f., 148, 157, 222,
    224, 249, 258, 288
  Reception in faith, 55f., 148, 150f.,
    275, 285
  Consecration of a Sacrament, 150f.
  Sacramental mode of speaking, 84
  Sacramental analogy or union, 57, 149
  Sacraments mark out the people of
    God, 63, 82, 224
Sacrifice of Christ, 11, 61, 74f., 80ff.,
    84f., 112, 115, 155, 169, 192f.,
    252, 257, 266
  of thanksgiving, 74f., 112, 145, 155f.
  of believers, 11, 40
  Old Testament sacrifices, 72, 190
Salvation, 6, 10, 12, 16f., 19f., 34f., 50,
    55f., 60, 69, 74, 78, 81, 97, 99,
    110, 121, 134, 136, 145, 147f.,
    153, 168, 176, 180f., 185, 190f.,
    196, 222f., 224, 234, 239f., 248
Sanctification, 13, 20, 45, 73, 81, 112f.,
    118, 120, 125, 161, 171, 182, 191,
    198ff., 234, 247ff., 290, 267
Satisfaction, recompense, reparation,
    etc., 16, 21, 50, 61, 69, 71, 76,
    79f., 84, 111, 114f., 142, 194, 198,
    233, 246, 248, 266, 285f., 288f.
Scholars in God's Household or School,
    5, 12, 53f., 146f., 247
Scriptures, Holy, 23, 40, 44, 52f., 86,
    98, 104, 118, 138, 144, 146ff., 158,
    185, 204, 223, 247, 258, 263, 284,
    286
Separation from the fellowship of the
    Church, 21, 49, 53, 63, 121, 160
Service of God, 6, 25, 28, 40, 104, 129,
    145, 167, 173f., 177, 180, 208,
    213, 239, 248, 260, 283, 286f.
Sin, 13f., 14, 16, 18, 23, 26, 37, 57f., 69f.,
    71f., 75f., 101f., 109, 113, 118,
    133f., 136, 142f., 151, 161f., 164f.,
    168, 175, 178f., 188f., 197, 200,
    202, 204ff., 208, 215f., 221f., 230,
    232f., 245, 248, 264f., 269, 274,
    283, 285, 287, 289
  Innate or original sin, 13, 16, 18, 23,
    57f., 69f., 75, 101, 113, 118, 133,
    168, 188f., 200, 204, 232f., 245,
    248, 264f., 285ff., 289f.
  Actual sin, 70, 189, 233
  Sin not a creature, 109f., 188f., 204f.
  Aggravation of sin, 221f., 274
Sovereignty of God, 210, 222, 231, 234,
    270
Surety, 14, 198

Teachers, 74, 111, 175, 247
Temples of the Spirit, 35, 91
Temptation, 37, 51, 76, 143, 168, 179,
    188, 200, 215, 223, 225, 233, 277,
    290
Thanksgiving, 41, 52, 69, 73, 80, 86ff.,
    93f., 99, 105, 129, 144f., 153, 167f.,
    179f., 190, 205, 209, 213f., 226,
    228f., 259, 276, 290
Toleration of false religion, 209
Tradition, 209, 239
Trial of God's children, 110, 143, 163
Trinity, Holy, 8, 73, 78, 81, 107, 168,
    186, 203, 225, 239, 263, 275, 288
Triplex munus, 10, 12, 111, 169, 192, 265
Triplex status, 99, 100, 101, 102, 284

Unbelief, 56, 101f.
Union with Christ, 12, 20, 60f., 62, 72,
    80, 84, 113, 120f., 124f., 150, 153,
    154ff., 160f., 172, 197, 200, 202f.,
    226, 246f., 249f., 251, 253, 266f.,
    268, 285, 288f.
Unity of the Church, 20, 78, 120f., 160,
    172, 197, 226

Vision of God, 202f.
Virgin Mary, 7, 12, 75, 113, 170, 191,
    265
Vivification, 289
Vocation, 40, 95, 102, 109, 140, 178, 218

Whoredom, spiritual, 28, 210
Word of God, 6, 8, 10, 33, 52f., 54, 59,
    64, 72ff., 80f., 89, 93f., 97, 99ff.,
    121, 130f., 138ff., 146ff., 149,
    155, 159, 161, 167, 174, 177,
    180f., 185, 187, 191f., 197ff., 207,
    209f., 212, 222ff., 226, 230f., 239,
    247, 249f., 258, 263, 266, 269f.,
    274ff., 284

Word of God—*cont.*
　Word and Spirit, 10, 52f., 74, 94, 185, 192, 197f., 199, 266
World, 8f., 11, 16, 18, 20, 25f., 30, 56, 95, 119, 136, 139, 160, 189, 193, 195, 232ff., 239, 246, 271
　Mirror, 8
　Salvation of the world, 16

Judgement of the world, 18
Works of God, 8, 30, 32, 107, 109, 130, 139f., 169, 185f., 207, 210, 231, 270
Worship, 26f., 38, 40, 52, 67, 84f., 89, 129, 136f., 174, 183, 186, 207, 209f., 212, 222, 229f., 269, 271, 290